Mastering Clojure

Understand the philosophy of the Clojure language
and dive into its inner workings to unlock its advanced
features, methodologies, and constructs

Akhil Wali

[PACKT]
PUBLISHING

open source*
community experience distilled

BIRMINGHAM - MUMBAI

Mastering Clojure

First published: March 2016

Production reference: 1180316

Published by Packt Publishing Ltd.
Livery Place
35 Livery Street
Birmingham B3 2PB, UK.

ISBN 978-1-78588-974-5

www.packtpub.com

Credits

Author
Akhil Wali

Reviewer
Matt Revelle

Commissioning Editor
Neil Alexander

Acquisition Editor
Aaron Lazar

Content Development Editor
Aishwarya Pandere

Technical Editor
Tanmayee Patil

Copy Editor
Merilyn Pereira

Project Coordinator
Nidhi Joshi

Proofreader
Safis Editing

Indexer
Rekha Nair

Graphics
Jason Monteiro

Production Coordinator
Melwyn Dsa

Cover Work
Melwyn D'sa

About the Author

Akhil Wali is a software developer. He has been writing code as a hobbyist since 1997 and professionally since 2010. He completed his post graduation from Santa Clara University in 2010, and he graduated from Visvesvaraya Technological University in 2008. His areas of work include business intelligence systems, ERP systems, search engines, and document collaboration tools. He mostly works with Clojure, JavaScript, and C#. Apart from computers, his interests include soccer, guitar solos, and finding out more about the universe.

I would like to thank two important women in my life for supporting me and inspiring me to write this book—my mother Renuka and my wife Megha. I also thank Matt Revelle and the Clojure community for their fantastic input and ideas.

About the Reviewer

Matt Revelle is a doctoral candidate in computer science at George Mason University, where he works on machine learning and social network dynamics. He started using Clojure in 2008 and it continues to be his preferred language for many projects and his daily work.

I would like to thank Akhil Wali and Nidhi Joshi for helping me to understand the purpose of this book and encouraging me to provide feedback in a timely fashion.

www.PacktPub.com

eBooks, discount offers, and more

Did you know that Packt offers eBook versions of every book published, with PDF and ePub files available? You can upgrade to the eBook version at www.PacktPub.com and as a print book customer, you are entitled to a discount on the eBook copy. Get in touch with us at customercare@packtpub.com for more details.

At www.PacktPub.com, you can also read a collection of free technical articles, sign up for a range of free newsletters and receive exclusive discounts and offers on Packt books and eBooks.

https://www2.packtpub.com/books/subscription/packtlib

Do you need instant solutions to your IT questions? PacktLib is Packt's online digital book library. Here, you can search, access, and read Packt's entire library of books.

Why subscribe?

- Fully searchable across every book published by Packt
- Copy and paste, print, and bookmark content
- On demand and accessible via a web browser

Table of Contents

Preface

Ever since the dawn of computers decades ago, there have been a number of programming languages created for the purpose of writing software. One of the earliest of these languages is Lisp, whose name is an abbreviation of the term "list processing". Lisp has evolved greatly over time, and there are now several dialects of Lisp. Each of these dialects emphasizes its own set of ideas and features. Clojure is one among these Lisps, and it focuses on immutability, concurrency, and parallelism. It emphasizes being simple, practical, and intuitive, which makes it easy to learn. It is said that you have never realized how a language can be powerful until you have programmed in a Lisp, and Clojure is no exception to this rule. A skilled Clojure programmer can easily and quickly create software that is both performant and scalable.

With the recent rise of parallel data processing and multicore architectures, functional programming languages have become more popular for creating software that is both provable and performant. Clojure brings functional programming to the Java Virtual Machine (JVM), and also to web browsers through ClojureScript. Like other functional programming languages, Clojure focuses on the use of functions and immutable data structures for writing programs. Clojure also adds a hint of Lisp through the use of symbolic expressions and a dynamic type system.

This book will walk you through the interesting features of the Clojure language. We will also discuss some of the more advanced and lesser known programming constructs in Clojure. Several libraries from the Clojure ecosystem that we can put to practical use in our own programs will also be described. You won't need to be convinced any more about the elegance and power of the Clojure language by the time you've finished this book.

This book wouldn't have materialized without the feedback from the technical reviewers and the effort of the content and editing teams at Packt Publishing.

What this book covers

Chapter 1, Working with Sequences and Patterns, describes several elementary programming techniques, such as recursion, sequences, and pattern matching.

Chapter 2, Orchestrating Concurrency and Parallelism, explains the various constructs available in the Clojure language for concurrent and parallel programming.

Chapter 3, Parallelization Using Reducers, introduces reducers, which are abstractions of collection types for parallel data processing.

Chapter 4, Metaprogramming with Macros, explains how we can use macros and quoting to implement our own programming constructs in Clojure.

Chapter 5, Composing Transducers, describes how we can define and compose data transformations using transducers.

Chapter 6, Exploring Category Theory, explores algebraic data structures, such as functors, monoids, and monads, from the pure functional programming world.

Chapter 7, Programming with Logic, describes how we can use logical relations to solve problems.

Chapter 8, Leveraging Asynchronous Tasks, explains how we can write code that is executed asynchronously.

Chapter 9, Reactive Programming, describes how we can implement solutions to problems using asynchronous event streams.

Chapter 10, Testing Your Code, covers several testing libraries that are useful in verifying our code. This chapter describes techniques such as test-driven development, behavior-driven development, and generative testing.

Chapter 11, Troubleshooting and Best Practices, describes techniques to debug your code as well as several good practices for developing Clojure applications and libraries.

What you need for this book

One of the pieces of software required for this book is the Java Development Kit (7 or above), which you can obtain from `http://www.oracle.com/technetwork/java/javase/downloads/`. JDK is necessary to run and develop applications on the Java platform. The other major software that you'll need is Leiningen (2.5.1 or above), which you can download and install from `http://github.com/technomancy/leiningen`.

Leiningen is a tool for managing Clojure projects and their dependencies. Throughout this book, we'll use a number of Clojure libraries. Leiningen will download these libraries, and also the Clojure language itself, for us, as required.

You'll also need a text editor or an integrated development environment (IDE). If you already have a text editor that you prefer, you can probably use it. Navigate to `http://dev.clojure.org/display/doc/Getting+Started` for a list of environment-specific plugins to write code in Clojure. If you don't have a preference, it is suggested that you use Eclipse with Counterclockwise (`http://doc.ccw-ide.org/`) or Light Table (`http://lighttable.com/`).

Some examples in this book will also require a web browser, such as Chrome (42 or above), Firefox (38 or above), or Microsoft Internet Explorer (9 or above).

Who this book is for

This book is for programmers or software architects who are familiar with Clojure and want to learn about the language's features in detail. It is also for readers who are eager to explore popular and practical Clojure libraries.

This book does not describe the syntax of the Clojure language. You are expected to be familiar with the language, but you need not be a Clojure expert. You are also expected to know how functions are used and defined in Clojure, and have some basic knowledge about Clojure data structures such as strings, lists, vectors, maps, and sets. You must also be able to compile ClojureScript programs to JavaScript and run them in an HTML page.

Conventions

In this book, you will find a number of text styles that distinguish between different kinds of information. Here are some examples of these styles and an explanation of their meaning.

Code words in text, database table names, folder names, filenames, file extensions, pathnames, dummy URLs, user input, and Twitter handles are shown as follows: "Hence, for trees that are represented as sequences, we should use the `seq-zip` function instead."

A block of code is set as follows:

```
(f/defun fibo
  ([0] 0N)
  ([1] 1N)
  ([n] (+ (fibo (- n 1))
          (fibo (- n 2)))))
```

When we wish to draw your attention to a particular part of a code block, the relevant lines or items are set in bold:

```
(f/defun fibo
  ([0] 0N)
  ([1] 1N)
  ([n] (+ (fibo (- n 1))
          (fibo (- n 2)))))
```

Any command-line input or output is written as follows:

```
$ lein repl
```

Another simple convention that we use is to always show the Clojure code that's entered in the REPL (read-evaluate-print-loop) starting with the user> prompt. In practice, this prompt will change depending on the Clojure namespace that we are currently using. However, for simplicity, code in the REPL always starts with the user> prompt in this book, as follows:

```
user> (cons 0 ())
(0)
user> (cons 0 nil)
(0)
user> (rest (cons 0 nil))
()
```

For convenience, the REPL output in this book is pretty-printed (using the clojure. pprint/pprint function). Objects that are printed in the REPL output are enclosed within the #< and > symbols. We must note that the output of the time form in your own REPL may not completely match the output shown in the code examples of this book. Rather, the use of time forms is meant to give you an idea of the scale of the time taken to execute a given expression. Similarly, the output of the code examples that use the rand-int function may not exactly match the output in your REPL.

Some examples in this book use ClojureScript, and the files for these examples will have a .cljs extension. Also, all macros used in these examples will have to be explicitly included using the :require-macros clause of the ns form. The HTML and CSS files associated with the ClojureScript examples in this book will not be shown in this book, but can always be found in the book's code bundle.

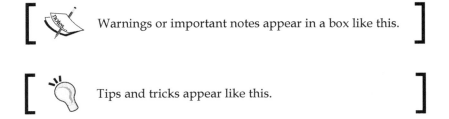

[Warnings or important notes appear in a box like this.]

[Tips and tricks appear like this.]

Reader feedback

Feedback from our readers is always welcome. Let us know what you think about this book—what you liked or disliked. Reader feedback is important for us as it helps us develop titles that you will really get the most out of.

To send us general feedback, simply e-mail feedback@packtpub.com, and mention the book's title in the subject of your message.

If there is a topic that you have expertise in and you are interested in either writing or contributing to a book, see our author guide at www.packtpub.com/authors.

Customer support

Now that you are the proud owner of a Packt book, we have a number of things to help you to get the most from your purchase.

Downloading the example code

You can download the example code files for this book from your account at http://www.packtpub.com. If you purchased this book elsewhere, you can visit http://www.packtpub.com/support and register to have the files e-mailed directly to you.

You can download the code files by following these steps:

1. Log in or register to our website using your e-mail address and password.
2. Hover the mouse pointer on the **SUPPORT** tab at the top.
3. Click on **Code Downloads & Errata**.
4. Enter the name of the book in the **Search** box.
5. Select the book for which you're looking to download the code files.
6. Choose from the drop-down menu where you purchased this book from.
7. Click on **Code Download**.

Once the file is downloaded, please make sure that you unzip or extract the folder using the latest version of:

- WinRAR / 7-Zip for Windows
- Zipeg / iZip / UnRarX for Mac
- 7-Zip / PeaZip for Linux

Errata

Although we have taken every care to ensure the accuracy of our content, mistakes do happen. If you find a mistake in one of our books—maybe a mistake in the text or the code—we would be grateful if you could report this to us. By doing so, you can save other readers from frustration and help us improve subsequent versions of this book. If you find any errata, please report them by visiting `http://www.packtpub.com/submit-errata`, selecting your book, clicking on the **Errata Submission Form** link, and entering the details of your errata. Once your errata are verified, your submission will be accepted and the errata will be uploaded to our website or added to any list of existing errata under the Errata section of that title.

To view the previously submitted errata, go to `https://www.packtpub.com/books/content/support` and enter the name of the book in the search field. The required information will appear under the **Errata** section.

Piracy

Piracy of copyrighted material on the Internet is an ongoing problem across all media. At Packt, we take the protection of our copyright and licenses very seriously. If you come across any illegal copies of our works in any form on the Internet, please provide us with the location address or website name immediately so that we can pursue a remedy.

Please contact us at `copyright@packtpub.com` with a link to the suspected pirated material.

We appreciate your help in protecting our authors and our ability to bring you valuable content.

Questions

If you have a problem with any aspect of this book, you can contact us at `questions@packtpub.com`, and we will do our best to address the problem.

1
Working with Sequences and Patterns

In this chapter, we'll revisit a few basic programming techniques, such as recursion and sequences, with Clojure. As we will see, Clojure focuses on the use of higher-order functions to abstract computation, like any other functional programming language. This design can be observed in most, if not all, of the Clojure standard library. In this chapter, we will cover the following topics:

- Exploring recursion
- Learning about sequences and laziness
- Examining zippers
- Briefly studying pattern matching

Defining recursive functions

Recursion is one of the central methodologies of computer science. It allows us to elegantly solve problems that have cumbersome non-recursive solutions. Yet, recursive functions are discouraged in quite a few imperative programming languages in favor of non-recursive functions. Clojure does no such thing and completely embraces recursion along with all its pros and cons. In this section, we will explore how to define recursive functions.

 The following examples can be found in `src/m_clj/c1/recur.clj` of the book's source code.

In general, a function can be made recursive by simply calling it again from within the body of the function. We can define a simple function to return the first n numbers of the Fibonacci sequence as shown in *Example 1.1*:

```
(defn fibo
  ([n]
   (fibo [0N 1N] n))
  ([xs n]
   (if (<= n (count xs))
     xs
     (let [x' (+ (last xs)
                 (nth xs (- (count xs) 2)))
           xs' (conj xs x')]
       (fibo xs' n)))))
```

Example 1.1: A simple recursive function

The Fibonacci sequence is a series of numbers that can be defined as follows:

The first element F_0 is 0 and the second element F_1 is 1.

The rest of the numbers are the sum of the previous two numbers, that is the nth Fibonacci number $F_n = F_{n-1} + F_{n-2}$.

In the previously defined `fibo` function, the last two elements of the list are determined using the `nth` and `last` functions, and the sum of these two elements is appended to the list using the `conj` function. This is done in a recursive manner, and the function terminates when the length of the list, determined by the `count` function becomes equal to the supplied value n. Also, the values `0N` and `1N`, which represent `BigInteger` types, are used instead of the values 0 and 1. This is done because using long or integer values for such a computation could result in an arithmetic overflow error. We can try out this function in the REPL shown as follows:

```
user> (fibo 10)
[0N 1N 1N 2N 3N 5N 8N 13N 21N 34N]
user> (last (fibo 100))
218922995834555169026N
```

The `fibo` function returns a vector of the first n Fibonacci numbers as expected. However, for larger values of n, this function will cause a stack overflow:

```
user> (last (fibo 10000))
StackOverflowError   clojure.lang.Numbers.lt (Numbers.java:219)
```

The reason for this error is that there were too many nested function calls. A call to any function requires an additional call stack. With recursion, we reach a point where all of the available stack space in a program is consumed and no more function calls can be performed. A *tail call* can overcome this limitation by using the existing call stack for a recursive call, which removes the need for allocating a new call stack. This is only possible when the return value of a function is the return value of a recursive call made by the function, in which case an additional call stack is not required to store the state of the function that performs the recursive call. This technique is termed as *tail call elimination*. In effect, a tail call optimized function consumes a constant amount of stack space.

In fact, the `fibo` function does indeed make a tail call, as the last expression in the body of the function is a recursive call. Still, it consumes stack space for each recursive call. This is due to the fact that the underlying virtual machine, the JVM, does not perform tail call elimination. In Clojure, tail call elimination has to be done explicitly using a `recur` form to perform a recursive call. The `fibo` function we defined earlier can be refined to be *tail recursive* by using a `recur` form, as shown in *Example 1.2*:

```
(defn fibo-recur
  ([n]
   (fibo-recur [0N 1N] n))
  ([xs n]
   (if (<= n (count xs))
     xs
     (let [x' (+ (last xs)
                 (nth xs (- (count xs) 2)))
           xs' (conj xs x')]
       (recur xs' n))))))
```

Example 1.2: A recursive function defined using recur

Effectively, the `fibo-recur` function can perform an infinite number of nested recursive calls. We can observe that this function does not blow up the stack for large values of n, shown as follows:

```
user> (fibo-recur 10)
[0N 1N 1N 2N 3N 5N 8N 13N 21N 34N]
user> (last (fibo-recur 10000))
207936...230626N
```

We should note that a call to `fibo-recur` can take quite a while to terminate for large values of n. We can measure the time taken for a call to `fibo-recur` to complete and return a value, using the `time` macro, as follows:

```
user> (time (last (fibo-recur 10000)))
"Elapsed time: 1320.050942 msecs"
207936...230626N
```

The `fibo-recur` function can also be expressed using the `loop` and `recur` forms. This eliminates the need for using a second function arity to pass the `[0N 1N]` value around, as shown in the `fibo-loop` function defined in *Example 1.3*:

```
(defn fibo-loop [n]
  (loop [xs [0N 1N]
         n n]
    (if (<= n (count xs))
      xs
      (let [x' (+ (last xs)
                  (nth xs (- (count xs) 2)))
            xs' (conj xs x')]
        (recur xs' n)))))
```

Example 1.3: A recursive function defined using loop and recur

Note that the `loop` macro requires a vector of bindings (pairs of names and values) to be passed as its first argument. The second argument to the `loop` form must be an expression that uses the `recur` form. This nested `recur` form calls the surrounding expression recursively by passing in the new values for the declared bindings in the `loop` form. The `fibo-loop` function returns a value that is equal to that returned by the `fibo-recur` function, from *Example 1.2*, shown as follows:

```
user> (fibo-loop 10)
[0N 1N 1N 2N 3N 5N 8N 13N 21N 34N]
user> (last (fibo-loop 10000))
207936...230626N
```

Another way to handle recursion is by using the `trampoline` function. The `trampoline` function takes a function as its first argument, followed by the values of the parameters to be passed to the supplied function. A `trampoline` form expects the supplied function to return another function, and in such a case, the returned function will be invoked. Thus, a `trampoline` form manages recursion by obtaining a return value, and invoking the returned value again if it's a function. Thus, the `trampoline` function avoids using any stack space. Each time the supplied function is invoked, it returns and the result gets stored in the process heap. For example, consider the function in *Example 1.4* that calculates the first n numbers of the Fibonacci sequence using a `trampoline`:

```
(defn fibo-trampoline [n]
  (letfn [(fibo-fn [xs n]
            (if (<= n (count xs))
              xs
              (let [x' (+ (last xs)
                          (nth xs (- (count xs) 2)))
                    xs' (conj xs x')]
                #(fibo-fn xs' n))))]
    (trampoline fibo-fn [0N 1N] n)))
```

Example 1.4: A recursive function defined using trampoline

In the `fib-trampoline` function, the internal `fibo-fn` function returns either a sequence, denoted by `xs`, or a closure that takes no arguments, represented by `#(fibo-fn xs' n)`. This function is equivalent to the `fibo-recur` function we defined earlier, even in terms of performance, shown as follows:

```
user> (fibo-trampoline 10)
[0N 1N 1N 2N 3N 5N 8N 13N 21N 34N]
user> (time (last (fibo-trampoline 10000)))
"Elapsed time: 1346.629108 msecs"
207936...230626N
```

Mutual recursion can also be handled effectively using a trampoline. In mutual recursion, two functions call each other in a recursive manner. For example, consider the function that utilizes two mutually recursive functions in *Example 1.5*:

```
(defn sqrt-div2-recur [n]
  (letfn [(sqrt [n]
            (if (< n 1)
              n
              (div2 (Math/sqrt n))))
          (div2 [n]
            (if (< n 1)
```

```
            n
            (sqrt (/ n 2)))))]
    (sqrt n)))
```

Example 1.5: A simple function that uses mutual recursion

The sqrt-div2-recur function from *Example 1.5* defines two mutually recursive functions internally, namely sqrt and div2, that repeatedly square root and halve a given value n until the calculated value is less than 1. The sqrt-div2-recur function declares these two functions using a letfn form and invokes the sqrt function. We can convert this to use a trampoline form as shown in *Example 1.6*:

```
(defn sqrt-div2-trampoline [n]
  (letfn [(sqrt [n]
            (if (< n 1)
              n
              #(div2 (Math/sqrt n))))
          (div2 [n]
            (if (< n 1)
              n
              #(sqrt (/ n 2))))]
    (trampoline sqrt n)))
```

Example 1.6: A function that uses mutual recursion using trampoline

In the previous sqrt-div2-trampoline function shown, the functions sqrt and div2 return closures instead of calling a function directly. The trampoline form in the body of the function calls the sqrt function while supplying the value n. Both the sqrt-div2-recur and sqrt-div2-trampoline functions take about the same time to return a value for the given value of n. Hence, using a trampoline form does not have any additional performance overhead, shown as follows:

```
user> (time (sqrt-div2-recur 10000000000N))
"Elapsed time: 0.327439 msecs"
0.5361105866719398
user> (time (sqrt-div2-trampoline 10000000000N))
"Elapsed time: 0.326081 msecs"
0.5361105866719398
```

As the preceding examples demonstrate, there are various ways to define recursive functions in Clojure. Recursive functions can be optimized using tail call elimination, by using recur, and mutual recursion, which is done using the trampoline function.

Thinking in sequences

A **sequence**, shortened as a **seq**, is essentially an abstraction of a list. This abstraction provides a unified model or interface to interact with a collection of items. In Clojure, all the primitive data structures, namely strings, lists, vectors, maps, and sets can be treated as sequences. In practice, almost everything that involves iteration can be translated into a sequence of computations. A collection is termed as **seqable** if it implements the abstraction of a sequence. We will learn everything there is to know about sequences in this section.

Sequences can also be *lazy*. A lazy sequence can be thought of as a possibly infinite series of computed values. The computation of each value is deferred until it is actually needed. We should note that the computation of a recursive function can easily be represented as a lazy sequence. For example, the Fibonacci sequence can be computed by lazily adding the last two elements in the previously computed sequence. This can be implemented as shown in *Example 1.7*.

 The following examples can be found in `src/m_clj/c1/seq.clj` of the book's source code.

```
(defn fibo-lazy [n]
  (->> [0N 1N]
       (iterate (fn [[a b]] [b (+ a b)]))
       (map first)
       (take n)))
```

Example 1.7: A lazy Fibonacci sequence

 The threading macro `->>` is used to pass the result of a given expression as the last argument to the next expression, in a repetitive manner for all expressions in its body. Similarly, the threading macro `->` is used to pass the result of a given expression as the first argument to the subsequent expressions.

The `fibo-lazy` function from *Example 1.7* uses the `iterate`, `map`, and `take` functions to create a lazy sequence. We will study these functions in more detail later in this section. The `fibo-lazy` function takes a single argument n, which indicates the number of items to be returned by the function. In the `fibo-lazy` function, the values `0N` and `1N` are passed as a vector to the `iterate` function, which produces a lazy sequence. The function used for this iteration creates a new pair of values b and `(+ a b)` from the initial values a and b.

Next, the map function applies the first function to obtain the first element in each resulting vector. A take form is finally applied to the sequence returned by the map function to retrieve the first n values in the sequence. The fibo-lazy function does not cause any error even when passed relatively large values of n, shown as follows:

```
user> (fibo-lazy 10)
(0N 1N 1N 2N 3N 5N 8N 13N 21N 34N)
user> (last (fibo-lazy 10000))
207936...230626N
```

Interestingly, the fibo-lazy function in *Example 1.7* performs significantly better than the recursive functions from *Example 1.2* and *Example 1.3*, as shown here:

```
user> (time (last (fibo-lazy 10000)))
"Elapsed time: 18.593018 msecs"
207936...230626N
```

Also, binding the value returned by the fibo-lazy function to a variable does not really consume any time. This is because this returned value is lazy and not evaluated yet. Also, the type of the return value is clojure.lang.LazySeq, as shown here:

```
user> (time (def fibo-xs (fibo-lazy 10000)))
"Elapsed time: 0.191981 msecs"
#'user/fibo-xs
user> (type fibo-xs)
clojure.lang.LazySeq
```

We can optimize the fibo-lazy function even further by using **memoization**, which essentially caches the value returned by a function for a given set of inputs. This can be done using the memoize function, as follows:

```
(def fibo-mem (memoize fibo-lazy))
```

The fibo-mem function is a memoized version of the fibo-lazy function. Hence, subsequent calls to the fibo-mem function for the same set of inputs will return values significantly faster, shown as follows:

```
user> (time (last (fibo-mem 10000)))
"Elapsed time: 19.776527 msecs"
207936...230626N
user> (time (last (fibo-mem 10000)))
"Elapsed time: 2.82709 msecs"
207936...230626N
```

Note that the `memoize` function can be applied to any function, and it is not really related to sequences. The function we pass to `memoize` must be free of side effects, or else any side effects will be invoked only the first time the memoized function is called with a given set of inputs.

Using the seq library

Sequences are a truly ubiquitous abstraction in Clojure. The primary motivation behind using sequences is that any domain with sequence-like data in it can be easily modelled using the standard functions that operate on sequences. This infamous quote from the Lisp world reflects on this design:

> *"It is better to have 100 functions operate on one data abstraction than 10 functions on 10 data structures."*

A sequence can be constructed using the `cons` function. We must provide an element and another sequence as arguments to the `cons` function. The `first` function is used to access the first element in a sequence, and similarly the `rest` function is used to obtain the other elements in the sequence, shown as follows:

```
user> (def xs (cons 0 '(1 2 3)))
#'user/xs
user> (first xs)
0
user> (rest xs)
(1 2 3)
```

 The `first` and `rest` functions in Clojure are equivalent to the `car` and `cdr` functions, respectively, from traditional Lisps. The `cons` function carries on its traditional name.

In Clojure, an empty list is represented by the literal `()`. An empty list is considered as a *truthy* value, and does not equate to `nil`. This rule is true for any empty collection. An empty list does indeed have a type – it's a list. On the other hand, the `nil` literal signifies the absence of a value, of any type, and is not a truthy value. The second argument that is passed to `cons` could be empty, in which case the resulting sequence would contain a single element:

```
user> (cons 0 ())
(0)
user> (cons 0 nil)
(0)
user> (rest (cons 0 nil))
()
```

An interesting quirk is that `nil` can be treated as an empty collection, but the converse is not true. We can use the `empty?` and `nil?` functions to test for an empty collection and a `nil` value, respectively. Note that `(empty? nil)` returns `true`, shown as follows:

```
user> (empty? ())
true
user> (empty? nil)
true
user> (nil? ())
false
user> (nil? nil)
true
```

 By the *truthy* value, we mean to say a value that will test positive in a conditional expression such as an `if` or a `when` form.

The `rest` function will return an empty list when supplied an empty list. Thus, the value returned by `rest` is always truthy. The `seq` function can be used to obtain a sequence from a given collection. It will return `nil` for an empty list or collection. Hence, the `head`, `rest` and `seq` functions can be used to iterate over a sequence. The `next` function can also be used for iteration, and the expression `(seq (rest coll))` is equivalent to `(next coll)`, shown as follows:

```
user> (= (rest ()) nil)
false
user> (= (seq ()) nil)
true
user> (= (next ()) nil)
true
```

The `sequence` function can be used to create a list from a sequence. For example, `nil` can be converted into an empty list using the expression `(sequence nil)`. In Clojure, the `seq?` function is used to check whether a value implements the sequence interface, namely `clojure.lang.ISeq`. Only lists implement this interface, and other data structures such as vectors, sets, and maps have to be converted into a sequence by using the `seq` function. Hence, `seq?` will return `true` only for lists. Note that the `list?`, `vector?`, `map?`, and `set?` functions can be used to check the concrete type of a given collection. The behavior of the `seq?` function with lists and vectors can be described as follows:

```
user> (seq? '(1 2 3))
true
user> (seq? [1 2 3])
```

```
false
user> (seq? (seq [1 2 3]))
true
```

Only lists and vectors provide a guarantee of sequential ordering among elements. In other words, lists and vectors will store their elements in the same order or sequence as they were created. This is in contrast to maps and sets, which can reorder their elements as needed. We can use the `sequential?` function to check whether a collection provides sequential ordering:

```
user> (sequential? '(1 2 3))
true
user> (sequential? [1 2 3])
true
user> (sequential? {:a 1 :b 2})
false
user> (sequential? #{:a :b})
false
```

The `associative?` function can be used to determine whether a collection or sequence associates a key with a particular value. Note that this function returns `true` only for maps and vectors:

```
user> (associative? '(1 2 3))
false
user> (associative? [1 2 3])
true
user> (associative? {:a 1 :b 2})
true
user> (associative? #{:a :b})
false
```

The behavior of the `associative?` function is fairly obvious for a map since a map is essentially a collection of key-value pairs. The fact that a vector is also associative is well justified too, as a vector has an implicit key for a given element, namely the index of the element in the vector. For example, the `[:a :b]` vector has two implicit keys, `0` and `1`, for the elements `:a` and `:b` respectively. This brings us to an interesting consequence – vectors and maps can be treated as functions that take a single argument, that is a key, and return an associated value, shown as follows:

```
user> ([:a :b] 1)
:b
user> ({:a 1 :b 2} :a)
1
```

Although they are not associative by nature, sets are also functions. Sets return a value contained in them, or `nil`, depending on the argument passed to them, shown as follows:

```
user> (#{1 2 3} 1)
1
user> (#{1 2 3} 0)
nil
```

Now that we have familiarized ourselves with the basics of sequences, let's have a look at the many functions that operate over sequences.

Creating sequences

There are several ways to create sequences other than using the `cons` function. We have already encountered the `conj` function in the earlier examples of this chapter. The `conj` function takes a collection as its first argument, followed by any number of arguments to add to the collection. We must note that `conj` behaves differently for lists and vectors. When supplied a list, the `conj` function adds the other arguments at the head, or start, of the list. In case of a vector, the `conj` function will insert the other arguments at the tail, or end, of the vector:

```
user> (conj [1 2 3] 4 5 6)
[1 2 3 4 5 6]
user> (conj '(1 2 3) 4 5 6)
(6 5 4 1 2 3)
```

The `concat` function can be used to join or *concatenate* any number of sequences in the order in which they are supplied, shown as follows:

```
user> (concat [1 2 3] [])
(1 2 3)
user> (concat [] [1 2 3])
(1 2 3)
user> (concat [1 2 3] [4 5 6] [7 8 9])
(1 2 3 4 5 6 7 8 9)
```

A given sequence can be reversed using the `reverse` function, shown as follows:

```
user> (reverse [1 2 3 4 5 6])
(6 5 4 3 2 1)
user> (reverse (reverse [1 2 3 4 5 6]))
(1 2 3 4 5 6)
```

The `range` function can be used to generate a sequence of values within a given integer range. The most general form of the `range` function takes three arguments—the first argument is the start of the range, the second argument is the end of the range, and the third argument is the step of the range. The step of the range defaults to 1, and the start of the range defaults to 0, as shown here:

```
user> (range 5)
(0 1 2 3 4)
user> (range 0 10 3)
(0 3 6 9)
user> (range 15 10 -1)
(15 14 13 12 11)
```

We must note that the `range` function expects the start of the range to be less than the end of the range. If the start of the range is greater than the end of the range and the step of the range is positive, the `range` function will return an empty list. For example, `(range 15 10)` will return `()`. Also, the `range` function can be called with no arguments, in which case it returns a lazy and infinite sequence starting at 0.

The `take` and `drop` functions can be used to take or drop elements in a sequence. Both functions take two arguments, representing the number of elements to take or drop from a sequence, and the sequence itself, as follows:

```
user> (take 5 (range 10))
(0 1 2 3 4)
user> (drop 5 (range 10))
(5 6 7 8 9)
```

To obtain an item at a particular position in the sequence, we should use the `nth` function. This function takes a sequence as its first argument, followed by the position of the item to be retrieved from the sequence as the second argument:

```
user> (nth (range 10) 0)
0
user> (nth (range 10) 9)
9
```

To repeat a given value, we can use the `repeat` function. This function takes two arguments and repeats the second argument the number of times indicated by the first argument:

```
user> (repeat 10 0)
(0 0 0 0 0 0 0 0 0 0)
user> (repeat 5 :x)
(:x :x :x :x :x)
```

The `repeat` function will evaluate the expression of the second argument and repeat it. To call a function a number of times, we can use the `repeatedly` function, as follows:

```
user> (repeat 5 (rand-int 100))
(75 75 75 75 75)
user> (repeatedly 5 #(rand-int 100))
(88 80 17 52 32)
```

In this example, the `repeat` form first evaluates the `(rand-int 100)` form, before repeating it. Hence, a single value will be repeated several times. Note that the `rand-int` function simply returns a random integer between `0` and the supplied value. On the other hand, the `repeatedly` function invokes the supplied function a number of times, thus producing a new value every time the `rand-int` function is called.

A sequence can be repeated an infinite number of times using the `cycle` function. As you might have guessed, this function returns a lazy sequence to indicate an infinite series of values. The `take` function can be used to obtain a limited number of values from the resulting infinite sequence, shown as follows:

```
user> (take 5 (cycle [0]))
(0 0 0 0 0)
user> (take 5 (cycle (range 3)))
(0 1 2 0 1)
```

The `interleave` function can be used to combine any number of sequences. This function returns a sequence of the first item in each collection, followed by the second item, and so on. This combination of the supplied sequences is repeated until the shortest sequence is exhausted of values. Hence, we can easily combine a finite sequence with an infinite one to produce another finite sequence using the `interleave` function:

```
user> (interleave [0 1 2] [3 4 5 6] [7 8])
(0 3 7 1 4 8)
user> (interleave [1 2 3] (cycle [0]))
(1 0 2 0 3 0)
```

Another function that performs a similar operation is the `interpose` function. The `interpose` function inserts a given element between the adjacent elements of a given sequence:

```
user> (interpose 0 [1 2 3])
(1 0 2 0 3)
```

The `iterate` function can also be used to create an infinite sequence. Note that we have already used the `iterate` function to create a lazy sequence in *Example 1.7*. This function takes a function `f` and an initial value `x` as its arguments. The value returned by the `iterate` function will have `(f x)` as the first element, `(f (f x))` as the second element, and so on. We can use the `iterate` function with any other function that takes a single argument, as follows:

```
user> (take 5 (iterate inc 5))
(5 6 7 8 9)
user> (take 5 (iterate #(+ 2 %) 0))
(0 2 4 6 8)
```

Transforming sequences

There are also several functions to convert sequences into different representations or values. One of the most versatile of such functions is the `map` function. This function *maps* a given function over a given sequence, that is, it applies the function to each element in the sequence. Also, the value returned by `map` is implicitly lazy. The function to be applied to each element must be the first argument to `map`, and the sequence on which the function must be applied is the next argument:

```
user> (map inc [0 1 2 3])
(1 2 3 4)
user> (map #(* 2 %) [0 1 2 3])
(0 2 4 6)
```

Note that `map` can accept any number of collections or sequences as its arguments. In this case, the resulting sequence is obtained by passing the first items of the sequences as arguments to the given function, and then passing the second items of the sequences to the given function, and so on until any of the supplied sequences are exhausted. For example, we can sum the corresponding elements of two sequences using the `map` and `+` functions, as shown here:

```
user> (map + [0 1 2 3] [4 5 6])
(4 6 8)
```

The `mapv` function has the same semantics of map, but returns a vector instead of a sequence, as shown here:

```
user> (mapv inc [0 1 2 3])
[1 2 3 4]
```

Another variant of the map function is the map-indexed function. This function expects that the supplied function will accept two arguments—one for the index of a given element and another for the actual element in the list:

```
user> (map-indexed (fn [i x] [i x]) "Hello")
([0 \H] [1 \e] [2 \l] [3 \l] [4 \o])
```

In this example, the function supplied to map-indexed simply returns its arguments as a vector. An interesting point that we can observe from the preceding example is that a string can be treated as a sequence of characters.

The mapcat function is a combination of the map and concat function. This function maps a given function over a sequence, and applies the concat function on the resulting sequence:

```
user> (require '[clojure.string :as cs])
nil
user> (map #(cs/split % #"\d") ["aa1bb" "cc2dd" "ee3ff"])
(["aa" "bb"] ["cc" "dd"] ["ee" "ff"])
user> (mapcat #(cs/split % #"\d") ["aa1bb" "cc2dd" "ee3ff"])
("aa" "bb" "cc" "dd" "ee" "ff")
```

In this example, we use the split function from the clojure.string namespace to split a string using a regular expression, shown as #"\d". The split function will return a vector of strings, and hence the mapcat function returns a sequence of strings instead of a sequence of vectors like the map function.

The reduce function is used to combine or *reduce* a sequence of items into a single value. The reduce function requires a function as its first argument and a sequence as its second argument. The function supplied to reduce must accept two arguments. The supplied function is first applied to the first two elements in the given sequence, and then applied to the previous result and the third element in the sequence, and so on until the sequence is exhausted. The reduce function also has a second arity, which accepts an initial value, and in this case, the supplied function is applied to the initial value and the first element in the sequence as the first step. The reduce function can be considered equivalent to loop-based iteration in imperative programming languages. For example, we can compute the sum of all elements in a sequence using reduce, as follows:

```
user> (reduce + [1 2 3 4 5])
15
user> (reduce + [])
0
user> (reduce + 1 [])
1
```

In this example, when the reduce function is supplied an empty collection, it returns 0, since (+) evaluates to 0. When an initial value of 1 is supplied to the reduce function, it returns 1, since (+ 1) returns 1.

A *list comprehension* can be created using the for macro. Note that a for form will be translated into an expression that uses the map function. The for macro needs to be supplied a vector of bindings to any number of collections, and an expression in the body. This macro binds the supplied symbol to each element in its corresponding collection and evaluates the body for each element. Note that the for macro also supports a :let clause to assign a value to a variable, and also a :when clause to filter out values:

```
user> (for [x (range 3 7)]
        (* x x))
(9 16 25 36)
user> (for [x [0 1 2 3 4 5]
            :let [y (* x 3)]
            :when (even? y)]
        y)
(0 6 12)
```

The for macro can also be used over a number of collections, as shown here:

```
user> (for [x ['a 'b 'c]
            y [1 2 3]]
        [x y])
([a 1] [a 2] [a 3] [b 1] [b 2] [b 3] [c 1] [c 2] [c 3])
```

The doseq macro has semantics similar to that of for, except for the fact that it always returns a nil value. This macro simply evaluates the body expression for all of the items in the given bindings. This is useful in forcing evaluation of an expression with side effects for all the items in a given collection:

```
user> (doseq [x (range 3 7)]
        (* x x))
nil
user> (doseq [x (range 3 7)]
        (println (* x x)))
9
16
25
36
nil
```

As shown in the preceding example, both the first and second `doseq` forms return `nil`. However, the second form prints the value of the expression `(* x x)`, which is a side effect, for all items in the sequence `(range 3 7)`.

The `into` function can be used to easily convert between types of collections. This function requires two collections to be supplied to it as arguments, and returns the first collection filled with all the items in the second collection. For example, we can convert a sequence of vectors into a map, and vice versa, using the `into` function, shown here:

```
user> (into {} [[:a 1] [:c 3] [:b 2]])
{:a 1, :c 3, :b 2}
user> (into [] {1 2 3 4})
[[1 2] [3 4]]
```

We should note that the `into` function is essentially a composition of the `reduce` and `conj` functions. As `conj` is used to fill the first collection, the value returned by the `into` function will depend on the type of the first collection. The `into` function will behave similar to `conj` with respect to lists and vectors, shown here:

```
user> (into [1 2 3] '(4 5 6))
[1 2 3 4 5 6]
user> (into '(1 2 3) '(4 5 6))
(6 5 4 1 2 3)
```

A sequence can be partitioned into smaller ones using the `partition`, `partition-all` and `partition-by` functions. Both the `partition` and `partition-all` functions take two arguments—one for the number of items n in the partitioned sequences and another for the sequence to be partitioned. However, the `partition-all` function will also return the items from the sequence, which have not been partitioned as a separate sequence, shown here:

```
user> (partition 2 (range 11))
((0 1) (2 3) (4 5) (6 7) (8 9))
user> (partition-all 2 (range 11))
((0 1) (2 3) (4 5) (6 7) (8 9) (10))
```

The `partition` and `partition-all` functions also accept a step argument, which defaults to the supplied number of items in the partitioned sequences, shown as follows:

```
user> (partition 3 2 (range 11))
((0 1 2) (2 3 4) (4 5 6) (6 7 8) (8 9 10))
user> (partition-all 3 2 (range 11))
((0 1 2) (2 3 4) (4 5 6) (6 7 8) (8 9 10) (10))
```

The `partition` function also takes a second sequence as an optional argument, which is used to pad the sequence to be partitioned in case there are items that are not partitioned. This second sequence has to be supplied after the step argument to the `partition` function. Note that the padding sequence is only used to create a single partition with the items that have not been partitioned, and the rest of the padding sequence is discarded. Also, the padding sequence is only used if there are any items that have not been partitioned. This can be illustrated in the following example:

```
user> (partition 3 (range 11))
((0 1 2) (3 4 5) (6 7 8))
user> (partition 3 3 (range 11 12) (range 11))
((0 1 2) (3 4 5) (6 7 8) (9 10 11))
user> (partition 3 3 (range 11 15) (range 11))
((0 1 2) (3 4 5) (6 7 8) (9 10 11))
user> (partition 3 4 (range 11 12) (range 11))
((0 1 2) (4 5 6) (8 9 10))
```

In this example, we first provide a padding sequence in the second statement as `(range 11 12)`, which only comprises of a single element. In the next statement, we supply a larger padding sequence, as `(range 11 15)`, but only the first item `11` from the padding sequence is actually used. In the last statement, we also supply a padding sequence but it is never used, as the `(range 11)` sequence is partitioned into sequences of 3 elements each with a step of `4`, which will have no remaining items.

The `partition-by` function requires a higher-order function to be supplied to it as the first argument, and will partition items in the supplied sequence based on the return value of applying the given function to each element in the sequence. The sequence is essentially partitioned by `partition-by` whenever the given function returns a new value, as shown here:

```
user> (partition-by #(= 0 %) [-2 -1 0 1 2])
((-2 -1) (0) (1 2))
user> (partition-by identity [-2 -1 0 1 2])
((-2) (-1) (0) (1) (2))
```

In this example, the second statement partitions the given sequence into sequences that each contain a single item as we have used the `identity` function, which simply returns its argument. For the `[-2 -1 0 1 2]` sequence, the `identity` function returns a new value for each item in the sequence and hence the resulting partitioned sequences all have a single element.

The `sort` function can be used to change the ordering of elements in a sequence. The general form of this function requires a function to compare items and a sequence of items to sort. The supplied function defaults to the `compare` function, whose behavior changes depending on the actual type of the items being compared:

```
user> (sort [3 1 2 0])
(0 1 2 3)
user> (sort > [3 1 2 0])
(3 2 1 0)
user> (sort ["Carol" "Alice" "Bob"])
("Alice" "Bob" "Carol")
```

If we intend to apply a particular function to each item in a sequence before performing the comparison in a `sort` form, we should consider using the `sort-by` function for a more concise expression. The `sort-by` function also accepts a function to perform the actual comparison, similar to the `sort` function. The `sort-by` function can be demonstrated as follows:

```
user> (sort #(compare (first %1) (first %2)) [[1 1] [2 2] [3 3]])
([1 1] [2 2] [3 3])
user> (sort-by first [[1 1] [2 2] [3 3]])
([1 1] [2 2] [3 3])
user> (sort-by first > [[1 1] [2 2] [3 3]])
([3 3] [2 2] [1 1])
```

In this example, the first and second statements both compare items after applying the `first` function to each item in the given sequence. The last statement passes the `>` function to the `sort-by` function, which returns the reverse of the sequence returned by the first two statements.

Filtering sequences

Sequences can also be *filtered*, that is transformed by removing some elements from the sequence. There are several standard functions to perform this task. The `keep` function can be used to remove values from a sequence that produces a `nil` value for a given function. The `keep` function requires a function and a sequence to be passed to it. The `keep` function will apply the given function to each item in the sequence and remove all values that produce `nil`, as shown here:

```
user> (keep #(if (odd? %) %) (range 10))
(1 3 5 7 9)
user> (keep seq [() [] '(1 2 3) [:a :b] nil])
((1 2 3) (:a :b))
```

In this example, the first statement removes all even numbers from the given sequence. In the second statement, the `seq` function is used to remove all empty collections from the given sequence.

A map or a set can also be passed as the first argument to the `keep` function since they can be treated as functions, as shown here:

```
user> (keep {:a 1, :b 2, :c 3} [:a :b :d])
(1 2)
user> (keep #{0 1 2 3} #{2 3 4 5})
(3 2)
```

The `filter` function can also be used to remove some elements from a given sequence. The `filter` function expects a predicate function to be passed to it along with the sequence to be filtered. The items for which the predicate function does not return a truthy value are removed from the result. The `filterv` function is identical to the filter function, except for the fact that it returns a vector instead of a list:

```
user> (filter even? (range 10))
(0 2 4 6 8)
user> (filterv even? (range 10))
[0 2 4 6 8]
```

Both the `filter` and `keep` functions have similar semantics. However, the primary distinction is that the `filter` function returns a subset of the original elements, whereas `keep` returns a sequence of non `nil` values that are returned by the function supplied to it, as shown in the following example:

```
user> (keep #(if (odd? %) %) (range 10))
(1 3 5 7 9)
user> (filter odd? (range 10))
(1 3 5 7 9)
```

Note that in this example, if we passed the `odd?` function to the `keep` form, it would return a list of `true` and `false` values, as these values are returned by the `odd?` function.

Also, a `for` macro with a `:when` clause is translated into an expression that uses the `filter` function, and hence a `for` form can also be used to remove elements from a sequence:

```
user> (for [x (range 10) :when (odd? x)] x)
(1 3 5 7 9)
```

A vector can be *sliced* using the `subvec` function. By sliced, we mean to say that a smaller vector is selected from the original vector depending on the values passed to the `subvec` function. The `subvec` function takes a vector as its first argument, followed by the index indicating the start of the sliced vector, and finally another optional index that indicates the end of the sliced vector, as shown here:

```
user> (subvec [0 1 2 3 4 5] 3)
[3 4 5]
user> (subvec [0 1 2 3 4 5] 3 5)
[3 4]
```

Maps can be filtered by their keys using the `select-keys` function. This function requires a map as the first argument and a vector of keys as a second argument to be passed to it. The vector of keys passed to this function indicates the key-value pairs to be included in the resulting map, as shown here:

```
user> (select-keys {:a 1 :b 2} [:a])
{:a 1}
user> (select-keys {:a 1 :b 2 :c 3} [:a :c])
{:c 3, :a 1}
```

Another way to select key-value pairs from a map is to use the `find` function, as shown here:

```
user> (find {:a 1 :b 2} :a)
[:a 1]
```

`take-while` and `drop-while` are analogous to the `take` and `drop` functions, and require a predicate to be passed to them, instead of the number of elements to take or drop. The `take-while` function takes elements as long as the predicate function returns a truthy value, and similarly the `drop-while` function will drop elements for the same condition:

```
user> (take-while neg? [-2 -1 0 1 2])
(-2 -1)
user> (drop-while neg? [-2 -1 0 1 2])
(0 1 2)
```

Lazy sequences

`lazy-seq` and `lazy-cat` are the most elementary constructs to create lazy sequences. The value returned by these functions will always have the type `clojure.lang.LazySeq`. The `lazy-seq` function is used to wrap a lazily computed expression in a `cons` form. This means that the rest of the sequence created by the `cons` form is lazily computed. For example, the `lazy-seq` function can be used to construct a lazy sequence representing the Fibonacci sequence as shown in *Example 1.8*:

```
(defn fibo-cons [a b]
  (cons a (lazy-seq (fibo-cons b (+ a b)))))
```

Example 1.8: A lazy sequence created using lazy-seq

The `fibo-cons` function requires two initial values, a and b, to be passed to it as the initial values, and returns a lazy sequence comprising the first value a and a lazily computed expression that uses the next two values in the sequence, that is, b and (+ a b). In this case, the `cons` form will return a lazy sequence, which can be handled using the `take` and `last` functions, as shown here:

```
user> (def fibo (fibo-cons 0N 1N))
#'user/fibo
user> (take 2 fibo)
(0N 1N)
user> (take 11 fibo)
(0N 1N 1N 2N 3N 5N 8N 13N 21N 34N 55N)
user> (last (take 10000 fibo))
207936...230626N
```

Note that the `fibo-cons` function from *Example 1.8* recursively calls itself without an explicit `recur` form, and yet it does not consume any stack space. This is because the values present in a lazy sequence are not stored in a call stack, and all the values are allocated on the process heap.

Another way to define a lazy Fibonacci sequence is by using the `lazy-cat` function. This function essentially concatenates all the sequences it is supplied in a lazy fashion. For example, consider the definition of the Fibonacci sequence in *Example 1.9*:

```
(def fibo-seq
  (lazy-cat [0N 1N] (map + fibo-seq (rest fibo-seq))))
```

Example 1.9: A lazy sequence created using lazy-cat

The `fibo-seq` variable from *Example 1.9* essentially calculates the Fibonacci sequence using a lazy composition of the `map`, `rest`, and `+` functions. Also, a sequence is required as the initial value, instead of a function as we saw in the definition of `fibo-cons` from *Example 1.8*. We can use the `nth` function to obtain a number from this sequence as follows:

```
user> (first fibo-seq)
0N
user> (nth fibo-seq 1)
1N
user> (nth fibo-seq 10)
55N
user> (nth fibo-seq 9999)
207936...230626N
```

As shown previously, `fibo-cons` and `fibo-seq` are concise and idiomatic representations of the infinite series of numbers in the Fibonacci sequence. Both of these definitions return identical values and do not cause an error due to stack consumption.

An interesting fact is that most of the standard functions that return sequences, such as `map` and `filter`, are inherently lazy. Any expression that is built using these functions is lazy, and hence never evaluated until needed. For example, consider the following expression that uses the `map` function:

```
user> (def xs (map println (range 3)))
#'user/xs
user> xs
0
1
2
(nil nil nil)
```

In this example, the `println` function is not called when we define the `xs` variable. However, once we try to print it in the REPL, the sequence is evaluated and the numbers are printed out by calling the `println` function. Note that `xs` evaluates to `(nil nil nil)` as the `println` function always returns `nil`.

Sometimes, it is necessary to eagerly evaluate a lazy sequence. The `doall` and `dorun` functions are used for this exact purpose. The `doall` function essentially forces evaluation of a lazy sequence along with any side effects of the evaluation. The value returned by `doall` is a list of all the elements in the given lazy sequence. For example, let's wrap the `map` expression from the previous example in a `doall` form, shown as follows:

```
user> (def xs (doall (map println (range 3))))
0
1
2
#'user/xs
user> xs
(nil nil nil)
```

Now, the numbers are printed out as soon as `xs` is defined, as we force evaluation using the `doall` function. The `dorun` function has similar semantics as the `doall` function, but it always returns `nil`. Hence, we can use the `dorun` function instead of `doall` when we are only interested in the side effects of evaluating the lazy sequence, and not the actual values in it. Another way to call a function with some side effects over all values in a collection is by using the `run!` function, which must be passed a function to call and a collection. The `run!` function always returns `nil`, just like the `dorun` form.

Using zippers

Now that we are well versed with sequences, let's briefly examine **zippers**. Zippers are essentially data structures that help in traversing and manipulating *trees*. In Clojure, any collection that contains nested collections is termed as a tree. A zipper can be thought of as a structure that contains location information about a tree. Zippers are not an extension of trees, but rather can be used to traverse and realize a tree.

The following namespaces must be included in your namespace declaration for the upcoming examples:

```
(ns my-namespace
  (:require [clojure.zip :as z]
            [clojure.xml :as xml]))
```

The following examples can be found in src/m_clj/c1/zippers.clj of the book's source code.

We can define a simple tree using vector literals, as shown here:

```
(def tree [:a [1 2 3] :b :c])
```

The vector `tree` is a tree, comprised of the nodes `:a`, `[1 2 3]`, `:b`, and `:c`. We can use the `vector-zip` function to create a zipper from the vector `tree` as follows:

```
(def root (z/vector-zip tree))
```

The variable `root` defined previously is a zipper and contains location information for traversing the given tree. Note that the `vector-zip` function is simply a combination of the standard `seq` function and the `seq-zip` function from the `clojure.zip` namespace. Hence, for trees that are represented as sequences, we should use the `seq-zip` function instead. Also, all other functions in the `clojure.zip` namespace expect their first argument to be a zipper.

To traverse the zipper, we must use the `clojure.zip/next` function, which returns the next node in the zipper. We can easily iterate over all the nodes in the zipper using a composition of the `iterate` and `clojure.zip/next` functions, as shown here:

```
user> (def tree-nodes (iterate z/next root))
#'user/tree-nodes
user> (nth tree-nodes 0)
[[:a [1 2 3] :b :c] nil]
user> (nth tree-nodes 1)
[:a {:l [], :pnodes ... }]
user> (nth tree-nodes 2)
[[1 2 3] {:l [:a], :pnodes ... }]
user> (nth tree-nodes 3)
[1 {:l [], :pnodes ... }]
```

As shown previously, the first node of the zipper represents the original tree itself. Also, the zipper will contain some extra information, other than the value contained in the current node, which is useful in navigating across the given tree. In fact, the return value of the next function is also a zipper. Once we have completely traversed the given tree, a zipper pointing to the root of the tree will be returned by the next function. Note that some information in a zipper has been truncated from the preceding REPL output for the sake of readability.

To navigate to the adjacent nodes in a given zipper, we can use the down, up, left, and right functions. All of these functions return a zipper, as shown here:

```
user> (-> root z/down)
[:a {:1 [], :pnodes ... }]
user> (-> root z/down z/right)
[[1 2 3] {:1 [:a], :pnodes ... }]
user> (-> root z/down z/right z/up)
[[:a [1 2 3] :b :c] nil]
user> (-> root z/down z/right z/right)
[:b {:1 [:a [1 2 3]], :pnodes ... }]
user> (-> root z/down z/right z/left)
[:a {:1 [], :pnodes ... }]
```

The down, up, left, and right functions change the location of the root zipper in the [:a [1 2 3] :b :c] tree, as shown in the following illustration:

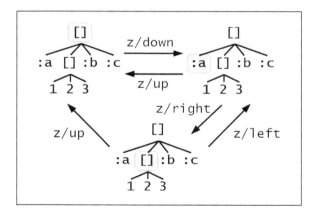

The preceding diagram shows a zipper at three different locations in the given tree. Initially, the location of the zipper is at the root of the tree, which is the entire vector. The down function moves the location to the first child node in the tree. The left and right functions move the location of the zipper to other nodes at the same level or depth in the tree. The up function moves the zipper to the parent of the node pointed to by the zipper's current location.

To obtain the node representing the current location of a zipper in a tree, we must use the `node` function, as follows:

```
user> (-> root z/down z/right z/right z/node)
:b
user> (-> root z/down z/right z/left z/node)
:a
```

To navigate to the extreme left or right of a tree, we can use the `leftmost` and `rightmost` functions, respectively, as shown here:

```
user> (-> root z/down z/rightmost z/node)
:c
user> (-> root z/down z/rightmost z/leftmost z/node)
:a
```

The `lefts` and `rights` functions return the nodes that are present to the left and right, respectively, of a given zipper, as follows:

```
user> (-> root z/down z/rights)
([1 2 3] :b :c)
user> (-> root z/down z/lefts)
nil
```

As the `:a` node is the leftmost element in the tree, the `rights` function will return all of the other nodes in the tree when passed a zipper that has `:a` as the current location. Similarly, the `lefts` function for the zipper at the `:a` node will return an empty value, that is `nil`.

The `root` function can be used to obtain the root of a given zipper. It will return the original tree used to construct the zipper, as shown here:

```
user> (-> root z/down z/right z/root)
[:a [1 2 3] :b :c]
user> (-> root z/down z/right r/left z/root)
[:a [1 2 3] :b :c]
```

The `path` function can be used to obtain the path from the root element of a tree to the current location of a given zipper, as shown here:

```
user> (def e (-> root z/down z/right z/down))
#'user/e
user> (z/node e)
1
user> (z/path e)
[[:a [1 2 3] :b :c]
 [1 2 3]]
```

In the preceding example, the path of the 1 node in `tree` is represented by a vector containing the entire tree and the subtree [1 2 3]. This means that to get to the 1 node, we must pass through the root and the subtree [1 2 3].

Now that we have covered the basics of navigating across trees, let's see how we can modify the original tree. The `insert-child` function can be used to insert a given element into a tree as follows:

```
user> (-> root (z/insert-child :d) z/root)
[:d :a [1 2 3] :b :c]
user> (-> root z/down z/right (z/insert-child 0) z/root)
[:a [0 1 2 3] :b :c]
```

We can also remove a node from the zipper using the `remove` function. Also, the `replace` function can be used to replace a given node in a zipper:

```
user> (-> root z/down z/remove z/root)
[[1 2 3] :b :c]
user> (-> root z/down (z/replace :d) z/root)
[:d [1 2 3] :b :c]
```

One of the most noteworthy examples of tree-like data is XML. Since zippers are great at handling trees, they also allow us to easily traverse and modify XML content. Note that Clojure already provides the `xml-seq` function to convert XML data into a sequence. However, treating an XML document as a sequence has many strange implications.

One of the main disadvantages of using `xml-seq` is that there is no easy way to get to the root of the document from a node if we are iterating over a sequence. Also, `xml-seq` only helps us iterate over the XML content; it doesn't deal with modifying it. These limitations can be overcome using zippers, as we will see in the upcoming example.

For example, consider the following XML document:

```
<countries>
  <country name="England">
    <city>Birmingham</city>
    <city>Leeds</city>
    <city capital="true">London</city>
  </country>
  <country name="Germany">
    <city capital="true">Berlin</city>
    <city>Frankfurt</city>
    <city>Munich</city>
  </country>
```

```
<country name="France">
  <city>Cannes</city>
  <city>Lyon</city>
  <city capital="true">Paris</city>
</country>
</countries>
```

The document shown above contains countries and cities represented as XML nodes. Each country has a number of cities, and a single city as its capital. Some information, such as the name of the country and a flag indicating whether a city is a capital, is encoded in the XML attributes of the nodes.

 The following example expects the XML content shown previously to be present in the `resources/data/sample.xml` file, relative to the root of your Leiningen project.

Let's define a function to find out all the capital cities in the document, as shown in *Example 1.10*:

```
(defn is-capital-city? [n]
  (and (= (:tag n) :city)
       (= "true" (:capital (:attrs n))))))

(defn find-capitals [file-path]
  (let [xml-root (z/xml-zip (xml/parse file-path))
        xml-seq (iterate z/next (z/next xml-root))]
    (->> xml-seq
         (take-while #(not= (z/root xml-root) (z/node %)))
         (map z/node)
         (filter is-capital-city?)
         (mapcat :content))))
```

Example 1.10: Querying XML with zippers

Firstly, we must note that the `parse` function from the `clojure.xml` namespace reads an XML document and returns a map representing the document. Each node in this map is another map with the `:tag`, `:attrs`, and `:content` keys associated with the XML node's tag name, attributes, and content respectively.

In *Example 1.10*, we first define a simple function, `is-capital-city?`, to determine whether a given XML node has the `city` tag, represented as `:city`. The `is-capital-city?` function also checks whether the XML node contains the `capital` attribute, represented as `:capital`. If the value of the `capital` attribute of a given node is the `"true"` string, then the `is-capital-city?` function returns `true`.

The `find-capitals` function performs most of the heavy lifting in this example. This function first parses XML documents present at the supplied path `file-path`, and then converts it into a zipper using the `xml-zip` function. We then iterate over the zipper using the `next` function until we arrive back at the root node, which is checked by the `take-while` function. We then map the `node` function over the resulting sequence of zippers using the `map` function, and apply the `filter` function to find the capital cities among all the nodes. Finally, we use the `mapcat` function to obtain the XML content of the filtered nodes and flatten the resulting sequence of vectors into a single list.

When supplied a file containing the XML content we described earlier, the `find-capitals` function returns the names of all capital cities in the document:

```
user> (find-capitals "resources/data/sample.xml")
("London" "Berlin" "Paris")
```

As demonstrated previously, zippers are apt for dealing with trees and hierarchical data such as XML. More generally, sequences are a great abstraction for collections and several forms of data, and Clojure provides us with a huge toolkit for dealing with sequences. There are several more functions that handle sequences in the Clojure language, and you are encouraged to explore them on your own.

Working with pattern matching

In this section, we will examine *pattern matching* in Clojure. Typically, functions that use conditional logic can be defined using the `if`, `when`, or `cond` forms. Pattern matching allows us to define such functions by declaring patterns of the literal values of their parameters. While this idea may appear quite rudimentary, it is a very useful and powerful one, as we shall see in the upcoming examples. Pattern matching is also a foundational programming construct in other functional programming languages.

In Clojure, there is no pattern matching support for functions and forms in the core language. However, it is a common notion among Lisp programmers that we can easily modify or extend the language using macros. Clojure takes this approach as well, and thus pattern matching is made possible using the `match` and `defun` macros. These macros are implemented in the `core.match` (https://github.com/clojure/core.match) and `defun` (https://github.com/killme2008/defun) community libraries. Both of these libraries are also supported on ClojureScript.

The following library dependencies are required for the upcoming examples:

```
[org.clojure/core.match "0.2.2"
  :exclusions [org.clojure/tools.analyzer.jvm]]
[defun "0.2.0-RC"]
```

Also, the following namespaces must be included in your namespace declaration:

```
(ns my-namespace
  (:require [clojure.core.match :as m]
            [defun :as f]))
```

The following examples can be found in `src/m_clj/c1/match.clj` of the book's source code.

Let's consider a simple example that we can model using pattern matching. The XOR logic function returns a true value only when its arguments are exclusive of each other, that is, when they have differing values. In other words, the XOR function will return false when both of its arguments have the same values. We can easily define such a function using the `match` macro, as shown in *Example 1.11*:

```
(defn xor [x y]
  (m/match [x y]
           [true true] false
           [false true] true
           [true false] true
           [false false] false))
```

Example 1.11: Pattern matching using the match macro

The `xor` function from *Example 1.11* simply matches its arguments, x and y, against a given set of patterns, such as `[true true]` and `[true false]`. If both the arguments are `true` or `false`, then the function returns `false`, or else it returns `true`. It's a concise definition that relies on the values of the supplied arguments, rather than the use of conditional forms such as `if` and `when`. The `xor` function can be defined alternatively, and even more concisely, by the `defun` macro, as shown in *Example 1.12*:

```
(f/defun xor
  ([true true] false)
  ([false true] true)
  ([true false] true)
  ([false false] false))
```

Example 1.12: Pattern match using the defun macro

The definition of the `xor` function that uses the `defun` macro simply declares the actual values as its arguments. The expression to be returned is thus determined by the values of its inputs. Note that the `defun` macro rewrites the definition of the `xor` function to use the `match` macro. Hence, all patterns supported by the `match` macro can also be used with the `defun` macro. Both the definitions of the `xor` function, from *Example 1.11* and *Example 1.12*, work as expected, as shown here:

```
user> (xor true true)
false
user> (xor true false)
true
user> (xor false true)
true
user> (xor false false)
false
```

The `xor` function will throw an exception if we try to pass values that have not been declared as a pattern:

```
user> (xor 0 0)
IllegalArgumentException No matching clause: [0 0] user/xor ...
```

We can define a simple function to compute the nth number of the Fibonacci sequence using the `defun` macro, as shown in *Example 1.13*:

```
(f/defun fibo
  ([0] 0N)
  ([1] 1N)
  ([n] (+ (fibo (- n 1))
          (fibo (- n 2)))))
```

Example 1.13: A recursive function with pattern matching

Note the use of the variable n in the function's pattern rules. This signifies that any value other than 0 and 1 will match with the pattern definition that uses n. The `fibo` function defined in *Example 1.13* does indeed calculate the nth Fibonacci sequence, as shown here:

```
user> (fibo 0)
0N
user> (fibo 1)
1N
user> (fibo 10)
55N
```

However, the definition of `fibo`, shown in *Example 1.13*, cannot be optimized by tail call elimination. This is due to the fact that the definition of `fibo` is tree recursive. By this, we mean to say that the expression `(+ (fibo ...) (fibo ...))` requires two recursive calls in order to be evaluated completely. In fact, if we replace the recursive calls to the `fibo` function with `recur` expressions, the resulting function won't compile. It is fairly simple to convert tree recursion into linear recursion, as shown in *Example 1.14*:

```
(f/defun fibo-recur
  ([a b 0] a)
  ([a b n] (recur b (+ a b) (dec n)))
  ([n] (recur 0N 1N n)))
```

Example 1.14: A tail recursive function with pattern matching

It is fairly obvious from the definition of the `fibo-recur` function, from *Example 1.14*, that it is indeed tail recursive. This function does not consume any stack space, and can be safely called with large values of n, as shown here:

```
user> (fibo-recur 0)
0N
user> (fibo-recur 1)
1N
user> (fibo-recur 10)
55N
user> (fibo-recur 9999)
207936...230626N
```

As the preceding examples show us, pattern matching is a powerful tool in functional programming. Functions that are defined using pattern matching are not only correct and expressive, but can also achieve good performance. In this respect, the `core.match` and `defun` libraries are indispensible tools in the Clojure ecosystem.

Summary

In this chapter, we introduced a few programming constructs that can be used in the Clojure language. We've explored recursion using the `recur`, `loop`, and `trampoline` forms. We've also studied the basics of sequences and laziness, while describing the various functions in the Clojure language that are used in creating, transforming, and filtering sequences. Next, we had a look at zippers, and how they can be used to idiomatically handle trees and hierarchical data such as XML. Finally, we briefly explored pattern matching using the `core.match` and `defun` libraries.

In the next chapter, we will explore concurrency and parallelism. We will study the various data structures and functions that allow us to leverage these concepts in Clojure in ample detail.

2
Orchestrating Concurrency and Parallelism

Let's now examine how concurrent and parallel programming are supported in Clojure. The term *concurrent programming* refers to managing more than one task at the same time. *Parallel programming* or *parallelism*, on the other hand, deals with executing multiple tasks at the same time. The distinction between these two terms is that concurrency is about how we structure and synchronize multiple tasks, and parallelism is more about running multiple tasks in parallel over multiple cores. The main advantages of using concurrency and parallelism can be elaborated as follows:

- Concurrent programs can perform multiple tasks simultaneously. For example, a desktop application can have a single task for handling user interaction and another task for handling I/O and network communication. A single processor can be shared among several tasks. Processor utilization is thus more effective in concurrent programs.

- Parallel programs take advantage of having multiple processor cores. This means that such programs can be made to run faster by executing them on a system with more processor cores. Also, tasks that are computationally expensive can be parallelized to complete in a lesser amount of time.

In this chapter, we will:

- Explore how we can create and synchronize tasks that run concurrently
- See how to deal with a shared state between concurrent tasks
- Examine how computations can be parallelized and how we can control the amount of parallelism used to perform these computations

Managing concurrent tasks

Clojure has a couple of handy constructs that allow us to define concurrent tasks. A *thread* is the most elementary abstraction of a task that runs in the background. In the formal sense, a thread is simply a sequence of instructions that can be scheduled for execution. A task that runs in the background of a program is said to execute on a separate thread. Threads will be scheduled for execution on a specific processor by the underlying operating system. Most modern operating systems allow a process to have several threads of execution. The technique of managing multiple threads in a single process is termed as *multithreading*.

While Clojure does support the use of threads, concurrent tasks can be modeled in more elegant ways using other constructs. Let's explore the different ways in which we can define concurrent tasks.

 The following examples can be found in `src/m_clj/c2/concurrent.clj` of the book's source code.

Using delays

A *delay* can be used to define a task whose execution is delayed, or *deferred*, until it is necessary. A delay is only run once, and its result is cached. We simply need to wrap the instructions of a given task in a `delay` form to define a delay, as shown in *Example 2.1*:

```
(def delayed-1
  (delay
   (Thread/sleep 3000)
   (println "3 seconds later ...")
   1))
```

Example 2.1: A delayed value

 The static `Thread/sleep` method suspends execution of the current thread of execution for a given number of milliseconds, which is passed as the first argument to this method. We can optionally specify the number of nanoseconds by which the current thread must be suspended as the second argument to the `Thread/sleep` method.

The `delay` form in *Example 2.1* simply sleeps for `3000` milliseconds, prints a string and returns the value `1`. However, it is not yet *realized*, in the sense that, it is has not been executed yet. The `realized?` predicate can be used to check whether a delay has been executed, as shown here:

```
user> (realized? delayed-1)
false
user> (realized? delayed-1)          ; after 3 seconds
false
```

 We can check whether a value is a delay using the `delay?` predicate.

The body expressions in a `delay` form will not be executed until the value returned by it is actually used. We can obtain the value contained in a delay by dereferencing it using the at-the-rate symbol (`@`):

```
user> @delayed-1
3 seconds later ...
1
user> (realized? delayed-1)
true
```

 Using the at-the-rate symbol (`@`) to dereference a value is the same as using the `deref` function. For example, the expression `@x` is equivalent to `(deref x)`.

The `deref` function also has a variant form that accepts three arguments—a value to dereference, the number of milliseconds to wait before timing out, and a value that will be returned in case of a timeout.

As shown previously, the expression `@delayed-1` returns the value `1`, after a pause of 3 seconds. Now, the call to `realized?` returns `true`. Also, the value returned by the expression `@delayed-1` will be cached, as shown here:

```
user> @delayed-1
1
```

It is thus evident that the expression `@delayed-1` will be blocked for 3 seconds, will print a string, and return a value only once.

 Another way to execute a delay is by using the `force` function, which takes a delay as an argument. This function executes a given delay if needed, and returns the value of the delay's inner expression.

Delays are quite handy for representing values or tasks that need not be executed until required. However, a delay will always be executed in the same thread in which it is dereferenced. In other words, delays are *synchronous*. Hence, delays aren't really a solution for representing tasks that run in the background.

Using futures and promises

As we mentioned earlier, threads are the most elementary way of dealing with background tasks. In Clojure, all functions implement the `clojure.lang.IFn` interface, which in turn extends the `java.lang.Runnable` interface. This means that any Clojure function can be invoked in a separate thread of execution. For example, consider the function in *Example 2.2*:

```
(defn wait-3-seconds []
  (Thread/sleep 3000)
  (println)
  (println "3 seconds later ...")))
```

Example 2.2: A function that waits for 3 seconds

The `wait-3-seconds` function in *Example 2.2* waits for `3000` milliseconds and prints a new line and a string. We can execute this function on a separate thread by constructing a `java.lang.Thread` object from it using the `Thread.` constructor. The resulting object can then be scheduled for execution in the background by invoking its `.start` method, as shown here:

```
user> (.start (Thread. wait-3-seconds))
nil
user>
3 seconds later ...

user>
```

The call to the `.start` method returns immediately to the REPL prompt. The `wait-3-seconds` function gets executed in the background, and prints to standard output in the REPL after 3 seconds. While using threads does indeed allow execution of tasks in the background, they have a couple shortcomings:

- There is no obvious way to obtain a return value from a function that is executed on a separate thread.

- Also, using the `Thread.` and `.start` functions is essentially interop with the underlying JVM. Thus, using these functions in a program's code would mean that the program could be run only on the JVM. We essentially lock our program into a single platform, and the program can't be run on any of the other platforms that Clojure supports.

A *future* is a more idiomatic way to represent a task that is executed in a separate thread. Futures can be concisely defined as values that will be realized in the future. A future represents a task that performs a certain computation and returns the result of the computation. We can create a future using the `future` form, as shown in *Example 2.3*:

```
(defn val-as-future [n secs]
  (future
    (Thread/sleep (* secs 1000))
    (println)
    (println (str secs " seconds later ..."))
    n))
```

Example 2.3: A future that sleeps for some time and returns a value

The `val-as-future` function defined in *Example 2.3* invokes a future that waits for the number of seconds specified by the argument `secs`, prints a new line and a string, and finally returns the supplied value n. A call to the `val-as-future` function will return a future immediately, and a string will be printed after the specified number of seconds, as shown here:

```
user> (def future-1 (val-as-future 1 3))
#'user/future-1
user>
3 seconds later ...

user>
```

The `realized?` and `future-done?` predicates can be used to check whether a future has completed, as shown here:

```
user> (realized? future-1)
true
user> (future-done? future-1)
true
```

 We can check whether a value is a future using the `future?` predicate.

A future that is being executed can be stopped by using the `future-cancel` function, which takes a future as its only argument and returns a Boolean value indicating whether the supplied future was cancelled, as depicted here:

```
user> (def future-10 (val-as-future 10 10))
#'user/future-10
user> (future-cancel future-10)
true
```

We can check whether a future has been cancelled using the `future-cancelled?` function. Also, dereferencing a future after it has been cancelled will cause an exception, as shown here:

```
user> (future-cancelled? future-10)
true
user> @future-10
CancellationException    java.util.concurrent.FutureTask.report
(FutureTask.java:121)
```

Now that we are familiar with the notion of representing tasks as futures, let's talk about how multiple futures can be synchronized. Firstly, we can use *promises* to synchronize two or more futures. A promise, created using the `promise` function, is simply a value that can be set only once. A promise is set, or *delivered*, using the `deliver` form. Subsequent calls to the `deliver` form on a promise that has been delivered will not have any effect, and will return `nil`. When a promise is not delivered, dereferencing it using the `@` symbol or the `deref` form will block the current thread of execution. Hence, a promise can be used with a future in order to pause the execution of the future until a certain value is available. The `promise` and `deliver` forms can be quickly demonstrated as follows:

```
user> (def p (promise))
#'user/p
user> (deliver p 100)
#<core$promise$reify__6363@1792b00: 100>
user> (deliver p 200)
nil
user> @p
100
```

As shown in the preceding output, the first call to the `deliver` form using the promise p sets the value of the promise to `100`, and the second call to the `deliver` form has no effect.

The `realized?` predicate can be used to check whether a promise instance has been delivered.

Another way to synchronize concurrent tasks is by using the `locking` form. The `locking` form allows only a single task to hold a lock variable, or a *monitor*, at any given point in time. Any value can be treated as a monitor. When a monitor is held, or *locked*, by a certain task, any other concurrent tasks that try to acquire the monitor are blocked until the monitor is available. We can thus use the `locking` form to synchronize two or more concurrent futures, as shown in *Example 2.4*:

```clojure
(defn lock-for-2-seconds []
  (let [lock (Object.)
        task-1 (fn []
                 (future
                   (locking lock
                     (Thread/sleep 2000)
                     (println "Task 1 completed"))))
        task-2 (fn []
                 (future
                   (locking lock
                     (Thread/sleep 1000)
                     (println "Task 2 completed"))))]
    (task-1)
    (task-2)))
```

Example 2.4: Using the locking form

The lock-for-2-seconds function in *Example 2.4* creates two functions, task-1 and task-2, which both invoke futures that try to acquire a monitor, represented by the variable lock. In this example, we use a boring java.lang.Object instance as a monitor for synchronizing two futures. The future invoked by the task-1 function sleeps for two seconds, whereas the future called by the task-2 function sleeps for a single second. The future called by the task-1 function is observed to complete first as the future invoked by the task-2 function will not be executed until the locking form in the future obtains the monitor lock, as shown in the following output:

```clojure
user> (lock-for-2-seconds)
[#<core$future_call$reify__6320@19ed4e9: :pending>
 #<core$future_call$reify__6320@ac35d5: :pending>]
user>
Task 1 completed
Task 2 completed
```

We can thus use the locking form to synchronize multiple futures. However, the locking form must be used sparingly as careless use of it could result in a deadlock among concurrent tasks. Concurrent tasks are generally synchronized to pass around a shared state. Clojure allows us to avoid using the locking form and any possible deadlocks through the use of reference types to represent shared state, as we will examine in the following section.

Managing state

A program can be divided into several parts which can execute concurrently. It is often necessary to share data or state among these concurrently running tasks. Thus, we arrive at the notion of having multiple observers for some data. If the data gets modified, we must ensure that the changes are visible to all observers. For example, suppose there are two threads that read data from a common variable. This data gets modified by one thread, and the change must be propagated to the other thread as soon as possible to avoid inconsistencies.

Programming languages that support mutability handle this problem by locking over a monitor, as we demonstrated with the `locking` form, and maintaining local copies of the data. In such languages, a variable is just a container for data. Whenever a concurrent task accesses a variable that is shared with other tasks, it copies the data from the variable. This is done in order to prevent unwanted overwriting of the variable by other tasks while a task is performing a computation on it. In case the variable is actually modified, a given task will still have its own copy of the shared data. If there are two concurrent tasks that access a given variable, they could simultaneously modify the variable and thus both of the tasks would have an inconsistent view of the data in the given variable. This problem is termed as a *race condition*, and must be avoided when dealing with concurrent tasks. For this reason, monitors are used to synchronize access to shared data. However, this methodology is not really *deterministic*, in the sense that we cannot easily reason about the actual data contained in a variable at a given point in time. This makes developing concurrent programs quite cumbersome in programming languages that use mutability.

Like other functional programming languages, Clojure tackles this problem using *immutability* — all values are immutable by default and cannot be changed. To model mutable state, there is the notion of *identity*, *state*, and *time*:

- An *identity* is anything that is associated with a changing state. At a given point in time, an identity has a single state.
- *State* is the value associated with an identity at a given point in time.
- *Time* defines an ordering between the states of an identity.

Programs that actually use state can thus be divided into two layers. One layer is purely functional and has nothing to do with state. The other layer constitutes parts of the program that actually require the use of mutable state. This decomposition allows us to isolate the parts of a program that actually require the use of mutable state.

There are several ways to define mutable state in Clojure, and the data structures used for this purpose are termed as *reference types*. A reference type is essentially a mutable reference to an immutable value. Hence, the reference has to be changed explicitly, and the actual value contained in a reference type cannot be modified in any way. Reference types can be characterized in the following ways:

- The change of state in some reference types can either be *synchronous* or *asynchronous*. For example, suppose we are writing data to a file. A synchronous write operation would block the caller until all data is written to the file. On the other hand, an asynchronous write operation would start off a background task to write all data to the file and return to the caller immediately.

- Mutation of a reference type can be performed in either a *coordinated* or an *independent* manner. By coordinated, we mean that state can only be modified within transactions that are managed by some underlying system, which is quite similar to the way a database works. A reference type that mutates independently, however, can be changed without the explicit use of a transaction.

- Changes in some state can be visible to only the thread in which the change occurs, or they could be visible to all threads in the current process.

We will now explore the various reference types that can be used to represent mutable state in Clojure.

Using vars

Vars are used to manage state that is changed within the scope of a thread. We essentially define vars that can have state, and then bind them to different values. The modified value of a var is only visible to the current thread of execution. Hence, vars are a form of the *thread-local* state.

 The following examples can be found in `src/m_clj/c2/vars.clj` of the book's source code.

Dynamic vars are defined using the `def` form with the `:dynamic` meta keyword. If we omit the `:dynamic` metadata, it would be the same as defining an ordinary variable, or a static var, using a `def` form. It's a convention that all dynamic var names must start and end with the asterisk character (`*`), but this is not mandatory. For example, let's define a dynamic variable shown as follows:

```
(def ^:dynamic *thread-local-state* [1 2 3])
```

The `*thread-local-state*` variable defined in *Example 2.5* represents a thread-local var that can change dynamically. We have initialized the var `*thread-local-state*` with the vector `[1 2 3]`, but it's not really required. In case an initial value is not supplied to a `def` form, then the resulting variable is termed as an *unbound* var. While the state of a var is confined to the current thread, its declaration is global to the current namespace. In other words, a var defined with the `def` form will be visible to all threads invoked from the current namespace, but the state of the variable is local to the thread in which it is changed. Thus, vars using the `def` form are also termed as *global vars*.

Normally, the `def` form creates a static var, which can only be redefined by using another `def` form. Static vars can also be redefined within a scope or context using the `with-redefs` and `with-redefs-fn` forms. A dynamic var, however, can be set to a new value after it has been defined by using the `binding` form, shown as follows:

```
user> (binding [*thread-local-state* [10 20]]
        (map #(* % %) *thread-local-state*))
(100 400)
user> (map #(* % %) *thread-local-state*)
(1 4 9)
```

In this example, the `binding` form changes the value contained in the `*thread-local-state*` var to the vector `[10 20]`. This causes the `map` form in the example to return a different value when called without a `binding` form surrounding it. Thus, the `binding` form can be used to temporarily change the state of the vars supplied to it.

The Clojure namespace system will resolve free symbols, or rather variable names, to their values. This process of resolving a variable name to a namespace qualified symbol is termed as *interning*. Also, a `def` form will first look for an existing global var depending on the symbol it is passed, and will create one if it hasn't been defined yet. The `var` form can be used to obtain the fully qualified name of a variable, instead of its current value, as shown here:

```
user> *thread-local-state*
[1 2 3]
user> (var *thread-local-state*)
#'user/*thread-local-state*
```

 Using the `#'` symbol is the same as using the `var` form. For example, `#'x` is equivalent to `(var x)`.

The `with-bindings` form is another way to rebind vars. This form accepts a map of var and value pairs as its first argument, followed by the body of the form, shown as follows:

```
user> (with-bindings {#'*thread-local-state* [10 20]}
        (map #(* % %) *thread-local-state*))
(100 400)
user> (with-bindings {(var *thread-local-state*) [10 20]}
        (map #(* % %) *thread-local-state*))
(100 400)
```

We can check if a var is bound to any value in the current thread of execution using the `thread-bound?` predicate, which requires a var to be passed as its only argument:

```
user> (def ^:dynamic *unbound-var*)
#'user/*unbound-var*
user> (thread-bound? (var *unbound-var*))
false
user> (binding [*unbound-var* 1]
        (thread-bound? (var *unbound-var*)))
true
```

We can also define vars that are not interned, or *local vars*, using the `with-local-vars` form. These vars will not be resolved by the namespace system, and have to be accessed manually using the `var-get` and `var-set` functions. These functions can thus be used to create and access mutable variables, as shown in *Example 2.5*.

Using the at-the-rate symbol (@) with a non-interned var is the same as using the `var-get` function. For example, if x is a non-interned var, @x is equivalent to `(var-get x)`.

```
(defn factorial [n]
  (with-local-vars [i n acc 1]
    (while (> @i 0)
      (var-set acc (* @acc @i))
      (var-set i (dec @i)))
    (var-get acc)))
```

Example 2.5: Mutable variables using the with-local-vars form

The `factorial` function defined in *Example 2.5* calculated the factorial of n using two mutable local vars i and acc, which are initialized with the values n and 1 respectively. Note that the code in this function exhibits an imperative style of programming, in which the state of the variables i and acc is manipulated using the `var-get` and `var-set` functions.

We can check whether a value has been created through a `with-local-vars` form using the `var?` predicate.

Using refs

A **Software Transactional Memory** (**STM**) system can also be used to model mutable state. STM essentially treats mutable state as a tiny database that resides in a program's memory. Clojure provides an STM implementation through *refs*, and they can only be changed within a transaction. Refs are a reference type that represent *synchronous* and *coordinated* state.

 The following examples can be found in `src/m_clj/c2/refs.clj` of the book's source code.

We can create a ref by using the `ref` function, which requires a single argument to indicate the initial state of the ref. For example, we can create a ref as follows:

```
(def state (ref 0))
```

The variable `state` defined here represents a ref with the initial value of `0`. We can dereference `state` using `@` or `deref` to obtain the value contained in it.

In order to modify a ref, we must start a transaction by using the `dosync` form. If two concurrent tasks invoke transactions using the `dosync` form simultaneously, then the transaction that completes first will update the ref successfully. The transaction which completes later will be retried until it completes successfully. Thus, I/O and other side-effects must be avoided within a `dosync` form, as it can be retried. Within a transaction, we can modify the value of a ref using the `ref-set` function. This function takes two arguments—a ref and the value that represents the new state of the ref. The `ref-set` function can be used to modify a ref as follows:

```
user> @state
0
user> (dosync (ref-set state 1))
1
user> @state
1
```

Initially, the expression `@state` returns `0`, which is the initial state of the ref `state`. The value returned by this expression changes after the call to `ref-set` within the `dosync` form.

We can obtain the latest value contained in a ref by using the `ensure` function. This function returns the latest value of a ref, and has to be called within a transaction. For example, the expression `(ensure state)`, when called within a transaction initiated by a `dosync` form, will return the latest value of the ref `state` in the transaction.

A more idiomatic way to modify a given ref is by using the `alter` and `commute` functions. Both these functions require a ref and a function to be passed to it as arguments. The `alter` and `commute` functions will apply the supplied function to the value contained in a given ref, and save the resulting value into the ref. We can also specify additional arguments to pass to the supplied function. For example, we can modify the state of the ref `state` using `alter` and `commute` as follows:

```
user> @state
1
user> (dosync (alter state + 2))
3
user> (dosync (commute state + 2))
5
```

The preceding transactions with the `alter` and `commute` forms will save the value `(+ @state 2)` into the ref `state`. The main difference between `alter` and `commute` is that a `commute` form must be preferred when the supplied function is *commutative*. This means two successive calls of the function supplied to a `commute` form must produce the same result regardless of the ordering among the two calls. Using the `commute` form is considered an optimization over the `alter` form in which we are not concerned with the ordering among concurrent transactions on a given ref.

The `ref-set`, `alter`, and `commute` functions all return the new value contained in the supplied ref. Also, these functions will throw an error if they are not called within a `dosync` form.

A mutation performed by the `alter` and `commute` forms can also be validated. This is achieved using the `:validator` key option when creating a ref, as shown here:

```
user> (def r (ref 1 :validator pos?))
#'user/r
user> (dosync (alter r (fn [_] -1)))
IllegalStateException Invalid reference state
clojure.lang.ARef.validate (ARef.java:33)
user> (dosync (alter r (fn [_] 2)))
2
```

As shown previously, the ref r throws an exception when we try to change its state to a negative value. This is because the pos? function is used to validate the new state of the ref. Note that the :validator key option can be used with other reference types as well. We can also set the validation function of a ref that was created without a :validator key option using the set-validator! function.

 The :validator key option and the set-validator! function can be used with *all* reference types. The supplied validation function must return false or throw an exception to indicate a validation error.

The *dining philosophers problem* depicts the use of synchronization primitives to share resources. The problem can be defined as follows: five philosophers are seated on a round table to eat spaghetti, and each philosopher requires two forks to eat from his plate of spaghetti. There are five forks on the table, placed in between the five philosophers. A philosopher will first have to pick up a fork from his left side as well as one from his right side before he can eat. When a philosopher cannot obtain the two forks to his left and right side, he must wait until both the forks are available. After a philosopher is done eating his spaghetti, he will think for some time, thereby allowing the other philosophers to use the forks that he used. The solution to this problem requires that all philosophers share the forks among them, and none of the philosophers starve due to being unable to get two forks. The five philosophers' plates and forks are placed on the table as illustrated in the following diagram:

A philosopher must obtain exclusive access to the forks on his left and right side before he starts eating. If both the forks are unavailable, the philosopher must wait for some time for either one of the forks to be free, and retry obtaining the forks. This way, each philosopher can access the forks in tandem with the other philosophers and avoid starvation.

Generally, this solution can be implemented by using synchronization primitives to access the available forks. Refs allow us to implement a solution to the dining philosophers problem without the use of any synchronization primitives. We will now demonstrate how we can implement and simulate a solution to this problem in Clojure. Firstly, we will have to define the states of a fork and a philosopher as refs, as shown in *Example 2.6*:

```
(defn make-fork []
  (ref true))

(defn make-philosopher [name forks food]
  (ref {:name name
        :forks forks
        :eating? false
        :food food}))
```

Example 2.6: The dining philosophers problem using refs

The `make-fork` and `make-philosopher` functions create refs to represent the states of a fork and a philosopher, respectively. A fork is simply the state of a Boolean value, indicating whether it is available or not. And a philosopher, created by the `make-philosopher` function, is a map encapsulated as a state, which has the following keys:

- The `:name` key contains the name of a philosopher that is a string value.
- The `:forks` key points to the forks on the left and the right side of a philosopher. Each fork will be a ref created by the `make-fork` function.
- The `:eating?` key indicates whether a philosopher is eating at the moment. It is a Boolean value.
- The `:food` key represents the amount of food available to a philosopher. For simplicity, we will treat this value as an integer.

Now, let's define some primitive operations to help in handling forks, as shown in *Example 2.7*:

```
(defn has-forks? [p]
  (every? true? (map ensure (:forks @p))))

(defn update-forks [p]
  (doseq [f (:forks @p)]
    (commute f not))
  p)
```

Example 2.7: The dining philosophers problem using refs (continued)

The `has-forks?` function defined previously checks whether both the forks that are placed to the left and right of a given philosopher ref p are available. The `update-forks` function will modify the state of both the associated forks of a philosopher ref p using a `commute` form, and returns the ref p. Obviously, these functions can only be called within a transaction created by the `dosync` form, since they use the `ensure` and `commute` functions. Next, we will have to define some functions to initiate transactions and invoke the `has-forks?` and `update-forks` functions for a given philosopher, as shown in *Example 2.8*:

```
(defn start-eating [p]
  (dosync
    (when (has-forks? p)
      (update-forks p)
      (commute p assoc :eating? true)
      (commute p update-in [:food] dec))))

(defn stop-eating [p]
  (dosync
    (when (:eating? @p)
      (commute p assoc :eating? false)
      (update-forks p))))

(defn dine [p retry-ms max-eat-ms max-think-ms]
  (while (pos? (:food @p))
    (if (start-eating p)
      (do
        (Thread/sleep (rand-int max-eat-ms))
        (stop-eating p)
        (Thread/sleep (rand-int max-think-ms)))
      (Thread/sleep retry-ms))))
```

Example 2.8: The dining philosophers problem using refs (continued)

The heart of the solution to the dining philosophers problem is the `start-eating` function in *Example 2.8*. This function will check whether both the forks on either side of a philosopher are available, using the `has-forks?` function. The `start-eating` function will then proceed to update the states of these forks by calling the `update-forks` function. The `start-eating` function will also change the state of the philosopher ref p by invoking `commute` with the `assoc` and `update-in` functions, which both return a new map. Since the `start-eating` function uses a `when` form, it will return `nil` when any of the philosophers' forks are unavailable. These few steps are the solution; in a nutshell, a philosopher will eat only when both his forks are available. .

The `stop-eating` function in *Example 2.8* reverses the state of a given philosopher ref after the `start-eating` function has been invoked on it. This function basically sets the `:eating` key of the map contained in the supplied philosopher ref `p` to `false` using a `commute` form, and then calls `update-forks` to reset the state of the associated forks of the philosopher ref `p`.

The `start-eating` and `stop-eating` function can be called repeatedly in a loop using a `while` form, as long as the `:food` key of a philosopher ref `p`, or rather the amount of available food, is a positive value. This is performed by the `dine` function in *Example 2.8*. This function will call the `start-eating` function on a philosopher ref `p`, and will wait for some time if the philosopher's forks are being used by any other philosophers. The amount of time that a philosopher waits for is indicated by the `retry-ms` argument that is passed to the dine function. If a philosopher's forks are available, he eats for a random amount of time, as indicated by the expression `(rand-int max-eat-ms)`. Then, the `stop-eating` function is called to reset the state of the philosopher ref `p` and the forks that it contains. Finally, the `dine` function waits for a random amount of time, which is represented by the `(rand-int max-think-ms)` expression, to indicate that a philosopher is thinking.

Let's now define some function and actually create some refs representing philosophers and associated forks, as shown in *Example 2.9*:

```
(defn init-forks [nf]
  (repeatedly nf #(make-fork)))

(defn init-philosophers [np food forks init-fn]
  (let [p-range (range np)
        p-names (map #(str "Philosopher " (inc %))
                     p-range)
        p-forks (map #(vector (nth forks %)
                              (nth forks (-> % inc (mod np))))
                     p-range)
        p-food (cycle [food])]
    (map init-fn p-names p-forks p-food)))
```

Example 2.9: The dining philosophers problem using refs (continued)

The `init-forks` function from *Example 2.9* will simply invoke the `make-fork` function a number of times, as indicated by its argument `nf`. The `init-philosophers` function will create `np` number of philosophers and associate each of them with a vector of two forks and a certain amount of food. This is done by mapping the function `init-fn`, which is a function that matches the arity of the `make-philosopher` function in *Example 2.6*, over a range of philosopher names `p-names` and forks `p-forks`, and an infinite range `p-food` of the value `food`.

We will now define a function to print the collective state of a sequence of philosophers. This can be done in a fairly simple manner using the `doseq` function, as shown in *Example 2.10*:

```
(defn check-philosophers [philosophers forks]
  (doseq [i (range (count philosophers))]
    (println (str "Fork:\t\t\t available=" @(nth forks i)))
    (if-let [p @(nth philosophers i)]
      (println (str (:name p)
                    ":\t\t eating=" (:eating? p)
                    " food=" (:food p))))))
```

Example 2.10: The dining philosophers problem using refs (continued)

The `check-philosophers` function in *Example 2.10* iterates through all of its supplied philosopher refs, represented by `philosophers`, and associated forks, represented by `forks`, and prints their state. The `if-let` form is used here to check if a dereferenced ref from the collection `philosophers` is not `nil`.

Now, let's define a function to concurrently invoke the `dine` function over a collection of philosopher. This function could also pass in values for the `retry-ms`, `max-eat-ms`, and `max-think-ms` arguments of the `dine` function. This is implemented in the `dine-philosophers` function in *Example 2.11*:

```
(defn dine-philosophers [philosophers]
  (doall (for [p philosophers]
            (future (dine p 10 100 100)))))
```

Example 2.11: The dining philosophers problem using refs (continued)

Finally, let's define five instances of philosophers and five associated forks for our simulation, using the `init-forks`, `init-philosophers`, and `make-philosopher` functions, as shown in *Example 2.12* as follows:

```
(def all-forks (init-forks 5))

(def all-philosophers
  (init-philosophers 5 1000 all-forks make-philosopher))
```

Example 2.12: The dining philosophers problem using refs (continued)

We can now use the `check-philosopher` function to print the state of the philosopher and fork refs created in *Example 2.12*, as shown here:

```
user> (check-philosophers all-philosophers all-forks)
Fork:                       available=true
Philosopher 1:              eating=false food=1000
Fork:                       available=true
Philosopher 2:              eating=false food=1000
```

```
Fork:                          available=true
Philosopher 3:                 eating=false food=1000
Fork:                          available=true
Philosopher 4:                 eating=false food=1000
Fork:                          available=true
Philosopher 5:                 eating=false food=1000
nil
```

Initially, all of the forks are available and none of the philosophers are eating. To start the simulation, we must call the `dine-philosophers` function on the philosopher refs `all-philosophers` and the fork refs `all-forks`, as shown here:

```
user> (def philosophers-futures (dine-philosophers all-philosophers))
#'user/philosophers-futures
user> (check-philosophers all-philosophers all-forks)
Fork:                          available=false
Philosopher 1:                 eating=true food=978
Fork:                          available=false
Philosopher 2:                 eating=false food=979
Fork:                          available=false
Philosopher 3:                 eating=true food=977
Fork:                          available=false
Philosopher 4:                 eating=false food=980
Fork:                          available=true
Philosopher 5:                 eating=false food=980
nil
```

After invoking the `dine-philosophers` function, each philosopher is observed to consume the allocated food, as shown in the output of the previous `check-philosophers` function. At any given point of time, one or two philosophers are observed to be eating, and the other philosophers will wait until they complete using the available forks. Subsequent calls to the `check-philosophers` function also indicate the same output, and the philosophers will eventually consume all of the allocated food:

```
user> (check-philosophers all-philosophers all-forks)
Fork:                          available=true
Philosopher 1:                 eating=false food=932
Fork:                          available=true
Philosopher 2:                 eating=false food=935
Fork:                          available=true
Philosopher 3:                 eating=false food=933
Fork:                          available=true
Philosopher 4:                 eating=false food=942
Fork:                          available=true
Philosopher 5:                 eating=false food=935
nil
```

We can pause the simulation by calling the `future-cancel` function, as shown here. Once the simulation is paused, it can be resumed by calling the `dine-philosophers` function again, as (`dine-philosophers all-philosophers`):

```
user> (map future-cancel philosophers-futures)
(true true true true true)
```

To summarize, the preceding example is a concise and working implementation of a solution to the dining philosophers problem using Clojure futures and refs.

Using atoms

Atoms are used to handle state that changes atomically. Once an atom is modified, its new value is reflected in all concurrent threads. In this way, atoms represent *synchronous* and *independent* state. Let's quickly explore the functions that can be used to handle atoms.

 The following examples can be found in `src/m_clj/c2/atoms.clj` of the book's source code.

We can define an atom using the `atom` function, which requires the initial state of the atom to be passed to it as the first argument, as shown here:

```
(def state (atom 0))
```

The `reset!` and `swap!` functions can be used to modify the state of an atom. The `reset!` function is used to directly set the state of an atom. This function takes two arguments—an atom and the value that represents the new state of the atom, as shown here:

```
user> @state
0
user> (reset! state 1)
1
user> @state
1
```

The `swap!` function requires a function and additional arguments to pass to the supplied function as arguments. The supplied function is applied to the value contained in the atom along with the other additional arguments specified to the `swap!` function. This function can thus be used to mutate an atom using a supplied function, as shown here:

```
user> @state
1
user> (swap! state + 2)
3
```

The call to the preceding `swap!` function sets the state of the atom to the result of the expression `(+ @state 2)`. The `swap!` function may call the function + multiple times due to concurrent calls to the `swap!` function on the atom `state`. Hence, functions that are passed to the `swap!` function must be free of I/O and other side effects.

 The `reset!` and `swap!` functions both return the new value contained in the supplied atom.

We can watch for any change in an atom, and other reference types as well, using the `add-watch` function. This function will call a given function whenever the state of an atom is changed. The `add-watch` function takes three arguments — a reference, a key and a *watch function*, that is, a function that must be called whenever the state of the supplied reference type is changed. The function that is supplied to the `add-watch` function must accept four arguments — a key, the reference that was changed, the old value of the reference, and the new value of the reference. The value of the key argument that is passed to the `add-watch` function gets passed to the `watch` function as its first argument. A `watch` function can also be unlinked from a given reference type using the `remove-watch` function. The `remove-watch` function accepts two arguments — a reference and a key that was specified while adding a `watch` function to the reference. *Example 2.13* depicts how we can track the state of an atom using a `watch` function:

```
(defn make-state-with-watch []
  (let [state (atom 0)
        state-is-changed? (atom false)
        watch-fn (fn [key r old-value new-value]
                   (swap! state-is-changed? (fn [_] true)))]
    (add-watch state nil watch-fn)
    [state
     state-is-changed?]))
```

Example 2.13: Using the add-watch function

The `make-state-with-watch` function defined in *Example 2.13* returns a vector of two atoms. The second atom in this vector initially contains the value `false`. Whenever the state of the first atom in the vector returned by the `make-state-with-watch` function is changed, the state of the second atom in this vector is changed to the value `true`. This can be verified in the REPL, as shown here:

```
user> (def s (make-state-with-watch))
#'user/s
user> @(nth s 1)
false
user> (swap! (nth s 0) inc)
1
user> @(nth s 1)
true
```

Thus, watch functions can be used with the `add-watch` function to track the state of atoms and other reference types.

[The `add-watch` function can be used with *all* reference types.]

Using agents

An *agent* is used to represent state that is associated with a queue of actions and a pool of worker threads. Any action that modifies the state of an agent must be sent to its queue, and the supplied function will be called by a thread selected from the agent's pool of worker threads. We can send actions asynchronously to agents as well. Thus, agents represent *asynchronous* and *independent* state.

[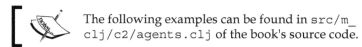 The following examples can be found in `src/m_clj/c2/agents.clj` of the book's source code.]

An agent is created using the `agent` function. For example, we can create an agent with an empty map as its initial value as follows:

```
(def state (agent {}))
```

We can modify the state of an agent by using the `send` and `send-off` functions. The `send` and `send-off` functions will send a supplied action and its additional arguments to an agent's queue in an asynchronous manner. Both these functions return the agent they are passed immediately.

The primary difference between the `send` and `send-off` functions is that the `send` function assigns actions to a thread selection from a pool of worker threads, whereas the `send-off` function creates a new dedicated thread to execute each action. Blocking actions that are sent to an agent using the `send` function could exhaust the agent's pool of threads. Thus, the `send-off` function is preferred for sending blocking actions to an agent.

To demonstrate the `send` and `send-off` functions, let's first define a function that returns a closure that sleeps for a certain amount of time, and then, call the `assoc` function, as shown in *Example 2.14*:

```
(defn set-value-in-ms [n ms]
  (fn [a]
    (Thread/sleep ms)
    (assoc a :value n)))
```

Example 2.14: A function that returns a closure which sleeps and calls assoc

A closure returned by the `set-value-in-ms` function, in *Example 2.14*, can be passed as an action to the `send` and `send-off` functions, as shown here:

```
user> (send state (set-value-in-ms 5 5000))
#<Agent@7fce18: {}>
user> (send-off state (set-value-in-ms 10 5000))
#<Agent@7fce18: {}>
user> @state
{}
user> @state ; after 5 seconds
{:value 5}
user> @state ; after another 5 seconds
{:value 10}
```

The calls to the preceding `send` and `send-off` functions will call the closures returned by the `set-value-in-ms` function, from *Example 2.14*, asynchronously over the agent `state`. The agent's state changes over a period of 10 seconds, which is required to execute the closures returned by the `set-value-in-ms` function. The new key-value pair `{:value 5}` is observed to be saved into the agent `state` after five seconds, and the state of the agent again changes to `{:value 10}` after another five seconds.

Any action that is passed to the `send` and `send-off` functions can use the `*agent*` var to access the agent through which the action will be executed.

The `await` function can be used to wait for all actions in an agent's queue to be completed, as shown here:

```
user> (send-off state (set-value-in-ms 100 3000))
#<Agent@af9ac: {:value 10}>
user> (await state)  ; will block
nil
user> @state
{:value 100}
```

The expression `(await state)` is observed to be blocked until the previous action that was sent to the agent `state` using the `send-off` function is completed. The `await-for` function is a variant of `await`, which waits for a certain number of milliseconds, indicated by its first argument, for all the actions on an agent, its second argument, to complete.

An agent also saves any error it encounters while performing the actions in its queue. An agent will throw the error it has encountered on any subsequent calls to the `send` and `send-off` functions. The error saved by an agent can be accessed using the `agent-error` function, and can be cleared using the `clear-agent-errors` function, as shown here:

```
user> (def a (agent 1))
#'user/a
user> (send a / 0)
#<Agent@5d29f1: 1>
user> (agent-error a)
#<ArithmeticException java.lang.ArithmeticException: Divide by zero>
user> (clear-agent-errors a)
1
user> (agent-error a)
nil
user> @a
1
```

An agent that has encountered an error can also be restarted using the `restart-agent` function. This function takes an agent as its first argument and the new state of the agent as its second argument. All actions that were sent to an agent while it was failed will be executed once the `restart-agent` is called on the agent. We can avoid this behavior by passing the `:clear-actions true` optional argument to the `restart-agent` function. In this case, any actions held in an agent's queue are discarded before it is restarted.

To create a pool of threads, or a *threadpool,* to use with an agent, we must call the static `newFixedThreadPool` method of the `java.util.concurrent.Executors` class by passing the desired number of threads in the pool as an argument, as follows:

```
(def pool (java.util.concurrent.Executors/newFixedThreadPool 10))
```

The pool of threads defined previously can be used to execute the actions of an agent by using the `send-via` function. This function is a variant of the `send` function that accepts a pool of threads, such as the `pool` defined previously, as its first argument, as shown here:

```
user> (send-via pool state assoc :value 1000)
#<Agent@8efada: {:value 100}>
user> @state
{:value 1000}
```

We can also specify the thread pools to be used by all agents to execute actions sent to them using the `send` and `send-off` functions using the `set-agent-send-executor!` and `set-agent-send-off-executor!` functions respectively. Both of these functions accept a single argument representing a pool of threads.

All agents in the current process can be stopped by invoking the `(shutdown-agents)`. The `shutdown-agents` function should only be called before exiting a process, as there is no way to restart the agents in a process after calling this function.

Now, let's try implementing the dining philosophers problem using agents. We can reuse most of the functions from the previous implementation of the dining philosophers problem that was based on refs. Let's define some functions to model this problem using agents, as shown in *Example 2.15*:

```
(defn make-philosopher-agent [name forks food]
  (agent {:name name
          :forks forks
          :eating? false
          :food food}))

(defn start-eating [max-eat-ms]
  (dosync (if (has-forks? *agent*)
            (do
              (-> *agent*
                  update-forks
                  (send assoc :eating? true)
                  (send update-in [:food] dec))
              (Thread/sleep (rand-int max-eat-ms))))))

(defn stop-eating [max-think-ms]
```

```
        (dosync (-> *agent*
                    (send assoc :eating? false)
                    update-forks))
      (Thread/sleep (rand-int max-think-ms)))

  (def running? (atom true))

  (defn dine [p max-eat-ms max-think-ms]
    (when (and p (pos? (:food p)))
      (if-not (:eating? p)
        (start-eating max-eat-ms)
        (stop-eating max-think-ms))
      (if-not @running?
        @*agent*
        @(send-off *agent* dine max-eat-ms max-think-ms))))

  (defn dine-philosophers [philosophers]
    (swap! running? (fn [_] true))
    (doall (for [p philosophers]
             (send-off p dine 100 100))))

  (defn stop-philosophers []
    (swap! running? (fn [_] false)))
```

Example 2.15: The dining philosophers problem using agents

In *Example 2.15*, the make-philosopher-agent function will create an agent representing a philosopher. The initial state of the resulting agent is a map of the keys :name, :forks, :eating?, and :food, as described in the previous implementation of the dining philosophers problem. Note that the forks in this implementation are still represented by refs.

The start-eating function in *Example 2.15* will start a transaction, check whether the forks placed to the left and right sides of a philosopher are available, changes the state of the forks and philosopher agent accordingly, and then suspends the current thread for some time to indicate that a philosopher is eating. The stop-eating function in *Example 2.15* will similarly update the state of a philosopher and the forks he had used, and then suspend the current thread for some time to indicate that a philosopher is thinking. Note that both the start-eating and stop-eating functions reuse the has-forks? and update-forks functions from *Example 2.7* of the previous implementation of the dining philosophers problem.

The `start-eating` and `stop-eating` functions are called by the `dine` function in *Example 2.15*. We can assume that this function will be passed as an action to a philosopher agent. This function checks the value of the `:eating?` key contained in a philosopher agent to decide whether it must invoke the `start-eating` or `stop-eating` function in the current call. Next, the `dine` function invokes itself again using the `send-off` function and dereferencing the agent returned by the `send-off` function. The `dine` function also checks the state of the atom `running?` and does not invoke itself through the `send-off` function in case the expression `@running` returns `false`.

The `dine-philosophers` function in *Example 2.15* starts the simulation by setting the value of the `running?` atom to `true` and then invoking the `dine` function asynchronously through the `send-off` function for all the philosopher agents passed to it, represented by `philosophers`. The function `stop-philosophers` simply sets the value of the `running?` atom to `false`, thereby stopping the simulation.

Finally, let's define five instances of forks and philosophers using the `init-forks` and `init-philosophers` functions from *Example 2.9*, shown in *Example 2.16* as follows:

```
(def all-forks (init-forks 5))

(def all-philosophers
  (init-philosophers 5 1000 all-forks make-philosopher-agent))
```

Example 2.16: The dining philosophers problem using agents (continued)

We can now start the simulation by calling the `dine-philosophers` function. Also, we can print the collective state of the fork and philosopher instances in the simulation using the `check-philosophers` function defined in *Example 2.10*, as follows:

```
user> (def philosophers-agents (dine-philosophers all-philosophers))
#'user/philosophers-agents
user> (check-philosophers all-philosophers all-forks)
Fork:                available=false
Philosopher 1:       eating=false food=936
Fork:                available=false
Philosopher 2:       eating=false food=942
Fork:                available=true
Philosopher 3:       eating=true food=942
Fork:                available=true
Philosopher 4:       eating=false food=935
Fork:                available=true
Philosopher 5:       eating=true food=943
nil
```

```
user> (check-philosophers all-philosophers all-forks)
Fork:                    available=false
Philosopher 1:           eating=true food=743
Fork:                    available=false
Philosopher 2:           eating=false food=747
Fork:                    available=true
Philosopher 3:           eating=false food=751
Fork:                    available=true
Philosopher 4:           eating=false food=741
Fork:                    available=true
Philosopher 5:           eating=false food=760
nil
```

As shown in the preceding output, all philosopher agents share the fork instances among themselves. In effect, they work in tandem to ensure that each philosopher eventually consumes all of their allocated food.

In summary, vars, refs, atoms, and agents can be used to represent mutable state that is shared among concurrently executing tasks.

Executing tasks in parallel

The simultaneous execution of several computations is termed as *parallelism*. The use of parallelism tends to increase the overall performance of a computation, since the computation can be partitioned to execute on several cores or processors. Clojure has a couple of functions that can be used for the parallelization of a particular computation or task, and we will briefly examine them in this section.

 The following examples can be found in `src/m_clj/c2/parallel.clj` of the book's source code.

Suppose we have a function that pauses the current thread for some time and then returns a computed value, as depicted in *Example 2.17*:

```
(defn square-slowly [x]
  (Thread/sleep 2000)
  (* x x))
```

Example 2.17: A function that pauses the current thread

The function `square-slowly` in *Example 2.17* requires a single argument x. This function pauses the current thread for two seconds and returns the square of its argument x. If the function `square-slowly` is invoked over a collection of three values using the `map` function, it takes three times as long to complete, as shown here:

```
user> (time (doall (map square-slowly (repeat 3 10))))
"Elapsed time: 6000.329702 msecs"
(100 100 100)
```

The previously shown `map` form returns a lazy sequence, and hence the `doall` form is required to realize the value returned by the map form. We could also use the `dorun` form to perform this realization of a lazy sequence. The entire expression is evaluated in about six seconds, which is thrice the time taken by the `square-slowly` function to complete. We can parallelize the application of the `square-slowly` function using the `pmap` function instead of `map`, as shown here:

```
user> (time (doall (pmap square-slowly (repeat 3 10))))
"Elapsed time: 2001.543439 msecs"
(100 100 100)
```

The entire expression now evaluates in the same amount of time required for a single call to the `square-slowly` function. This is due to the `square-slowly` function being called in parallel over the supplied collection by the `pmap` form. Thus, the `pmap` form has the same semantics as that of the `map` form, except that it applies the supplied function in parallel.

The `pvalues` and `pcalls` forms can also be used to parallelize computations. The `pvalues` form evaluates the expressions passed to it in parallel, and returns a lazy sequence of the resulting values. Similarly, the `pcalls` form invokes all functions passed to it, which must take no arguments, in parallel and returns a lazy sequence of the values returned by these functions:

```
user> (time (doall (pvalues (square-slowly 10)
                            (square-slowly 10)
                            (square-slowly 10))))
"Elapsed time: 2007.702703 msecs"
(100 100 100)
user> (time (doall (pcalls #(square-slowly 10)
                           #(square-slowly 10)
                           #(square-slowly 10))))
"Elapsed time: 2005.683279 msecs"
(100 100 100)
```

As shown in the preceding output, both expressions that use the `pvalues` and `pcalls` forms take the same amount of time to evaluate as a single call to the `square-slowly` function.

 The `pmap`, `pvalues`, and `pcalls` forms *all* return lazy sequences that have to be realized using the `doall` or `dorun` form.

Controlling parallelism with thread pools

The `pmap` form schedules parallel execution of the supplied function on the default threadpool. If we wish to configure or tweak the threadpool used by `pmap`, the `claypoole` library (https://github.com/TheClimateCorporation/claypoole) is a good option. This library provides an implementation of the `pmap` form that must be passed a configurable threadpool. We will now demonstrate how we can use this library to parallelize a given function.

The following library dependencies are required for the upcoming examples:

```
[com.climate/claypoole "1.0.0"]
```

Also, the following namespaces must be included in your namespace declaration:

```
(ns my-namespace
  (:require [com.climate.claypoole :as cp]
            [com.climate.claypoole.lazy :as cpl]))
```

The `pmap` function from the `com.climate.claypoole` namespace is essentially a variant of the standard `pmap` function to which we supply a threadpool instance to be used in parallelizing a given function. We can also supply the number of threads to be used by this variant of the `pmap` function in order to parallelize a given function, as shown here:

```
user> (time (doall (cpl/pmap 2 square-slowly [10 10 10])))
"Elapsed time: 4004.029789 msecs"
(100 100 100)
```

As previously shown, the `pmap` function from the `claypoole` library can be used to parallelize the `square-slowly` function that we defined earlier in *Example 2.17* over a collection of three values. These three elements are computed over in two batches, in which each batch will parallely apply the `square-slowly` function over two elements in two separate threads. Since the `square-slowly` function takes two seconds to complete, the total time taken to compute over the collection of three elements is around four seconds.

We can create an instance of a pool of threads using the `threadpool` function from the `claypoole` library. This threadpool instance can then be passed to the `pmap` function from the `claypoole` library. The `com.climate.claypoole` namespace also provides the `ncpus` function that returns the number of physical processors available to the current process. We can create a threadpool instance and pass it to this variant of the `pmap` function as shown here:

```
user> (def pool (cp/threadpool (cp/ncpus)))
#'user/pool
user> (time (doall (cpl/pmap pool square-slowly [10 10 10])))
"Elapsed time: 4002.05885 msecs"
(100 100 100)
```

Assuming that we are running the preceding code on a computer system that has two physical processors, the call to the `threadpool` function shown previously will create a threadpool of two threads. This threadpool instance can then be passed to the `pmap` function as shown in the preceding example.

 We can fall back to the standard behavior of the `pmap` function by passing the `:builtin` keyword as the first argument to the `com.climate.claypoole/pmap` function. Similarly, if the keyword `:serial` is passed as the first argument to the `claypoole` version of the `pmap` function, the function behaves like the standard `map` function.

The `threadpool` function also supports a couple of useful key options. Firstly, we can create a pool of non-daemon threads using the `:daemon false` optional argument. Daemon threads are killed when the process exits, and all threadpools created by the `threadpool` function are pools of daemon threads by default. We can also name a threadpool using the `:name` key option of the `threadpool` function. The `:thread-priority` key option can be used to indicate the priority of the threads in the new threadpool.

Tasks can also be prioritized using the `pmap`, `priority-threadpool`, and `with-priority` forms from the `claypoole` library. A priority threadpool is created using the `priority-threadpool` function, and this new threadpool can be used along with the `with-priority` function to assign a priority to a task that must be parallelized using `pmap`, as shown here:

```
user> (def pool (cp/priority-threadpool (cp/ncpus)))
#'user/pool
user> (def task-1 (cp/pmap (cp/with-priority pool 1000)
                           square-slowly [10 10 10]))
#'user/task-1
user> (def task-2 (cp/pmap (cp/with-priority pool 0)
                           square-slowly [5 5 5]))
#'user/task-2
```

Tasks with higher priority are assigned to threads first. Hence, the task represented by `task-1` will be assigned to a thread of execution before the task represented by `task-2` in the previous output.

To gracefully deallocate a given threadpool, we can call the `shutdown` function from the `com.climate.claypoole` namespace, which accepts a threadpool instance as its only argument. The `shutdown!` function from the same namespace will forcibly shut down the threads in a threadpool. The `shutdown!` function can also be called using the `with-shutdown!` macro. We specify the threadpools to be used for a series of computations as a vector of bindings to the `with-shutdown!` macro. This macro will implicitly call the `shutdown!` function on all of the threadpools that it has created once all the computations in the body of this macro are completed. For example, we can define a function to create a threadpool, use it for a computation, and finally, shut down the threadpool, using the `with-shutdown!` function as shown in *Example 2.18*:

```
(defn square-slowly-with-pool [v]
  (cp/with-shutdown! [pool (cp/threadpool (cp/ncpus))]
    (doall (cp/pmap pool square-slowly v))))
```

Example 2.18: Using a priority threadpool

The `square-slowly-with-pool` function defined in *Example 2.18* will create a new threadpool, represented by `pool`, and then use it to call the `pmap` function. The `shutdown!` function is implicitly called once the `doall` form completely evaluates the lazy sequence returned by the `pmap` function.

The `claypoole` library also supports *unordered parallelism*, in which results of individual threads of computation are used as soon as they are available in order to minimize latency. The `com.climate.claypoole/upmap` function is an unordered parallel version of the `pmap` function.

The `com.climate.claypoole` namespace also provides several other functions that use threadpools, as described here:

- The `com.climate.claypoole/pvalues` function is a threadpool-based implementation of the `pvalues` function. It will evaluate its arguments in parallel using a supplied threadpool and return a lazy sequence.

- The `com.climate.claypoole/pcalls` function is a threadpool-based version of the `pcalls` function, which invokes several no-argument functions to return a lazy sequence.

- A future that uses a given threadpool can be created using the `com.climate.claypoole/future` function.

- We can evaluate an expression in a parallel fashion over the items in a given collection using the `com.climate.claypoole/pfor` function.

- The `upvalues`, `upcalls`, and `upfor` functions in the `com.climate.claypoole` namespace are unordered parallel versions of the `pvalues`, `pcalls`, and `pfor` functions, respectively, from the same namespace.

It is quite evident that the `pmap` function from the `com.climate.claypoole` namespace will eagerly evaluate the collection it is supplied. This may be undesirable when we intend to call `pmap` over an infinite sequence. The `com.climate.claypoole.lazy` namespace provides versions of `pmap` and other functions from the `com.climate.claypoole` namespace that preserve the laziness of a supplied collection. The lazy version of the `pmap` function can be demonstrated as follows:

```
user> (def lazy-pmap (cpl/pmap pool square-slowly (range)))
#'user/lazy-pmap
user> (time (doall (take 4 lazy-pmap)))
"Elapsed time: 4002.556548 msecs"
(0 1 4 9)
```

The previously defined `lazy-pmap` sequence is a lazy sequence created by mapping the `square-slowly` function over the infinite sequence (range). As shown previously, the call to the `pmap` function returns immediately, and the first four elements of the resulting lazy sequence are realized in parallel using the `doall` and `take` functions.

To summarize, Clojure has the `pmap`, `pvalues`, and `pcalls` primitives to deal with parallel computations. If we intend to control the amount of parallelism utilized by these functions, we can use the `claypoole` library's implementations of these primitives. The `claypoole` library also supports other useful features such as prioritized threadpools and unordered parallelism.

Summary

We have explored various constructs that can be used to create concurrent and parallel tasks in Clojure. You learned to handle shared mutable state through the use of reference types, namely vars, refs, atoms and agents. As we described earlier, the dining philosophers problem can be easily implemented using refs and agents. You also studied how tasks can be executed in parallel. Lastly, we explored the `claypoole` library, which allows us to control the amount of parallelism used for a given computation.

In the next chapter, we will continue our exploration of parallelism in Clojure through the use of reducers.

3
Parallelization Using Reducers

Reducers are another way of looking at collections in Clojure. In this chapter, we will study this particular abstraction of collections, and how it is quite orthogonal to viewing collections as sequences. The motivation behind reducers is to increase the performance of computations over collections. This performance gain is achieved mainly through parallelization of such computations.

As we have seen in *Chapter 1, Working with Sequences and Patterns*, sequences and laziness are a great way to handle collections. The Clojure standard library provides several functions to handle and manipulate sequences. However, abstracting a collection as a sequence has an unfortunate consequence; any computation performed over all the elements of a sequence is inherently sequential. Also, all of the standard sequence functions create a new collection that is similar to the collection passed to these functions. Interestingly, performing a computation over a collection without creating a similar collection, even as an intermediary result, is quite useful. For example, it is often required to reduce a given collection to a single value through a series of transformations in an iterative manner. This sort of computation does not necessarily require the intermediary results of each transformation to be saved.

A consequence of iteratively computing values from a collection is that we cannot parallelize it in a straightforward way. Modern *MapReduce* frameworks handle this kind of computation by pipelining the elements of a collection through several transformations in parallel, and finally, reducing the results into a single result. Of course, the result could as well be a new collection. A drawback of this methodology is that it produces concrete collections as intermediate results of each transformation, which is rather wasteful. For example, if we wanted to filter out values from a collection, the MapReduce strategy would require creating empty collections to represent values that are left out of the reduction step to produce the final result.

This incurs unnecessary memory allocation and also creates additional work for the reduction step, which produces the final result. Hence, there's a scope for optimizing these sorts of computations.

This brings us to the notion of treating computations over collections as *reducers* to attain better performance. Of course, this doesn't mean that reducers are a replacement for sequences. Sequences and laziness are great for abstracting computations that create and manipulate collections, while reducers are a specialized high-performance abstraction of collections in which a collection needs to be piped through several transformations, and finally, combined to produce the final result. Reducers achieve a performance gain in the following ways:

- Reducing the amount of memory allocated to produce the desired result
- Parallelizing the process of reducing a collection into a single result, which could be an entirely new collection

The `clojure.core.reducers` namespace provides several functions to process collections using reducers. Let's now examine how reducers are implemented and a few examples that demonstrate how reducers can be used.

Using reduce to transform collections

Sequences and functions that operate on sequences preserve the sequential ordering between elements. Lazy sequences avoid the unnecessary realization of elements in a collection until they are required for a computation, but the realization of these values is still performed in a sequential manner. However, this characteristic of sequential ordering may not be desirable for all computations performed over it. For example, it's not possible to map a function over a vector and then lazily realize values in the resulting collection out of order; since the `map` function converts the supplied collection into a sequence. Also, functions such as `map` and `filter` are lazy, but still sequential by nature.

What's wrong with sequences?

One of the limitations of sequences is that they are realized in *chunks*. Let's study a simple example to illustrate what this means. Consider a unary function, as shown in *Example 3.1*, which we intend to map over a given vector. The function must compute a value from the one it is supplied, and also perform a side effect so that we can observe its application over the elements in a collection.

The following examples can be found in `src/m_clj/c3/reducers.clj` of the book's source code.

```
(defn square-with-side-effect [x]
  (do
    (println (str "Side-effect: " x))
    (* x x)))
```

Example 3.1: A simple unary function

The `square-with-side-effect` function simply returns the square of a number x using the * function. This function also prints the value of x using a `println` form whenever it is called. Suppose this function is mapped over a given vector. The resulting collection would have to be realized completely if a computation has to be performed over it, even if all the elements from the resulting vector are not required. This can be demonstrated as follows:

```
user> (def mapped (map square-with-side-effect [0 1 2 3 4 5]))
#'user/mapped
user> (reduce + (take 3 mapped))
Side-effect: 0
Side-effect: 1
Side-effect: 2
Side-effect: 3
Side-effect: 4
Side-effect: 5
5
```

As shown previously, the `mapped` variable contains the result of mapping the `square-with-side-effect` function over a vector. If we try to sum the first three values in the resulting collection using the `reduce`, `take`, and + functions, all the values in the [0 1 2 3 4 5] vector are printed as a side effect, as shown in the preceding output. This means that the `square-with-side-effect` function was applied to all the elements in the initial vector, despite the fact that only the first three elements were actually required by the `reduce` form. Of course, this can be solved using the `seq` function to convert the vector to a sequence before mapping the `square-with-side-effect` function over it. But then, we lose the ability to efficiently access elements in a random order in the resulting collection.

To understand why this actually happens, we first need to understand how the standard `map` function is actually implemented. A simplified definition of the `map` function is shown in *Example 3.2*:

```
(defn map [f coll]
  (cons (f (first coll))
        (lazy-seq (map f (rest coll)))))
```

Example 3.2: A simplified definition of the map function

The definition of `map` in *Example 3.2* is a simplified and rather incomplete one, as it doesn't check for an empty collections and cannot be used over multiple collections. That aside, this definition of `map` does indeed apply a function `f` to all the elements in a collection `coll`. This is implemented using a composition of the `cons`, `first`, `rest`, and `lazy-seq` forms.

This implementation can be interpreted as "applying the function `f` to the first element in the collection `coll`, and then mapping `f` over the rest of the collection in a lazy manner". An interesting consequence of this implementation is that the `map` function has the following characteristics:

- The ordering among elements in the collection `coll` is preserved.
- This computation is performed recursively.
- The `lazy-seq` form is used to perform the computation in a lazy manner.
- The use of the `first` and `rest` forms indicate that `coll` must be a sequence, and the `cons` form will also produce a result that is a sequence. Hence, the `map` function accepts a sequence and builds a new one.

However, none of these properties of sequences are needed to transform a given collection into a result that is not a sequence. Another characteristic of lazy sequences is how they are realized. By the term realized, we mean to say a given lazy sequence is evaluated to produce concrete values. Lazy sequences are realized in *chunks*. Each chunk is comprised of 32 elements, and this is done as an optimization. Sequences that behave this way are termed as *chunked sequences*. Of course, not all sequences are chunked, and we can check whether a given sequence is chunked using the `chunked-seq?` predicate. The `range` function returns a chunked sequence, as shown here:

```
user> (first (map #(do (print \!) %) (range 70)))
!!!!!!!!!!!!!!!!!!!!!!!!!!!!!!!!
0
user> (nth (map #(do (print \!) %) (range 70)) 32)
!!!!!!!!!!!!!!!!!!!!!!!!!!!!!!!!!!!!!!!!!!!!!!!!!!!!!!!!!!!!!!!!!!!!
32
```

Both the statements in the preceding output select a single element from a sequence returned by the `map` function. The function passed to the `map` function in both the preceding statements prints the `!` character and returns the value supplied to it. In the first statement, the first 32 elements of the resulting sequence are realized even though only the first element is required. Similarly, the second statement is observed to realize the first 64 elements of the resulting sequence when the element at the 32nd position is obtained using the `nth` function. But again, realizing a collection in chunks isn't required to perform a computation over the elements in the collection.

Chunked sequences have been an integral part of Clojure since version 1.1.

If we are to handle such computations efficiently, we cannot build on functions that return sequences, such as map and filter. Incidentally, the reduce function does not necessarily produce a sequence. It also has a couple of other interesting properties:

- The reduce function actually lets the supplied collection define how it is computed over or reduced. Thus, reduce is *collection independent*.

- Also, the reduce function is versatile enough to build a single value or an entirely new collection as well. For example, using reduce with the * or + functions will create a single valued result, while using it with the cons or concat functions can create a new collection as a result. Thus, reduce can *build anything*.

To summarize, the reduce function can be used as a premise to generalize any computation or transformation that has to be applied on a collection.

Introducing reducers

A collection is said to be *reducible* when it defines its behavior with the reduce function. The binary function used by the reduce function along with a collection is also termed as a *reducing function*. A reducing function requires two arguments — one to represent the accumulated result of the reduction, and another to represent an input value that has to be combined into the result. Several reducing functions can be composed into one, which effectively changes how the reduce function processes a given collection. This composition is done using *reducing function transformers*, or simply *reducers*.

The use of sequences and laziness can be compared to using reducers to perform a given computation by Rich Hickey's infamous pie-maker analogy. Suppose a pie-maker has been supplied a bag of apples, with an intent to *reduce* the apples to a pie. There are a couple transformations needed to perform this task. First, the stickers on all the apples have to be removed, as in we *map* a function to "take the sticker off" over the apples in the collection. Also, all the rotten apples will have to be removed, which is analogous to using the filter function to remove elements from a collection. Instead of performing this work herself, the pie-maker delegates it to her assistant. The assistant could first take the stickers off of all the apples, thus producing a new collection, and then take out the rotten apples to produce another new collection, which illustrates the use of lazy sequences. But then, the assistant would be doing unnecessary work by removing the stickers from the rotten apples, which will have to be discarded later.

On the other hand, the assistant could delay this work until the actual reduction of the processed apples into a pie is performed. Once the work is actually needed to be performed, the assistant will compose the two tasks of *mapping* and *filtering* the collection of apples, thus avoiding any unnecessary work. This case depicts the use of reducers to compose and transform the tasks needed to effectively reduce the collection of apples into a pie. Thus, the use of intermediary collections between each transformation is avoided, which is an optimization in terms of memory allocations performed to produce the result.

Of course, a smart assistant would simply discard the rotten apples first, which is essentially filtering the apples before mapping them. However, not all recipes are that trivial, and moreover, we can achieve a more interesting optimization through the use of reducers—parallelism. By using reducers, we create a *recipe* of tasks to reduce a collection of apples into a pie that can be parallelized. Also, all processing is delayed until the final reduction, instead of dealing with collections as intermediary results of each task. This is the gist of how reducers achieve performance though function composition and parallelization.

The following namespaces must be included in your namespace declaration for the upcoming examples:

```
(ns my-namespace
    (:require [clojure.core.reducers :as r]))
```

The `clojure.core.reducers` namespace requires Java 6 with the `jsr166y.jar` JAR or Java 7+ for fork/join support.

Let's now briefly explore how reducers are actually implemented. Functions that operate on sequences use the `clojure.lang.ISeq` interface to abstract the behavior of a collection. In the case of reducers, the common interface that we must build upon is that of a reducing function. As we mentioned earlier, a reducing function is a two-arity function in which the first argument is the accumulated result so far and the second argument is the current input that has to be combined with the first argument. The process of performing a computation over a collection and producing some result can be generalized into three distinct cases. They can be described as follows:

- A new collection with the same number of elements as the collection it is supplied needs to be produced. This *one-to-one* case is analogous to using the `map` function.

- The computation *shrinks* the supplied collection by removing elements from it. This can be done using the `filter` function.

- The computation could also be *expansive*, in which case it produces a new collection that contains an increased number of elements. This is like what the mapcat function does.

These cases depict the different ways in which a collection can be transformed into the desired result. Any computation, or reduction, over a collection can be thought of as an arbitrary sequence of such transformations. These transformations are represented by *transformers*, which are essentially functions that transform a reducing function. They can be implemented as shown in *Example 3.3*:

```
(defn mapping [f]
  (fn [rf]
    (fn [result input]
      (rf result (f input)))))

(defn filtering [p?]
  (fn [rf]
    (fn [result input]
      (if (p? input)
        (rf result input)
        result))))

(defn mapcatting [f]
  (fn [rf]
    (fn [result input]
      (reduce rf result (f input))))))
```

Example 3.3: Transformers

The mapping, filtering, and mapcatting functions in *Example 3.3* represent the core logic of the map, filter, and mapcat functions respectively. All of these functions are transformers that take a single argument and return a new function. The returned function transforms a supplied reducing function, represented by rf, and returns a new reducing function, created using the expression (fn [result input] ...). Functions returned by the mapping, filtering, and mapcatting functions are termed as *reducing function transformers*.

The mapping function applies the f function to the current input, represented by the input variable. The value returned by the function f is then combined with the accumulated result, represented by result, using the reducing function rf. This transformer is a frighteningly pure abstraction of the standard map function that applies a function f over a collection. The mapping function makes no assumptions of the structure of the collection it is supplied or how the values returned by the function f are combined to produce the final result.

Similarly, the `filtering` function uses a predicate `p?` to check whether the current input of the reducing function `rf` must be combined into the final result, represented by `result`. If the predicate is not true, then the reducing function will simply return the value `result` without any modification. The `mapcatting` function uses the `reduce` function to combine the value `result` with the result of the expression `(f input)`. In this transformer, we can assume that the function `f` will return a new collection and the reducing function `rf` will somehow combine two collections.

One of the foundations of the `reducers` library is the `CollReduce` protocol defined in the `clojure.core.protocols` namespace. This protocol abstracts the behavior of a collection when it is passed as an argument to the `reduce` function, and is declared as shown in *Example 3.4*:

```
(defprotocol CollReduce
  (coll-reduce [coll rf init]))
```

Example 3.4: The CollReduce protocol

The `clojure.core.reducers` namespace defines a `reducer` function that creates a reducible collection by dynamically extending the `CollReduce` protocol, as shown in *Example 3.5*:

```
(defn reducer
  ([coll xf]
   (reify
     CollReduce
     (coll-reduce [_ rf init]
       (coll-reduce coll (xf rf) init)))))
```

Example 3.5: The reducer function

The `reducer` function combines a collection `coll` and a reducing function transformer `xf`, which is returned by the `mapping`, `filtering`, and `mapcatting` functions, to produce a new reducible collection. When `reduce` is invoked on a reducible collection, it will ultimately ask the collection to reduce itself using the reducing function returned by the expression `(xf rf)`. Using this mechanism, several reducing functions can be composed into a single computation to be performed over a given collection. Also, the `reducer` function needs to be defined only once, and the actual implementation of `coll-reduce` is provided by the collection supplied to the `reducer` function.

Now, we can redefine the `reduce` function to simply invoke the `coll-reduce` function implemented by a given collection, as shown in *Example 3.6*:

```
(defn reduce
  ([rf coll]
   (reduce rf (rf) coll))
```

```
([rf init coll]
 (coll-reduce coll rf init)))
```
Example 3.6: Redefining the reduce function

As shown in *Example 3.6*, the reduce function delegates the job of reducing a collection to the collection itself using the coll-reduce function. Also, the reduce function will use the reducing function rf to also supply the init argument when it is not specified. An interesting consequence of this definition of reduce is that the function rf must produce an *identity value* when supplied no arguments. The standard reduce function also uses the CollReduce protocol to delegate the job of reducing a collection to the collection itself, but will also fall back on the default definition of reduce in case the supplied collection does not implement the CollReduce protocol.

 Since Clojure 1.4, the reduce function allows a collection to define how it reduced using the clojure.core.CollReduce protocol. Clojure 1.5 introduced the clojure.core.reducers namespace that extends the use of this protocol.

All of the standard Clojure collections, namely lists, vectors, sets, and maps, implement the CollReduce protocol. The reducer function can be used to build a sequence of transformations to be applied to a collection when it is passed as an argument to the reduce function. This can be demonstrated as follows:

```
user> (r/reduce + 0 (r/reducer [1 2 3 4] (mapping inc)))
14
user> (reduce + 0 (r/reducer [1 2 3 4] (mapping inc)))
14
```

In the preceding output, the mapping function is used with the inc function to create a reducing function transformer that increments all the elements in a given collection. This transformer is then combined with a vector using the reducer function to produce a reducible collection. The call to reduce in both of the preceding statements is transformed into the expression (reduce + [2 3 4 5]), thus producing the result 14. We can now redefine the map, filter, and mapcat functions using the reducer function, as shown in *Example 3.7*:

```
(defn map [f coll]
  (reducer coll (mapping f)))
(defn filter [p? coll]
  (reducer coll (filtering p?)))
(defn mapcat [f coll]
  (reducer coll (mapcatting f)))
```
Example 3.7: Redefining the map, filter and mapcat functions using the reducer form

As shown in *Example 3.7*, the map, filter, and mapcat functions are now simply compositions of the reducer form with the mapping, filtering, and mapcatting transformers respectively.

 The definitions of CollReduce, reducer, reduce, map, filter, and mapcat as shown in this section are simplified versions of their actual definitions in the clojure.core.reducers namespace.

The definitions of the map, filter, and mapcat functions shown in *Example 3.7* have the same shape as the standard versions of these functions, as shown here:

```
user> (r/reduce + (r/map inc [1 2 3 4]))
14
user> (r/reduce + (r/filter even? [1 2 3 4]))
6
user> (r/reduce + (r/mapcat range [1 2 3 4]))
10
```

Hence, the map, filter, and mapcat functions from the clojure.core.reducers namespace can be used in the same way as the standard versions of these functions. The reducers library also provides a take function that can be used as a replacement for the standard take function. We can use this function to reduce the number of calls to the square-with-side-effect function (from *Example 3.1*) when it is mapped over a given vector, as shown here:

```
user> (def mapped (r/map square-with-side-effect [0 1 2 3 4 5]))
#'user/mapped
user> (reduce + (r/take 3 mapped))
Side-effect: 0
Side-effect: 1
Side-effect: 2
Side-effect: 3
5
```

Thus, using the map and take functions from the clojure.core.reducers namespace as shown here avoids applying the square-with-side-effect function to all five elements in the vector [0 1 2 3 4 5] as only the first three are required.

The `reducers` library also provides variants of the standard `take-while`, `drop`, `flatten`, and `remove` functions, which are based on reducers. Effectively, functions based on reducers will require a lesser number of allocations than sequence-based functions, thus leading to an improvement in performance. For example, consider the `process` and `process-with-reducer` functions shown in *Example 3.8*:

```
(defn process [nums]
  (reduce + (map inc (map inc (map inc nums)))))

(defn process-with-reducer [nums]
  (reduce + (r/map inc (r/map inc (r/map inc nums)))))
```

Example 3.8: Functions to process a collection of numbers using sequences and reducers

The `process` function in *Example 3.8* applies the `inc` function over a collection of numbers represented by `nums` using the `map` function. The `process-with-reducer` function performs the same action, but uses the reducer variant of the `map` function. The `process-with-reducer` function will take a lesser amount of time to produce its result from a large vector when compared to the `process` function, as shown here:

```
user> (def nums (vec (range 1000000)))
#'user/nums
user> (time (process nums))
"Elapsed time: 471.217086 msecs"
500002500000
user> (time (process-with-reducer nums))
"Elapsed time: 356.767024 msecs"
500002500000
```

The `process-with-reducer` function gets a slight performance boost as it requires a lesser number of memory allocations than the `process` function. We should note that the available memory should be large enough to load the entire file, or else we could run out of memory. The performance of this computation can be improved by a greater scale if we can somehow parallelize it, and we shall examine how this can be done in the following section.

Using fold to parallelize collections

A collection that implements the CollReduce protocol is still sequential by nature. Using the reduce function with CollReduce does have a certain amount of performance gain, but it still processes elements in a collection in a sequential order. The most obvious way to improve the performance of a computation that is performed over a collection is parallelization. Such computations can be parallelized if we ignore the ordering of elements in a given collection to produce the result of the computation. In the reducers library, this is implemented based on the *fork/join model* of parallelization from the java.util.concurrent namespace. The fork/join model essentially partitions a collection over which a computation has to be performed into two halves and processes each partition in parallel. This halving of the collection is done in a recursive manner. The granularity of the partitions affects the overall performance of a computation modeled using fork/join. This means that if a fork/join strategy is used to recursively partition a collection into smaller collections that contain a single element each, the overhead of the mechanics of fork/join would actually bring down the overall performance of the computation.

A fork/join based method of parallelization is actually implemented in the clojure.core.reducers namespace using the ForkJoinTask and ForkJoinPool classes from the java.util. concurrent namespace in Java 7. In Java 6, it is implemented in the ForkJoinTask and ForkJoinPool classes of the jsr166y namespace. For more information on the Java fork/join framework, visit https://docs.oracle.com/javase/tutorial/essential/concurrency/forkjoin.html.

The parallelization of such computations using reducers is quite different from how it is handled in MapReduce-based libraries. In case of reducers, the elements are first reduced through a number of transformations into a smaller number of elements and then finally, combined to create the result. This contrasts with how a MapReduce strategy models such a computation, in which the elements of a collection are mapped through several transformations and a final reduction step is used to produce the final result. This distinguishes the MapReduce model of parallel computation with the *reduce-combine* model used by the reducers library. This methodology of parallelization using a reduce-combine strategy is implemented by the fold function in the clojure.core.reducers namespace.

In Clojure, the `fold` function refers to a parallelizable computation, which is very different from the traditional fold left (`foldl`) and fold right (`foldr`) functions in other functional programming languages such as Haskell and Erlang. The `reduce` function in Clojure actually has the same sequential nature and semantics as the `foldl` function in other languages.

The `fold` function parallelizes a given computation over a collection using fork/join based threads. It implements the reduce-combine strategy that we previously described and executes the `reduce` function in parallel over equally partitioned segments of a given collection. The results produced by these parallel executions of the `reduce` function are finally combined using a *combining function*. Of course, if the supplied collection is too small to actually gain any performance through fork/join based parallelization, a `fold` form will simply call the `reduce` function on a single thread of execution. The `fold` function thus represents a *potentially parallelizable* computation over a collection. Due to this nature of `fold`, we should avoid performing IO and other side effects based on sequential ordering when using the `fold` form.

The `fold` function allows a collection to define how it is *folded* into the result, which is similar to the semantics of the `reduce` function. A collection is said to be *foldable* if it implements the `CollFold` protocol from the `clojure.core.reducers` namespace. The `reducers` library extends the `CollFold` protocol for the standard vector and map collection types. The parallelization of these implementations of `CollFold` is done using fork/join based parallelism. The definition of the `CollFold` protocol is shown in *Example 3.9*:

```
(defprotocol CollFold
  (coll-fold [coll n cf rf]))
```

Example 3.9: The CollFold protocol

The `CollFold` protocol defines a `coll-fold` function, which requires four arguments—a collection `coll`, the number of elements `n` in each segment or partition of the collection, a combining function `cf`, and a reducing function `rf`. A foldable collection must implement this protocol, as well as the `clojure.core.protocols.CollReduce` protocol, as a call to `fold` on a given collection may fall back to a single-threaded execution of the `reduce` function.

To create a foldable collection from a collection and a reduction function transformer, the reducers library defines a `folder` function with similar semantics as the `reducer` function. This function is implemented as shown in *Example 3.10*:

```
(defn folder
  ([coll xf]
   (reify
     CollReduce
     (coll-reduce [_ rf init]
       (coll-reduce coll (xf rf) init))
     CollFold
     (coll-fold [_ n cf rf]
       (coll-fold coll n cf (xf rf)))))))
```

Example 3.10: The folder function

The `folder` function creates a new foldable and reducible collection from the collection `coll` and the reduction function transformer `xf`. This composition of the `xf` and `rf` functions is analogous to that performed by the `reducer` function described in *Example 3.5*. Apart from the `xf` and `rf` functions, the `coll-fold` function also requires a combining function `cf` with which the results of the potentially parallel executions of the `reduce` function are combined. Similar to the `reduce` function, the `fold` function passes on the responsibility of actually folding a given collection to the collections implementation of the `coll-fold` function. An implementation of the `fold` function is described in *Example 3.11*:

```
(defn fold
  ([rf coll]
   (fold rf rf coll))
  ([cf rf coll]
   (fold 512 cf rf coll))
  ([n cf rf coll]
   (coll-fold coll n cf rf)))
```

Example 3.11: The fold function

As shown in *Example 3.11*, the `fold` function calls the `coll-fold` function of the collection `coll` using the reducing function `rf` and the combining function `cf`. The `fold` function can also specify the number of elements n in each segment processed by the `reduce` function, which defaults to `512` elements. We can also avoid specifying the combining function `cf` to the `fold` function, in which case the reducing function `rf` itself will be used as the combining function.

An interesting aspect of the combining and reducing functions used by the `fold` form is that they must be *associative* in nature. This guarantees that the result of the `fold` function will be independent of the order in which the elements in a given collection are combined to produce the given result. This allows us to parallelize the execution of the `fold` function over segments of a given collection. Also, analogous to the reducing function required by the `reduce` form, the `fold` function requires the combining and reducing functions to produce an *identity value* when invoked with no arguments. In functional programming, a function that is both associative and provides an identity value is termed as a **monoid**. The `clojure.core.reducers` namespace provides the `monoid` function, described in *Example 3.12*, to create such a function that can be used as the combining function or the reducing function supplied to a `fold` form:

```
(defn monoid
  [op ctor]
  (fn
    ([] (ctor))
    ([a b] (op a b)))))
```

Example 3.12: The monoid function

The `monoid` function shown in *Example 3.12* produces a function that calls a function `op` when supplied with two arguments `a` and `b`. When the function returned by the `monoid` function is called with no arguments, it will produce an identity value of the operation by simply calling the `ctor` function with no arguments. This function allows us to easily create a combining function to be used with the `fold` function from any arbitrary functions `ctor` and `op`.

We can now redefine the map, `filter`, and `mapcat` operations as compositions of the `folder` function and the `mapping`, `filtering`, and `mapcatting` transformers defined in *Example 3.3*, as shown in *Example 3.13*:

```
(defn map [f coll]
  (folder coll (mapping f)))

(defn filter [p? coll]
  (folder coll (filtering p?)))

(defn mapcat [f coll]
  (folder coll (mapcatting f)))
```

Example 3.13: Redefining the map, filter and mapcat functions using the folder form

The definitions of folder, fold, monoid, map, filter, and mapcat as shown in this section are simplified versions of their actual definitions in the clojure.core.reducers namespace.

The reducers library also defines the foldcat function. This function is a high-performance variant of the reduce and conj functions. In other words, the evaluation of the expression (foldcat coll) will be significantly faster than that of the expression (reduce conj [] coll), where coll is a reducible or foldable collection. Also, the collection returned by the foldcat function will be a foldable collection.

Let's now use the fold and map functions to improve the performance of the process and process-with-reducer functions from *Example 3.8*. We can implement this as shown in *Example 3.14*:

```
(defn process-with-folder [nums]
  (r/fold + (r/map inc (r/map inc (r/map inc nums)))))
```

Example 3.14: A function to process a collection of numbers using a fold form

The performance of the process-with-folder function with a large vector can be compared to the process and process-with-reducer functions, as shown here:

```
user> (def nums (vec (range 1000000)))
#'user/nums
user> (time (process nums))
"Elapsed time: 474.240782 msecs"
500002500000
user> (time (process-with-reducer nums))
"Elapsed time: 364.945748 msecs"
500002500000
user> (time (process-with-folder nums))
"Elapsed time: 241.057025 msecs"
500002500000
```

It is observed from the preceding output that the process-with-folder function performs significantly better than the process and process-with-reducer functions due to its inherent use of parallelism. In summary, reducers improve the performance of a computation that has to be performed over a collection using fork/join-based parallelism.

Processing data with reducers

We will now study a simple example that depicts the use of reducers in efficiently processing large collections. For this example, we will use the iota library (https://github.com/thebusby/iota) to handle large memory-mapped files. The usage of the iota library with large files is encouraged as an efficient alternative to using concrete collections. For example, loading the records in a 1 GB TSV file as strings into a Clojure vector would consume over 10 GB of memory due to the inefficient storage of Java strings. The iota library avoids this by efficiently indexing and caching the contents of a large file, and this is done with much lower amount of memory overhead when compared to using concrete collections.

The following library dependencies are required for the upcoming examples:

```
[iota "1.1.2"]
```

Also, the following namespaces must be included in your namespace declaration:

```
(ns my-namespace
  (:require [iota :as i]
            [clojure.string :as cs]
            [clojure.core.reducers :as r]))
```

The following examples can be found in src/m_clj/c3/io.clj of the book's source code.

Suppose we have a large TSV file that contains several thousands of records. Each record represents a person, and can be assumed to have five fields, as shown in the following data:

```
brown   brian   :m   :child    :east
smith   bill    :f   :child    :south
jones   jill    :f   :parent   :west
```

Each record contains two strings and three keywords. The first two string fields of a record represent the last and first name of a person, the third column is a keyword that indicates the gender of a person, and the fourth column is a keyword that identifies a person as a parent or a child. Finally, the fifth column is a keyword that represents an arbitrary direction.

The following example expects the content shown previously to be present in the file resources/data/sample.tsv, relative to the root of your Leiningen project.

The `seq` and `vec` functions from the `iota` library can be used to create a sequence and a vector representation of a memory-mapped file. These objects can then be used to access the file in a performant way. Both of the `seq` and `vec` functions require a file path to be passed to them as the first argument. The `vec` function will index the supplied file in *chunks*, and we can specify the size of each chunk as the second argument to the `vec` function. The `seq` function performs buffered reads of the supplied file as required, similar to the way a lazy sequence is realized. The size of the buffer used by this resulting sequence can be specified as the second argument to the `seq` function. Both the `seq` and `vec` functions split the contents of a file by a predefined byte-separator into records represented as strings. These functions also accept an optional third argument to indicate the byte separator between records in the supplied file. The `vec` function is slower than the `seq` function as it must index the records in the file, which can be demonstrated as follows:

```
user> (time (def file-as-seq (i/seq "resources/data/sample.tsv")))
"Elapsed time: 0.905326 msecs"
#'user/file-as-seq
user> (time (def file-as-vec (i/vec "resources/data/sample.tsv")))
"Elapsed time: 4.95506 msecs"
#'user/file-as-vec
```

Both the statements shown here load the `sample.tsv` file into Clojure data structures. As expected, the `vec` function takes a bit more time than the `seq` function to return a value. The values returned by `seq` and `vec` can be treated just like any other collection. Naturally, iterating over a vector returned by the `vec` function is much faster than using a sequence, as shown here:

```
user> (time (def first-100-lines (doall (take 100 file-as-seq))))
"Elapsed time: 63.470598 msecs"
#'user/first-100-lines
user> (time (def first-100-lines (doall (take 100 file-as-vec))))
"Elapsed time: 0.984128 msecs"
#'user/first-100-lines
```

We will now demonstrate a couple of ways to query the data in the `sample.tsv` file using reducers and the `iota` library. We will need to first define a function that converts a collection of records into collections of columnar values from their string-based representations. This can be implemented using the reducer based `map` and `filter` functions, as shown in the `into-records` function in *Example 3.15*:

```
(defn into-records [file]
  (->> file
       (r/filter identity)
       (r/map #(cs/split % #"[\t] "))))
```

Example 3.15: A function to convert a memory-mapped file into a reducible collection

Now, let's say we need to compute the total number of females from the records in the `sample.tsv` file. We can implement a function to perform this computation using the `map` and `fold` functions, as shown in the `count-females` function in *Example 3.16*:

```
(defn count-females [coll]
  (->> coll
       (r/map #(-> (nth % 2)
                   ({":m" 0 ":f" 1})))
       (r/fold +)))
```

Example 3.16: A function to count the number of females in a collection of persons

We can query the total number of females in the `file-as-seq` and `file-as-vec` collections by composing the `into-records` and `count-females` functions. This can be done using the `->` threading form, as shown here:

```
user> (-> file-as-seq into-records count-females)
10090
user> (-> file-as-vec into-records count-females)
10090
```

Similarly, the reducer-based `map` and `filter` functions can be used to fetch the first names of all the children with the same last name or family in a given collection, as implemented by the `get-children-names-in-family` function in *Example 3.17*:

```
(defn get-children-names-in-family [coll family]
  (->> coll
       (r/filter #(and (= (nth % 0) family)
                       (= (nth % 3) ":child")))
       (r/map #(nth % 1))
       (into [])))
```

Example 3.17: A function to get the first names of all children in a collection of persons

The `into-records` and `get-children-names-in-family` functions can be composed together to query the first names of all children with the last name `"brown"` from the available data, as shown here:

```
user> (-> file-as-seq into-records
          (get-children-names-in-family "brown"))
["sue" "walter" ... "jill"]
user> (-> file-as-vec into-records
          (get-children-names-in-family "brown"))
["sue" "walter" ... "jill"]
```

The `iota` library provides a couple more useful functions to handle large text files:

- The `numbered-vec` function will create a vector representing a memory-mapped file in which each string representing a record will be prepended with its position in the given file.

- The `subvec` function of the `iota` library can be used to *slice* records from a memory-mapped file returned by the `vec` and `numbered-vec` functions. Its semantics are identical to the standard `subvec` function that operates on vectors.

Reducers and the `iota` library allow us to idiomatically and efficiently handle text files containing a large number of byte-separated records. There are also several other libraries and frameworks in the Clojure ecosystem that use reducers to handle large amounts of data, and the reader is encouraged to explore these libraries and frameworks on their own.

Summary

In this chapter, we explored the `clojure.core.reducers` library in detail. We had a look at how reducers are implemented and also how we can use reducers to handle large collections of data in an efficient manner. We also briefly studied the `iota` library that can be used with reducers to handle large amounts of data stored in text files.

In the following chapter, we will explore Clojure macros.

4
Metaprogramming with Macros

Programmers often stumble into situations where they would like to add features or constructs to their programming language of choice. Generally, if a feature would have to be added to a language, the language's compiler or interpreter would need some modification. Alternatively, Clojure (and other Lisps as well) uses *macros* to solve this problem. The term *metaprogramming* is used to describe the ability to generate or manipulate a program's source code by using another program. Macros are a metaprogramming tool that allow programmers to easily add new features to their programming language.

Lisps are not the only languages with support for macro-based metaprogramming. For example, in C and C++, macros are handled by the compiler's preprocessor. In these languages, before a program is compiled, all macro calls in the program's source code are replaced by their definitions. In this sense, macros are used to generate code through a form of text substitution during the compilation phase of a program. On the other hand, Lisps allow programmers to transform or rewrite code when macros are interpreted or compiled. Macros can thus be used to concisely encapsulate recurring patterns in code. Of course, this can be done in languages without macros, as well, without much hassle. But macros allow us to encapsulate patterns in code in a clean and concise manner. As we will see ahead in this chapter, there's nothing equivalent to Lisp macros in other programming languages in terms of clarity, flexibility, and power. Lisps are truly leaps ahead of other programming languages in terms of metaprogramming capabilities.

The rabbit hole of macros in Lisps goes deep enough that there are entire books that talk about them. *Mastering Clojure Macros* by *Colin Jones* is one among these, and this publication describes the various patterns in which macros can be used in great detail. In this chapter, we will explore the foundational concepts behind macros and their usage. We will:

- First, have a look at the basics of reading, evaluating, and transforming code in Clojure.

- Later on, we will examine how macros can be defined and used, and also study several examples based on macros. We will also describe how we can handle platform-specific code using *reader conditionals*.

Understanding the reader

The reader is responsible for interpreting Clojure code. It performs several steps to translate source code in textual representation into executable machine code. In this section, we will briefly describe these steps performed by the reader to illustrate how the reader works.

Clojure and other languages from the Lisp family are **homoiconic**. In a homoiconic language, the source code of a program is represented as a plain data structure. This means that all the code written in a Lisp language is simply a bunch of nested lists. Thus, we can manipulate programs' code just like any other list of values. Clojure has a few more data structures, such as vectors and maps in its syntax, but they can be handled just as easily. In languages that are not homoiconic, any expression or statement in a program has to be translated into an internal data structure termed as a *parse tree*, or *syntax tree*, when the program is compiled or interpreted. In Lisps, however, an expression is already in the form of a syntax tree, since a tree is really just another name for a nested list. In other words, there is no distinction between an expression and the syntax tree it produces. One might also opine that this design tricks programmers into writing code directly as a syntax tree. This distinguishing aspect of Lisps is succinctly captured by the following axiom: *Code is Data*.

Let's first take a look at the most rudimentary representation of code and data in Lisps—an **s-expression**. Any expression comprises of *values* and *symbols*, where the symbols represent variables being used. A nested list of symbols is known as a *symbolic expression*, *s-expression*, or *sexp*. All source code in Clojure is represented as s-expressions. A symbolic expression is formally defined as:

- An atom, which refers to a single symbol or literal value.
- A combination of two s-expressions x and y, represented as (x . y). Here, the dot (.) is used to signify a `cons` operation.

Using this recursive definition, a list of symbols (x y z) is represented by the s-expression, (x . (y . (z . nil))) or (x . (y . z)). When an s-expression is used to represent source code, the first element of the expression represents the function used, and the rest of the elements are the arguments to the function. Of course, this is just a theoretical representation and not really Clojure code. This representation is also called *prefix notation*. This recursive structure of s-expressions is flexible enough to represent both code as well as data. In fact, s-expressions are more-or-less the only form of syntax in Clojure (and other Lisps). For example, if we wanted to add two numbers, we would use an expression with the + function as the first symbol, followed by the values to be added. Similarly, if we wanted to define a function, we would have to write an expression with defn or def as the first symbol in the expression. In Clojure and other Lisps, we also represent data such as lists, vectors, and maps using s-expressions.

Let's look at a simple example that depicts how Clojure code is interpreted. The expression (-> [0 1 2] first inc) that uses a threading macro (->) will be interpreted in three distinct steps. This expression will be read, *macroexpanded*, and evaluated to the value 1, as illustrated here:

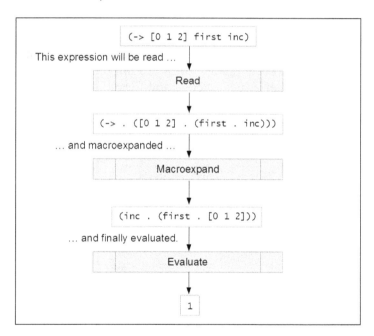

The reader will first parse textual representations of s-expressions from a Clojure program's source code. Once a program's source code is read into s-expressions, all macro calls in the code are replaced by their definitions. This transformation of macro calls in a program is called *macroexpansion*. Lastly, the resulting s-expressions from the macroexpansion phase are evaluated by the Clojure runtime. In the evaluation phase, bytecode is generated from the supplied expressions, loaded into memory, and executed. In short, code in a program's source code is read, transformed through macros, and finally evaluated. Also, macroexpansion happens immediately after a program's source code is parsed, thus allowing the program to internally transform itself before it is evaluated. This transformation of code is exactly what macros are used to achieve.

> In Clojure, the reader only reads code and performs macroexpansion. The generation of bytecode is done by the analyzer and the emitter, and this generated bytecode is evaluated by the JVM.

All Clojure code is translated to *reader forms* and *special forms* before it is evaluated. Special forms are constructs, such as `quote` and `let*`, that are implemented directly as bytecode for the underlying runtime, such as the JVM for Clojure or the Rhino JavaScript runtime for ClojureScript. Interestingly, Clojure source code is composed mostly of reader forms, and these reader forms are implemented in Clojure itself. The reader also transforms certain characters and forms called *reader macros* as soon as they are read. There are several reader macros in the Clojure language, as described in the following table:

Reader macro	Usage
`\x`	This is a character literal.
`;`	This is used to comment. It ignores the rest of the line.
`(.method o)`	This is a native method call. It is rewritten to a dot (`.`) form as (`. o method`). Also, `o` must be a native object.
`@x` or `@( ... )`	This is the dereference operator. It is used with reference types and is rewritten to a `deref` form.
`^{ ... }`	This is the metadata map to be used with a form. It is rewritten to a `with-meta` form.
`'x` or `'( ... )`	This is a quote.
`` `x `` or `` `( ... ) ``	This is a syntax quote.
`~x` or `~( ... )`	This is used to unquote.
`~@x` or `~@( ... )`	This is a splicing unquote.

Reader macro	Usage
#_x or #_(...)	This ignores the next form. #_ should be preferred over the comment form to comment out code, since comment actually returns nil.
#'x	This is a var quote. It is equivalent to (var x).
#=x or #=(...)	This will read-evaluate an expression.
#?(...)	This is a reader conditional form.
#?@(...)	This is a reader conditional splicing form.

We have encountered quite a few of the preceding reader macros in the previous chapters. We will demonstrate the usage of several reader forms that are used with macros in this chapter.

 At the time of writing this book, Clojure does not support user-defined reader macros.

Now that we have familiarized ourselves with the Clojure reader and how code is interpreted, let's explore the various metaprogramming constructs that help us read and evaluate code.

Reading and evaluating code

Let's have a look at how code can be parsed and evaluated in Clojure. The most elementary way to convert text into an expression is by using the read function. This function accepts a java.io.PushbackReader instance as its first argument, as shown here:

```
user> (read (-> "(list 1 2 3)"
            .toCharArray
            java.io.CharArrayReader.
            java.io.PushbackReader.))
(list 1 2 3)
```

 These examples can be found in src/m_clj/c4/read_and_eval.clj of the book's source code.

In this example, a string containing a valid expression is first converted into an instance of `java.io.PushbackReader` and then passed to the `read` function. It seems like a lot of unnecessary work to read a string, but it is due to the fact that the `read` function deals with streams and readers, and not strings. If no arguments are passed to the `read` function, it will create a reader from the standard input and prompt the user to enter an expression to be parsed. The `read` function has several other options as well, and you are encouraged to explore these options in the REPL on their own.

A simpler way to read an expression from a string is by using the `read-string` function. This function accepts a string as its only argument and converts the supplied string into an expression, as shown here:

```
user> (read-string "(list 1 2 3)")
(list 1 2 3)
```

The `read` and `read-string` forms can only convert strings into valid expressions. If we have to evaluate an expression, we must use the `eval` function, as shown here:

```
user> (eval '(list 1 2 3))
(1 2 3)
user> (eval (list + 1 2 3))
6
user> (eval (read-string "(+ 1 2 3)"))
6
```

In the first statement in the preceding output, we prevent the expression `(list 1 2 3)` from being evaluated before it is passed to the `eval` function using the quote operator (`'`). This technique is termed as *quoting* and we shall explore more of it later in this chapter. The `eval` function evaluates the expression `(list 1 2 3)` to the list `(1 2 3)`. Similarly, in the second statement, the expression `(list + 1 2 3)` is first evaluated as `(+ 1 2 3)` by the reader, and then the `eval` function evaluates this list to the value `6`. In the third statement, the string `"(+ 1 2 3)"` is first parsed by the `read-string` function and then evaluated by the `eval` function.

The read-evaluate macro (`#=`) can be used to force the `read` and `read-string` functions to evaluate an expression when it is parsed, as shown here:

```
user> (read (-> "#=(list 1 2 3)"
                .toCharArray
                java.io.CharArrayReader.
                java.io.PushbackReader.))
(1 2 3)
user> (read-string "#=(list 1 2 3)")
(1 2 3)
```

In the preceding output, the `#=` reader macro evaluates the expression (list 1 2 3) when it is read by the `read` and `read-string` functions. If the `#=` macro was not used, both statements would return the expression (list 1 2 3) in verbatim. We can also use the `#=` macro without using `read` or `read-string`, in which case it would be equivalent to calling the `eval` function. Also, the calls to the `#=` macro can be nested any number of times, as shown here:

```
user> #=(list + 1 2 3)
6
user> (read-string "#=(list + 1 2 3)")
(+ 1 2 3)
user> (read-string "#=#=(list + 1 2 3)")
6
```

The `#=` macro makes it easy to evaluate expressions while they are being read. Oh wait! This is a potential security hazard as the `read` and `read-string` functions are evaluating arbitrary strings, even if they contain any malicious code. Thus, evaluation of code while it is being parsed is deemed unsafe. As a solution to this problem, the `*read-eval*` var can be set to `false` to prevent usage of the `#=` macro, as shown here:

```
user> (binding [*read-eval* false]
         (read-string (read-string "#=(list 1 2 3)")))
RuntimeException EvalReader not allowed when *read-eval* is false.
clojure.lang.Util.runtimeException (Util.java:221)
```

Thus, use of the `#=` macro in strings passed to the `read` and `read-string` functions will throw an error if `*read-eval*` is set to `false`. Obviously, the default value of this var is `true`. For this reason, we must avoid using the `#=` macro, or set the `*read-eval*` var to `false`, while processing the user input.

Another way to read and evaluate arbitrary strings is by using the `load-string` function. This function has the same arity as the `read-string` function, and is equivalent to calling the `eval` and `read-string` forms, as shown here:

```
user> (load-string "(+ 1 2 3)")
6
```

There are a couple of semantic differences between using the `load-string` form and a composition of the `eval` and `read-string` forms. Firstly, the behavior of the `load-string` function is not affected by the changing `*read-eval*` var, and is thus unsafe for use with arbitrary user input.

A more important difference is that the `read-string` function only parses the first expression it encounters in the string that it has passed. The `load-string` function will parse and evaluate all expressions passed to it, as shown here:

```
user> (eval (read-string "(println 1) (println 2)"))
1
nil
user> (load-string "(println 1) (println 2)")
1
2
nil
```

In the preceding output, the `read-string` form skips the second `println` form in the string that it is passed, thus printing the value 1 only. The `load-string` form, however, parses and evaluates both the `println` forms it is passed as a string, and prints both the values 1 and 2.

The `load-reader` function is analogous to the `read` function, in the sense that it accepts a `java.io.PushbackReader` instance, from which it has to read and evaluate forms, as an argument. Another variant of `load-string` is the `load-file` function, to which we can pass the path of a file that contains source code. The `load-file` function will parse the file in the path that it is passed and evaluate all forms present in it.

> Note that the `*file*` var can be used to obtain the path of the current file being executed.

So far, we have seen how code can be parsed and evaluated by the Clojure reader. There are several constructs that can be used to perform these tasks. However, evaluating arbitrary strings is not really a good idea, as the code being evaluated is insecure and may be malicious. In practice, we should always set the `*read-eval*` variable to `false` in order to prevent the evaluation of arbitrary code by functions such as `read` and `read-string`. Next, we will explore how *quoting* and *unquoting* can be used to transform expressions.

Quoting and unquoting code

We will now explore *quoting* and *unquoting*, which are techniques used to generate expressions based on a predefined template for an expression. These techniques are foundational in creating macros, and they help structure the code of a macro to look more like its macroexpanded form.

The following examples can be found in `src/m_clj/c4/` `quoting.clj` of the book's source code.

The `quote` form simply returns an expression without evaluating it. This may seem trivial, but preventing the evaluation of an expression is actually something that is not possible in all programming languages. The `quote` form is abbreviated using the apostrophe character (`'`). If we *quote* an expression, it is returned in verbatim, as shown here:

```
user> 'x
x
user> (quote x)
x
```

The `quote` form is quite historic in Lisp. It is one of the seven primitive operators in the original Lisp language, as described in John McCarthy's paper. Incidentally, `quote` is one among the rare special forms that are implemented in Java and not in Clojure itself. The `quote` form is used to handle variable names, or *symbols*, as values. In a nutshell, using the `quote` form, we can treat a given expression as a list of symbols and values. After all, *Code is Data*.

 An apostrophe (`'`) represents a quoted expression only when it appears as the first character in the expression. For example, `x'` is just a variable name.

A syntax quote, written as a backtick character (`` ` ``), will quote an expression and allows *unquoting* to be performed within it. This construct allows us to create expressions just like quoting, but also has the added benefit of letting us interpolate values and execute arbitrary code in a quoted form. This has the effect of treating a predefined expression as a template with some parts left blank to be filled in later. An expression within a syntax quoted form can be unquoted using the tidal character (`~`). Unquoting an expression will evaluate it and insert the result into the surrounding syntax quoted form. A *splicing unquote*, written as `~@`, can be used to evaluate an expression that returns a list and use the returned list of values as arguments for a form. This is something like what the `apply` form does, except that it's within the context of a syntax quote. We must note that both of these unquoting operations (`~` and `~@`) can only be used within a syntax quoted form. We can try out these operations in the REPL, as shown here:

```
user> (def a 1)
#'user/a
user> `(list ~a 2 3)
```

```
(clojure.core/list 1 2 3)
user> `(list ~@[1 2 3])
(clojure.core/list 1 2 3)
```

As shown here, unquoting the variable a in the preceding syntax quoted list form
returns the expression (list 1 2 3). Similarly, using a splicing unquote with the
vector [1 2 3] returns the same list. On the other hand, unquoting a variable in a
quoted form will expand the unquote reader macro (~) to a clojure.core/unquote
form, as shown here:

```
user> (def a 1)
#'user/a
user> `(list ~a 2 3)
(clojure.core/list 1 2 3)
user> '(list ~a 2 3)
(list (clojure.core/unquote a) 2 3)
```

A more interesting difference between using a quote and a syntax quote is that the
latter will resolve all variable names to namespace-qualified names. This applies to
function names as well. For example, let's look at the following expressions:

```
user> `(vector x y z)
(clojure.core/vector user/x user/y user/z)
user> `(vector ~'x ~'y ~'z)
(clojure.core/vector x y z)
```

As shown in the preceding output, the variables x, y, and z are resolved to user/x,
user/y, and user/z respectively by the syntax quoted form, since user is the current
namespace. Also, the vector function is translated to its namespace-qualified name,
shown as clojure.core/vector. The unquote and quote operations in succession,
shown as ~', can be used to bypass the resolution of a symbol to a namespace-
qualified name.

Quoting is supported on data structures other than lists, such as vectors, sets, and
maps, as well. The effect of a syntax quote is the same on all of the data structures;
it allows expressions to be unquoted within it, thus transforming the quoted form.
Also, quoted forms can be nested, as in a quoted forms can contain other quoted
forms. In such a case, the deepest quoted form is processed first. Consider the
following quoted vectors:

```
user> `[1 :b ~(+ 1 2)]
[1 :b 3]
user> `[1 :b '~(+ 1 2)]
[1 :b (quote 3)]
user> `[1 ~'b ~(+ 1 2)]
[1 b 3]
```

There are a lot of interesting aspects that can be inferred from the preceding output. Firstly, keywords are apparently not interned to namespace-qualified names such as symbols. In fact, this behavior is exhibited by any value that evaluates to itself, such as keywords, `nil`, `true`, and `false`, when used in a syntax quoted form. Other than that, unquoting followed by quoting an expression in a syntax quote, shown as `'~(+ 1 2)`, will evaluate the expression and wrap it in a quote. Conversely, unquoting a quoted symbol, shown as `~'b`, will prevent it from being resolved to a namespace-qualified name as we mentioned earlier. Let's take a look at another example that uses nested quoting, as shown here:

```
user> (def ops ['first 'second])
#'user/ops
user> `{:a (~(nth ops 0) ~'xs)
        :b (~(nth ops 1) ~'xs)}
{:b (second xs),
 :a (first xs)}
```

In the preceding output, the variables `first`, `second`, and `xs` are prevented from being interned to a namespace-qualified names using the quote (`'`) and unquote (`~`) operations in tandem. Anyone who's used older Lisps is probably cringing at this point. In practice, usage of the `~'` operation should actually be avoided. This is because preventing the resolution of a variable to a namespace-qualified name isn't really a good idea. In fact, unlike Clojure, some Lisps completely disallow it. It causes a peculiar problem called *symbol capture*, which we will see ahead while we explore macros.

Transforming code

As previously described in this chapter, it's trivial to read and evaluate code in Clojure using the `read` and `eval` functions and their variants. Instead of evaluating code right after it is parsed, we can use macros to first transform code programmatically using quoting and unquoting, and then evaluate it. Thus, macros help us define our own constructs that rewrite and transform expressions passed to them. In this section, we will explore the basics of creating and using macros.

Expanding macros

Macros need to be *expanded* when they are called. All Clojure code is read, macroexpanded, and evaluated by the reader as we described earlier. Let's now take a look at how macroexpansion is performed. As you may have guessed already, this is done using plain Clojure functions.

Interestingly, the reader of the Clojure runtime also uses these functions to process a program's source code. As an example, we will examine how the -> threading macro is macroexpanded. The -> macro can be used as shown here:

```
user> (-> [0 1 2] first inc)
1
user> (-> [0 1 2] (-> first inc))
1
user> (-> (-> [0 1 2] first) inc)
1
```

 These examples can be found in src/m_clj/c4/macroexpand.clj of the book's source code.

All of the three expressions using the -> macro in the preceding output will be evaluated to the value 1. This is due to the fact that they are all macroexpanded to produce the same final expression. How can we claim that? Well, we can prove it using the macroexpand-1, macroexpand, and clojure.walk/macroexpand-all functions. The macroexpand function returns the complete macroexpansion of a form, as shown here:

```
user> (macroexpand '(-> [0 1 2] first inc))
(inc (first [0 1 2]))
```

The expression using the -> threading macro is thus transformed to the expression (inc (first [0 1 2])), which evaluates to the value 1. In this way, the macroexpand function allows us to inspect the macroexpanded form of an expression.

The macroexpand-1 function returns the first expansion of a macro. In fact, the macroexpand function simply applies the macroexpand-1 function repeatedly until no more macroexpansion can be performed. We can inspect how the expression (-> [0 1 2] (-> first inc)) is macroexpanded using these functions:

```
user> (macroexpand-1 '(-> [0 1 2] (-> first inc)))
(-> [0 1 2] first inc)
user> (macroexpand '(-> [0 1 2] (-> first inc)))
(inc (first [0 1 2]))
```

The macroexpand function has a small limitation. It only repeatedly macroexpands an expression until the first form in the expression is a macro. Hence, the macroexpand function will not completely macroexpand the expression (-> (-> [0 1 2] first) inc), as shown here:

```
user> (macroexpand-1 '(-> (-> [0 1 2] first) inc))
(inc (-> [0 1 2] first))
user> (macroexpand '(-> (-> [0 1 2] first) inc))
(inc (-> [0 1 2] first))
```

As shown in the preceding example, the macroexpand function will return the same macroexpansion as macroexpand-1. This is because the second call to the -> macro is not the first form in the result of the first macroexpansion for the previous expression. In such cases, we can use the macroexpand-all function from the clojure.walk namespace to macroexpand a given expression regardless of the positions of macro calls in it, as shown here:

```
user> (clojure.walk/macroexpand-all '(-> (-> [0 1 2] first) inc))
(inc (first [0 1 2]))
```

Thus, all three expressions using the -> macro as examples are macroexpanded to the same expression (inc (first [0 1 2])), which is evaluated to the value 1.

 The macroexpand-1, macroexpand, and clojure.walk/ macroexpand-all functions will have no effect on an expression that does not contain any macros.

The macroexpand-1 and macroexpand functions are indispensable tools for debugging user-defined macros. Additionally, the clojure.walk/macroexpand-all function can be used in situations where the macroexpand function does not completely macroexpand a given expression. The Clojure reader also uses these functions for macroexpanding a program's source code.

Creating macros

Macros are defined using the defmacro form. A macro name, a vector of arguments for the macro, an optional doc-string, and the body of the macro have to be passed to this form. We can also specify multiple arities for a macro. Its similarity to the defn form is quite obvious. Unlike a defn form, however, a macro defined using the defmacro form will not evaluate the arguments passed to it. In other words, the arguments passed to a macro are implicitly quoted. For example, we can create a couple of macros to rewrite an s-expression in infix and postfix notation, as shown in *Example 4.1*.

```
(defmacro to-infix [expr]
  (interpose (first expr) (rest expr)))

(defmacro to-postfix [expr]
  (concat (rest expr) [(first expr)]))
```

Example 4.1: Macros to transform a prefix expression

These examples can be found in `src/m_clj/c4/defmacro.clj` of the book's source code.

Each of the macros in *Example 4.1* describes an elegant way to rewrite an expression `expr` by treating it as a generic sequence. The function being called in the expression `expr` is extracted using the `first` form, and its arguments are obtained using the `rest` form. To convert the expression to its infix form, we use the `interpose` function. Similarly, the `postfix` form of the expression `expr` is generated using the `concat` form. We can use the `macroexpand` function to inspect the expression generated by the `to-infix` and `to-postfix` macros, as shown here:

```
user> (macroexpand '(to-infix (+ 0 1 2)))
(0 + 1 + 2)
user> (macroexpand '(to-postfix (+ 0 1 2)))
(0 1 2 +)
```

 The expression x + y is said to be written in an *infix* notation. The *prefix* notation of this expression is + x y, and its *postfix* notation is x y +.

In this way, by transforming expressions we can effectively modify the language. It's that simple! The basis of the `to-infix` and `to-postfix` macros in *Example 4.1* are that we can treat the terms of an expression as a sequence of elements and manipulate them by using sequence functions such as `interpose` and `concat`. Of course, the preceding example was simple enough such that we could avoid the use of quoting altogether. The `defmacro` form can also be used in combination with quoting to easily rewrite more complex expressions. The same rule can be applied to *any* form of Clojure code.

Interestingly, macros are internally represented as functions, and this can be verified by dereferencing the fully qualified name of a macro and using the `fn?` function, as shown here:

```
user> (fn? @#'to-infix)
true
user> (fn? @#'to-postfix)
true
```

At the time of writing this book, ClojureScript only supports macros written in Clojure. Macros have to be referenced using the `:require-macros` keyword in a ClojureScript namespace declaration, as shown here:

```
(ns my-cljs-namespace
  (:require-macros [my-clj-macro-namespace :as macro]))
```

The `symbol` and `gensym` functions can be used to create temporary variables for use within the body of a macro. The `symbol` function returns a symbol from a name and an optional namespace, as shown here:

```
user> (symbol 'x)
x
user> (symbol "x")
x
user> (symbol "my-namespace" "x")
my-namespace/x
```

We can check whether a value is a symbol using the `symbol?` predicate.

The `gensym` function can be used to create a unique symbol name. We can specify a prefix to be used for the returned symbol name to the `gensym` function. The prefix is defaulted to a capital G character followed by two underscores (`G__`). The `gensym` function can also be used to create a new unique keyword. We can try out the `gensym` function in the REPL, as shown here:

```
user> (gensym)
G__8090
user> (gensym 'x)
x8081
user> (gensym "x")
x8084
user> (gensym :x)
:x8087
```

As shown here, the `gensym` function creates a new symbol every time it is called. In a syntax quoted form, we can use an automatic symbol name created from a prefixed name and the `gensym` function by using the hash character (#), shown as follows:

```
user> `(let [x# 10] x#)
(clojure.core/let [x__8561__auto__ 10]
  x__8561__auto__)
```

```
user> (macroexpand `(let [x# 10] x#))
(let* [x__8910__auto__ 10]
  x__8910__auto__)
```

 The let form is, in fact, a macro defined using the let* special form.

As shown in the preceding expression, all occurrences of the *auto-gensym* variable x# in the syntax quoted form are replaced with an automatically generated symbol name. We should note that only symbols, and not strings or keywords, can be used as a prefix for an auto-gensym symbol.

By generating unique symbols in this way, we can create *hygenic macros*, which avoid the possibility of *symbol capture* or *variable capture*, which is an interesting problem that arises with the use of dynamically scoped variables and macros. To illustrate this problem, consider the macros defined in *Example 4.2*:

```
(defmacro to-list [x]
  `(list ~x))

(defmacro to-list-with-capture [x]
  `(list ~'x))
```

Example 4.2: Macros to depict symbol capture

The macros in *Example 4.2* create a new list using a list form and the value x. Of course, we wouldn't really need to use a macro here, but it is only done for the sake of demonstrating symbol capture. The to-list-with-capture macro *captures* the variable x from the surrounding scope by the use of the ~' operation. If we use a let form to bind the variable name x with a value, we will get different results on calling the to-list and to-list-with-capture macros, as shown here:

```
user> (let [x 10]
        (to-list 20))
(20)
user> (let [x 10]
        (to-list-with-capture 20))
(10)
```

The to-list-with-capture function seems to dynamically obtain the value of x from the surrounding scope, and not from the parameter passed to it. As you may have guessed, this can lead to a number of subtle and bizarre bugs. In Clojure, the solution to this problem is simple; a syntax quoted form will resolve all free symbols to namespace-qualified names. This can be verified by macroexpanding the expression that uses the to-list function in the preceding example.

Let's say we would like to use a temporary variable using a `let` form with a macro that performs the same task as the `to-list` macro from *Example 4.2*. This may seem rather unnecessary, but it is only being done to demonstrate how symbols are resolved by a syntax quote. Such a macro can be implemented as shown in *Example 4.3*:

```
(defmacro to-list-with-error [x]
  `(let [y ~x]
     (list y)))
```

Calling the `to-list-with-error` macro will result in an error due to the use of the free symbol `y`, as shown here:

```
user> (to-list-with-error 10)
CompilerException java.lang.RuntimeException:
Can't let qualified name: user/y
```

This error can be quite annoying, as we simply intended to use a temporary variable in the body of the `to-list-with-error` macro. This error occurred because it is not clear where the variable `y` is resolved from. To get around this error, we can declare the variable `y` as an auto-gensym variable, as shown in *Example 4.4*:

```
(defmacro to-list-with-gensym [x]
  `(let [y# ~x]
     (list y#)))
```

Example 4.4: A macro that uses a let form and an auto-gensym variable

The `to-list-with-gensym` macro works as expected without any error, as shown here:

```
user> (to-list-with-gensym 10)
(10)
```

We can also inspect the expression generated by the `to-list-with-gensym` macro using the `macroexpand` and `macroexpand-1` forms, and the reader is encouraged to try this in the REPL.

To summarize, macros defined using the `defmacro` form can be used to rewrite and transform code. Syntax quote and auto-gensym variables can be used to write hygenic macros that avoid certain problems that can arise due the use of dynamic scope.

Syntax quote can actually be implemented as a user defined macro. Libraries such as `syntax-quote` (https://github.com/hiredman/syntax-quote) and `backtick` (https://github.com/brandonbloom/backtick) demonstrate how syntax quote can be implemented through macros.

Encapsulating patterns in macros

In Clojure, macros can be used to rewrite expressions in terms of functions and special forms. However, in languages such as Java and C#, there is a lot of additional syntax added to the language for handling special forms. For example, consider the `if` construct in these languages, which is used to check whether an expression is true or not. This construct does have some special syntax. If a recurring pattern of usage of the `if` construct is found in a program written in these languages, there is no obvious way to automate this pattern. Languages such as Java and C# have the concept of *design patterns* that encapsulate these sort of patterns. But without the ability to rewrite expressions, encapsulating patterns in these languages can get a bit incomplete and cumbersome. The more special forms and syntax we add to a language, the harder it gets to programmatically generate code for the language. On the other hand, macros in Clojure and other Lisps can easily rewrite expressions to automate recurring patterns in code. Also, there is more-or-less no special syntax for code in Lisps, as code and data are one and the same. In a way, macros in Lispy languages allow us to concisely encapsulate design patterns by extending the language with our own hand-made constructs.

Let's explore a few examples that demonstrate how macros can be used to encapsulate patterns. The `->` and `->>` threading macros in Clojure are used to compose several functions together by passing in an initial value. In other words, the initial value is *threaded* through the various forms that are passed as arguments to the `->` and `->>` macros. These macros are defined in the `clojure.core` namespace as part of the Clojure language, as shown in *Example 4.5*.

The following examples can be found in `src/m_clj/c4/threading.clj` of the book's source code.

```
(defmacro -> [x & forms]
  (loop [x x
         forms forms]
    (if forms
      (let [form (first forms)
            threaded (if (seq? form)
                       (with-meta
                         `(~(first form) ~x ~@(next form))
```

```
                        (meta form))
                     (list form x))]
          (recur threaded (next forms)))
     x)))


(defmacro ->> [x & forms]
  (loop [x x
         forms forms]
    (if forms
      (let [form (first forms)
            threaded (if (seq? form)
                       (with-meta
                         `(~(first form) ~@(next form) ~x)
                         (meta form))
                       (list form x))]
        (recur threaded (next forms)))
      x)))
```

Example 4.5: The -> and ->> threading macros

The ‑> and ‑>> macros in *Example 4.5* use a loop form to recursively thread a value x through the expressions represented by forms. The first symbol in a form, that is the function being called, is determined using the first function. The arguments to be passed in this function, other than x, are extracted using the next function. If a form is just a function name without any additional arguments, we create a new form using the expression (list form x). The with-meta form is used to preserve any metadata specified with form. The ‑> macro passes x as the first argument, whereas ‑>> passes x as the last argument. This is done in a recursive manner for all the forms passed to these macros. Interestingly, syntax quoted forms are used sparingly by both of the ‑> and ‑>> macros. We can actually refactor out some parts of these macros into functions. This adds a slight advantage as functions can be tested quite easily compared to macros. The ‑> and ‑>> threading macros can be refactored as shown in *Example 4.6* and *Example 4.7*:

```
(defn thread-form [first? x form]
  (if (seq? form)
    (let [[f & xs] form
          xs (conj (if first? xs (vec xs)) x)]
      (apply list f xs))
    (list form x)))

(defn threading [first? x forms]
  (reduce #(thread-form first? %1 %2)
          x forms))
```

Example 4.6: Refactoring the -> and ->> threading macros

The `thread-form` function in *Example 4.6* positions the value x in the expression form using the `conj` function. The premise here is that the `conj` function will add an element in the head of a list and at the end or tail of a vector. The `first?` argument is used to indicate whether the value x has to be passed as the first argument to `form`. The `threading` function simply applies the `thread-form` function to all the expressions passed to it, represented by `forms`. The macros `->` and `->>` can now be implemented using the `threading` function as shown in *Example 4.7*:

```
(defmacro -> [x & forms]
  (threading true x forms))

(defmacro ->> [x & forms]
  (threading false x forms))
```

Example 4.7: Refactoring the -> and ->> threading macros (continued)

The threading macros defined in *Example 4.7* work just as well as the ones in *Example 4.5*, and we can verify this in the REPL. This is left as an exercise for the reader.

A common pattern of usage of the `let` form is to repeatedly rebind a variable to new values by passing it through several functions. This kind of pattern can be encapsulated using the `as->` threading macro, which is defined as shown in *Example 4.8*.

```
(defmacro as-> [expr name & forms]
  `(let [~name ~expr
         ~@(interleave (repeat name) forms)]
     ~name))
```

Example 4.8: Refactoring the -> and ->> threading macros

Let's skip past explaining the details of the `as->` macro through words and simply describe the code it generates using the `macroexpand` function, as shown here:

```
user> (macroexpand '(as-> 1 x (+ 1 x) (+ x 1)))
(let* [x 1
       x (+ 1 x)
       x (+ x 1)]
  x)
user> (as-> 1 x (+ 1 x) (+ x 1))
3
```

The `as->` macro binds its first argument to a symbol represented by its second argument and generates a `let*` form as a result. This allows us to define expressions that have to be threaded over in terms of an explicit symbol. One might even say it's a more flexible way to perform the threading of a value through several expressions, as compared to using the `->` and `->>` macros.

The `as->` form has been introduced in Clojure 1.5 along with several other threading macros.

Thus, macros are great tools in automating or encapsulating patterns in code. Several commonly used forms in the Clojure language are actually defined as macros, and we can just as easily define our own macros.

Using reader conditionals

It is often necessary to interoperate with native objects in Clojure and its dialects such as ClojureScript. We can define platform-specific code using *reader conditionals*. Let's now briefly take a look at how we can use reader conditionals.

 Reader conditionals have been introduced in Clojure 1.7. Prior to version 1.7, platform-specific Clojure/ClojureScript code had to be managed using the `cljx` library (`https://github.com/lynaghk/cljx`).

The *reader conditional form*, written as `#?( ... )`, allows us to define platform-specific code using the `:cljs`, `:clj`, `:clr`, and `:default` keywords. The *reader conditional splicing form*, written as `#?@( ... )`, has semantics similar to a reader conditional form. It can be used to splice a list of platform-specific values or expressions into a form. Both these conditional forms are processed when code is read, instead of when it is macroexpanded.

Since Clojure 1.7, the `read-string` function has a second arity in which we can specify a map as an argument. This map can have two keys, `:read-cond` and `:features`. When a string containing a conditional form is passed to the `read-string` function, platform-specific code can be generated by specifying the platform as a set of keywords, represented by `:cljs`, `:clj`, or `:clr`, with the `:features` key in the map of options. In this case, the keyword `:allow` must be specified for the key `:read-cond` in the map passed to the `read-string` function, or else an exception will be thrown. We can try out the reader conditional form with the `read-string` function in the REPL as shown here:

```
user> (read-string {:read-cond :allow :features #{:clj}}
                   "#?(:cljs \"ClojureScript\" :clj \"Clojure\")")
"Clojure"
user> (read-string {:read-cond :allow :features #{:cljs}}
                   "#?(:cljs \"ClojureScript\" :clj \"Clojure\")")
"ClojureScript"
```

These examples can be found in `src/m_clj/c4/reader_conditionals.cljc` of the book's source code.

Similarly, we can read a conditional splicing form into an expression with the `read-string` function as shown here:

```
user> (read-string {:read-cond :allow :features #{:clr}}
                   "[1 2 #?@(:cljs [3 4] :default [5 6])]")
[1 2 5 6]
user> (read-string {:read-cond :allow :features #{:clj}}
                   "[1 2 #?@(:cljs [3 4] :default [5 6])]")
[1 2 5 6]
user> (read-string {:read-cond :allow :features #{:cljs}}
                   "[1 2 #?@(:cljs [3 4] :default [5 6])]")
[1 2 3 4]
```

We can also prevent the transformation of conditional forms by specifying the `:preserve` keyword with the `:read-cond` key in the optional map passed to the `read-string` function, as shown here:

```
user> (read-string {:read-cond :preserve}
                   "[1 2 #?@(:cljs [3 4] :clj [5 6])]")
[1 2 #?@(:cljs [3 4] :clj [5 6])]
```

However, wrapping conditional forms in a string is not really something we should be doing in practice. Generally, we should write all platform-specific code as reader conditional forms in source files with the `.cljc` extension. Once the top-level forms defined in the `.cljc` file are processed by the Clojure reader, we can use them just like any other reader forms. For example, consider the macro written using a reader conditional form in *Example 4.9*:

```
(defmacro get-milliseconds-since-epoch []
  `(.getTime #?(:cljs (js/Date.)
                :clj (java.util.Date.)))))
```

Example 4.9: A macro using a reader conditional

The `get-milliseconds-since-epoch` macro in *Example 4.9* calls the `.getTime` method on a new `java.util.Date` instance when called from the Clojure code. Also, this macro calls the `.getTime` method on a new JavaScript `Date` object when used in ClojureScript code. We can macroexpand a call to the `get-milliseconds-since-epoch` macro from the Clojure REPL to generate JVM-specific code, as shown here:

```
user> (macroexpand '(get-milliseconds-since-epoch))
(. (java.util.Date.) getTime)
```

Thus, reader conditionals help in encapsulating platform-specific code to be used in code that is agnostic of the underlying platform.

Avoiding macros

Macros are an extremely flexible way of defining our own constructs in Clojure. However, careless use of macros in a program can become complicated and lead to a number of strange bugs that are hidden from plain sight. As described in the book, *Programming Clojure* by *Stuart Halloway* and *Aaron Bedra*, the usage of macros in Clojure has two thumb rules:

- **Don't write macros**: Anytime we try to use a macro, we must think twice whether we could perform the same task using a function.

- **Write macros if it's the only way to encapsulate a pattern**: A macro must be used only if it is easier or more convenient than calling a function.

What's the problem with macros? Well, macros complicate a program's code in several ways:

- Macros cannot be composed like functions as they are not really values. It's not possible to pass a macro as an argument to the map or apply forms, for example.

- Macros cannot be tested as easily as functions. Though it can be done programmatically, the only way to test macros is by using macroexpansion functions and quoting.

- In some cases, code that calls a macro may have been written as a macro itself, thus adding more complexity to our code.

- Hidden bugs caused by problems such as symbol capture make macros a little tricky. Debugging macros isn't really easy either, especially in a large codebase.

For these reasons, macros have to be used carefully and responsibly. In fact, if we can solve a problem using macros as well functions, we should always prefer the solution that uses functions. If the use of a macro is indeed required, we should always strive to refactor out as much code as possible from a macro into a function.

That aside, macros make programming a lot of fun as they allow us to define our own constructs. They allow a degree of freedom and liberty that is not really possible in other languages. You may hear a lot of seasoned Clojure programmers tell you that macros are evil and you should never use them, but don't let that stop you from exploring what is possible with macros. Once you encounter and tackle some of the problems that arise with the use of macros, you will have enough experience to be able to decide when macros can be used appropriately.

Summary

We have explored how metaprogramming is possible with Clojure in this chapter. We discussed how code is read, macroexpanded, and evaluated, as well as the various primitive constructs that implement these operations. Macros can be used to encapsulate patterns in code, as we demonstrated in the various examples in this chapter. Toward the end of the chapter, we also talked about reader conditionals and pointed out the various complications that arise with the use of macros.

In the following chapter, we will explore how transducers can be used to process any data regardless of the source of the data.

5
Composing Transducers

Let's get back to our journey of performing computations over data in Clojure. We've already discussed how *reducers* can be used to process collections in *Chapter 3, Parallelization Using Reducers*. Transducers are, in fact, a generalization of reducers that are independent of the source of data. Also, reducers are more about parallelization, while transducers are more focused on generalizing data transformations without restricting us to any particular source of data. Transducers capture the essence of the standard functions that operate on sequences, such as `map` and `filter`, for several sources of data. They allow us to define and compose transformations of data regardless of how the data is supplied to us.

Incidentally, in the context of physics, a transducer is a device that converts a signal from one form of energy into another form. In a way, Clojure transducers can be thought of as ways to capture the *energy* in functions, such as `map` and `filter`, and convert between different sources of data. These sources include collections, streams, and asynchronous channels. Transducers can also be extended to other sources of data. In this chapter, we will focus on how transducers can be used for sequences and collections, and will reserve discussing transducers with asynchronous channels until we talk about the `core.async` library in *Chapter 8, Leveraging Asynchronous Tasks*. Later in this chapter, we will study how transducers are implemented in Clojure.

Understanding transducers

Transducers are essentially a stack of transformations that can be composed and applied to *any* representation of data. They allow us to define transformations that are agnostic of implementation-specific details about the source of the supplied data. Transducers also have a significant performance benefit. This is attributed to the avoidance of unnecessary memory allocations for arbitrary containers, such as sequences or other collections, to store intermediate results between transformations.

Transducers have been introduced in Clojure 1.7.

Transformations can be composed without the use of transducers as well. This can be done using the `comp` and `partial` forms. We can pass any number of transformations to the `comp` function, and the transformation returned by the `comp` function will be a composition of the supplied transformations in the right-to-left order. In Clojure, a transformation is conventionally denoted as `xf` or `xform`.

 The following examples can be found in `src/m_clj/c5/transduce.clj` of the book's source code.

For example, the expression `(comp f g)` will return a function that applies the function `g` to its input and then applies the function `f` to the result. The `partial` function will bind a function to any number of arguments and return a new function. The `comp` function can be used with a `partial` form to compose the `map` and `filter` functions, as shown here:

```
user> (def xf-using-partial (comp
                              (partial filter even?)
                              (partial map inc)))
#'user/xf-using-partial
user> (xf-using-partial (vec (range 10)))
(2 4 6 8 10)
```

In the preceding output, the `partial` function is used to bind the `inc` and `even?` functions to the `map` and `filter` functions respectively. The functions returned by both the `partial` forms shown above will expect a collection to be passed to them. Thus, they represent transformations that can be applied to a given collection. These two transformations are then composed with the `comp` function to create a new function `xf-using-partial`. This function is then applied to a vector of numbers to return a sequence of even numbers. There are a few issues with this code:

- The filtering of even numbers using the `even?` function is performed after applying the `inc` function. This proves that the transformations passed to the `comp` function are applied in the right-to-left order, which is the reverse of the order in which they are specified. This can be a little inconvenient at times.

- The value returned by the `xf-using-partial` function is a list and not a vector. This is because the `map` and `filter` function both return lazy sequences, which are ultimately converted into lists. Thus, the use of the `vec` function has no effect on the type of collection returned by the `xf-using-partial` function.

- Also, the transformation (partial map inc) applied by the xf-using-partial function will create a new sequence. This resulting sequence is then passed to the transformation (partial filter even?). The intermediate use of a sequence is both unnecessary and wasteful in terms of memory if we have several transformations that must be composed.

This brings us to transducers, which address the preceding problems related to composing transformations using the comp and partial forms. In the formal sense, a transducer is a function that modifies a *step function*. This step function is analogous to a reducing function in the context of reducers. A step function combines an input value with the accumulated result of a given computation. A transducer accepts a step function as an argument and produces a modified version of it. In fact, the xf and xform notations are also used to represent a transducer; because a transducer is also a transformation, it transforms a step function. While it may be hard to illustrate without any code, this modification of a step function performed by a transducer actually depicts how some input data is consumed by a given computation to produce a result. Several transducers can also be composed together. In this way, transducers can be thought of as a unified model to process data.

Several of the standard Clojure functions return a transducer when they are called with a single argument. These functions either:

- Accept a function along with a collection as arguments. Examples of such functions are map, filter, mapcat, and partition-by.

- Accept a value indicating the number of elements, usually specified as n, along with a collection. This category includes functions such as take, drop, and partition-all.

 Visit http://clojure.org/transducers for the complete list of standard functions that implement transducers.

The use of transducers can be aptly depicted by Rich Hickey's baggage loading example. Suppose we intend to load several bags into an airplane. The bags will be supplied in pallets, which can be thought of as collections of bags. There are several steps that have to be performed to load the bags into the airplane. Firstly, the bags must be unbundled from the supplied pallets. Next, we must check whether a bag contains any food, and not process it any further if it does. Finally, all the bags must be weighed and labeled in case they are heavy. Note that these steps needed to load the bags into the airplane do not specify how the pallets are supplied to us, or how the labeled bags from the final step are transported to the plane.

We can model the process of loading the bags into the plane as shown in the
`process-bags` function in *Example 5.1*, as follows:

```
(declare unbundle-pallet)
(declare non-food?)
(declare label-heavy)

(def process-bags
  (comp
    (partial map label-heavy)
    (partial filter non-food?)
    (partial mapcat unbundle-pallet)))
```

Example 5.1: Loading bags into an airplane

The functions `unbundle-pallet`, `non-food?`, and `label-heavy` in *Example 5.1*
represent the three steps of loading bags into an airplane. These functions are
applied to a collection of bags using the `map`, `filter`, and `mapcat` functions. Also,
they can be composed using the `comp` and `partial` functions in a right-to-left order.
As we described earlier, the `map`, `filter`, and `mapcat` functions will all produce
sequences on being called, hence creating intermediate collections of bags between
the three transformations. This intermediate use of sequences is analogous to putting
all the bags on trollies after the step is performed. The supplied input and the final
result would both be a bag of trollies. The use of trollies not only incurs additional
work between the steps of our process, but the steps are now convoluted with the
use of trollies. Thus, we would have to redefine these steps if we had to use, say,
conveyer belts instead of trollies to transport the baggage. This means that the `map`,
`filter`, and `mapcat` functions would have to be implemented again if we intend
to produce a different type of collection as a final result. Alternatively, we can use
transducers to implement the `process-bags` function without specifying the type of
collection of either the input or the result, as shown in *Example 5.2*:

```
(def process-bags
  (comp
    (mapcat unbundle-pallet)
    (filter non-food?)
    (map label-heavy)))
```

Example 5.2: Loading bags into an airplane using transducers

The `process-bags` function in *Example 5.2* shows how transducers can be used to compose the `unbundle-pallet`, `non-food?`, and `label-heavy` functions in a left-to-right order. Each of the expressions passed to the `comp` function in *Example 5.2* return a transducer. This implementation of the `process-bags` function does not create any intermediary collections when it is executed.

Producing results from transducers

Transducers are only recipes for computations, and are not capable of performing any actual work on their own. A transducer can produce results when coupled with a source of data. There's also another vital piece of the puzzle, that is, the step function. To combine a transducer, a step function, and a source of data, we must use the `tranduce` function.

The step function passed to `transduce` is also used to create the initial value of the result to be produced. This initial value of the result can also be specified as an argument to the `transduce` function. For example, the `transduce` function can be used with the `conj` form is shown as follows:

```
user> (def xf (map inc))
#'user/xf
user> (transduce xf conj [0 1 2])
[1 2 3]
user> (transduce xf conj () [0 1 2])
(3 2 1)
```

The `inc` function is coupled with the `map` function to create a transducer `xf`, as shown previously. The `transduce` function can be used to produce either a list or a vector from the transducer `xf` using the `conj` function. The order of elements in the results of both the `transduce` forms shown previously is different due to the fact that the `conj` function will add an element to the head of a list, as opposed to adding it at the end of a vector.

We can also compose several transducers together using the `comp` function, as shown here:

```
user> (def xf (comp
                (map inc)
                (filter even?)))
#'user/xf
user> (transduce xf conj (range 10))
[2 4 6 8 10]
```

The transducer xf in the preceding output encapsulates the application of the inc and even? functions using the map and filter forms respectively. This transducer will produce a vector of even numbers when used with the transduce and conj forms. Note that the inc function is indeed applied to the supplied collection (range 10), or else the value 10 would not show up in the final result. This computation using the transducer xf can be illustrated as follows:

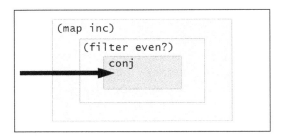

The preceding diagram depicts how the transformations (map inc), (filter even?), and conj are composed in the transformation xf. The map form is applied first, followed by the filter form, and finally the conj form. In this manner, transducers can be used to compose a series of transformations for any source of data.

Another way to produce a collection from a transducer is by using the into function. The result of this function depends on the initial collection supplied to it as the first argument, as shown here:

```
user> (into [] xf (range 10))
[2 4 6 8 10]
user> (into () xf (range 10))
(10 8 6 4 2)
```

The standard sequence function can also be used to produce a lazy sequence from a transducer. Of course, the returned lazy sequence will be converted to a list in the REPL, as shown here:

```
user> (sequence xf (range 10))
(2 4 6 8 10)
```

So far, we've composed transducers to produce collections with a finite number of elements. An infinite series of values could also be produced by a transducer when used with the sequence function. The eduction function can be used to represent this sort of computation. This function will transform a collection, specified as its last argument, to any number of transformations passed to it in right-to-left order. An eduction form may also require a fewer number of allocations compared to using a sequence.

For example, if we were to retrieve the 100th element in a sequence using the nth function, the first 99 elements would have to be realized and also discarded later as they are not needed. On the other hand, an eduction form can avoid this overhead. Consider the declaration of simple-eduction in *Example 5.3*:

```
(def simple-eduction (eduction (map inc)
                               (filter even?)
                               (range)))
```

Example 5.3: Using the eduction function

The collection simple-eduction shown in *Example 5.3* will first filter out even values using the even? predicate from the infinite range (range) and then increment the resulting values using the inc function. We can retrieve elements from the collection simple-eduction using the nth function. The same computation can also be modeled using lazy sequences, but transducers perform much better, as shown here:

```
user> (time (nth simple-eduction 100000))
"Elapsed time: 65.904434 msecs"
200001
user> (time (nth (map inc (filter even? (range))) 100000))
"Elapsed time: 159.039363 msecs"
200001
```

The eduction form using a transducer performs twice as fast compared to a sequence! From the output shown previously, it is quite clear that transducers perform significantly better than lazy sequences for composing a number of transformations. In summary, transducers created using functions such as map and filter can be easily composed to produce collections using functions such as transduce, into, and eduction. We can also use transducers with other sources of data such as streams, asynchronous channels, and observables.

Comparing transducers and reducers

Both transducers and reducers, which were discussed in *Chapter 3, Parallelization Using Reducers,* are ways to improve the performance of computations performed over collections. While transducers are a generalization of data processing for multiple data sources, there are a few other subtle differences between transducers and reducers, which are described as follows:

- Transducers are implemented as part of the Clojure language in the clojure.core namespace. However, reducers must be explicitly included in a program, as they are implemented in the clojure.core.reducers namespace.

- Transducers only create a collection when producing the final result of a series of transformations. There are no intermediary collections required to store the results of a transformation that constitutes a transducer. On the other hand, reducers produce intermediate collections to store results, and only avoid the creation of unnecessary empty collections.

- Transducers deal with efficient composition of a series of transformations. This is quite orthogonal to how reducers squeeze out performance from a computation performed over a collection through the use of parallelization. Transducers perform significantly better than both the `reduce` functions from the `clojure.core` and `clojure.core.reducers` namespaces. Of course, using the `clojure.core.reducers/fold` function is still a good way to implement a computation that can be parallelized.

These contrasts between transducers and reducers describe how these two methodologies of processing data are different. In practice, the performance of these techniques depends on the actual computation being implemented. Generally, if we intend to implement an algorithm to process data in a performant way, we should use transducers. On the other hand, if we are dealing with a lot of data in the memory with no need for I/O and laziness, we should use reducers. The reader is encouraged to compare the performance of the `transduce` function with that of the `reduce` and `fold` functions of the `clojure.core.reducers` library for different computations and data sources.

Transducers in action

In this section, we will examine how transducers are implemented. We will also get a basic idea of how our own *transducible* source of data can be implemented.

Managing volatile references

Some transducers can internally use state. It turns out that the existing reference types, such as atoms and refs, aren't fast enough for the implementation of transducers. To circumvent this problem, transducers also introduce a new *volatile* reference type. A volatile reference represents a mutable variable that will not be copied into the thread-local cache. Also, volatile references are not atomic. They are implemented in Java using the `volatile` keyword with a `java.lang.Object` type.

 The following examples can be found in `src/m_clj/c5/` `volatile.clj` of the book's source code.

We can create a new volatile reference using the `volatile!` function. The value contained in the volatile state can then be retrieved using the @ reader macro or a `deref` form. The `vreset!` function can be used to set the state of a volatile reference, as shown here:

```
user> (def v (volatile! 0))
#'user/v
user> @v
0
user> (vreset! v 1)
1
```

In the preceding output, we encapsulate the value 0 in a volatile state, and then set its state to 1 using the `vreset!` function. We can also mutate the state contained in a volatile reference using the `vswap!` function. We will have to pass a volatile reference and a function to be applied to the value contained in the reference to this function. We can also specify any other arguments for the supplied function as additional arguments to the `vswap!` function. The `vswap!` function can be used to change the state of the volatile reference v that we previously defined, as shown here:

```
user> (vswap! v inc)
2
user> (vswap! v + 3)
5
```

The first call to the `vswap!` function in the preceding output uses the `inc` function to increment the value stored in the reference v. Similarly, the subsequent call to the `vswap!` function adds the value 3 to the new value in the volatile reference v, thus producing the final value 5.

 We can check whether a value is a volatile using the `volatile?` predicate.

One may argue that the volatile reference type has the same semantics as that of an atom. The `vreset!` and `vswap!` functions have the exact same shape as the `reset!` and `swap!` functions that are used with atoms. However, there is an important difference between a volatile reference and an atom. Unlike an atom, a volatile reference does not guarantee atomicity of operations performed on it. Hence, it's recommended to use volatile references in a single thread.

Creating transducers

As a transducer modifies a supplied step function, let's first define what a step function actually does. The following aspects need to be considered:

- The step function must be able to provide an initial value to the transformation it models. In other words, the step function must have an *identity* form that takes no arguments.

- Inputs must be combined with the result accumulated so far by the computation. This is analogous to how a reducing function combines an input value with an accumulated result to produce a new result. The arity of this form is also the same as that of a reducing function; it requires two arguments to represent the current input and the accumulated result.

- The step function must also be able to complete the computation of the modeled process to return something. This can be implemented as a function that accepts a single argument that represents the accumulated result.

Thus, a step function is represented as a function with three arities, as described previously. *Early termination* may also be needed by some transducers to abruptly stop a computational process based on certain conditions.

Now, let's look at how some of the standard functions in the `clojure.core` namespace are implemented with transducers. The `map` function returns a transducer when called with a single argument.

 The following examples can be found in `src/m_clj/c5/implementing_transducers.clj` of the book's source code.

The following *Example 5.4* describes how the `map` function is implemented:

```clojure
(defn map
  ([f]
   (fn [step]
     (fn
       ([] (step))
       ([result] (step result))
       ([result input]
        (step result (f input))))))
  ([f coll]
   (sequence (map f) coll)))
```

Example 5.4: The map function

The 1-arity form of the `map` function returns a function that accepts a step function, represented by `step`, and returns another step function. The returned step function has three different arities, just like we described earlier in this section. The essence of the `map` function is described by the expression (`step result (f input)`), which translates to "apply the function `f` on the current input `input` and combine it with the accumulated result `result` using the function `step`". The returned step function also has two other arities — one that takes no arguments and another that takes one argument. These arities correspond to the other two cases of a step function that we described earlier.

The second arity of the `map` function, which returns a collection and not a transducer, is merely a composition of the `sequence` function and the transducer returned by the expression (`map f`). The actual creation of a collection is done by the `sequence` function. The 1-arity form of the `map` function only describes how the function `f` is applied over a transducible context such as a collection.

Similarly, the `filter` function can be implemented using a transducer, as shown in *Example 5.5*, as follows:

```
(defn filter
  ([p?]
   (fn [step]
     (fn
       ([] (step))
       ([result] (step result))
       ([result input]
        (if (p? input)
          (step result input)
          result)))))
  ([p? coll]
   (sequence (filter p?) coll)))
```

Example 5.5: The filter function

The premise in the implementation of the `filter` function is that a predicate `p?` is used to conditionally combine the accumulated result and the current input, which are represented by `result` and `input` respectively. If the expression (`p? input`) does not return a truthy value, the accumulated result is returned without any modification. Similar to the map function in *Example 5.4*, the 2-arity form of the filter function is implemented using a `sequence` form and a transducer.

To handle early termination in transducers, we must use the `reduced` and `reduced?` functions. Calling reduce or a step function on a value that has been wrapped in a `reduced` form will simply return the contained value. The `reduced?` function checks whether a value is already *reduced*, that is, wrapped in a `reduced` form. The `reduced` and `reduced?` forms both accept a single argument, as shown here:

```
user> (def r (reduced 0))
#'user/r
user> (reduced? r)
true
```

Consider the following function `rf` in *Example 5.6* that uses a `reduced` form to ensure that the accumulated result is never more than 100 elements:

```
(defn rf [result input]
  (if (< result 100)
    (+ result input)
    (reduced :too-big)))
```

Example 5.6: Using the reduced function

The function `rf` merely sums up all inputs to produce a result. If the `rf` function is passed to the `reduce` function along with a sufficiently large collection, the `:too-big` value is returned as the final result, as shown here:

```
user> (reduce rf (range 3))
3
user> (reduce rf (range 100))
:too-big
```

A value wrapped in a `reduced` form can be extracted using the `unreduced` function or the `@` reader macro. Also, the `ensure-reduced` function can be used instead of `reduced` to avoid re-applying a `reduced` form to a value that has already been reduced.

The standard `take-while` function can be implemented using a `reduced` form and a transducer, as shown in the following *Example 5.7*:

```
(defn take-while [p?]
  (fn [step]
    (fn
      ([] (step))
      ([result] (step result))
      ([result input]
       (if (p? input)
         (step result input)
         (reduced result))))))
```

Example 5.7: The take-while function

Note that only the 1-arity form of the take-while function is described in *Example 5.7*. The step function returned by the take-while function uses the expression (p? input) to check if the accumulated result has to be combined with the current input. If the p? predicate does not return a truthy value, the accumulated result is returned by wrapping it in a reduced form. This prevents any other transformations, which may be composed with the transformation returned by the take-while function, from modifying the accumulated result any further. In this way, the reduced form can be used to wrap the result of a transducer and perform early termination based on some conditional logic.

Let's look at how a stateful transducer is implemented. The take function returns a transducer that maintains an internal state. This state is used to keep a track of the number of items that have been processed so far, since the take function must only return a certain number of items from a collection or any other transducible context by definition. *Example 5.8* describes how the take function is implemented using a volatile reference to maintain state:

```
(defn take [n]
  (fn [step]
    (let [nv (volatile! n)]
      (fn
        ([] (step))
        ([result] (step result))
        ([result input]
         (let [n @nv
               nn (vswap! nv dec)
               result (if (pos? n)
                        (step result input)
                        result)]
           (if (not (pos? nn))
             (ensure-reduced result)
             result)))))))
```

Example 5.8: The take function

The transducer returned by the take function will first create a volatile reference nv from the supplied value n to track the number of items to be processed. The returned step function then decrements the volatile reference nv and combines the result with the input using the step function. This is done repeatedly until the value contained in the reference nv is positive. Once all n items have been processed, the result is wrapped in an ensure-reduced form to signal early termination. Here, the ensure-reduced function is used to prevent wrapping the value result in another reduced form, since the expression (step result input) could return a value that is already reduced.

Finally, let's take a quick look at how the transduce function is implemented, as shown in *Example 5.9*:

```
(defn transduce
  ([xform f coll] (transduce xform f (f) coll))
  ([xform f init coll]
   (let [xf (xform f)
         ret (if (instance? clojure.lang.IReduceInit coll)
               (.reduce ^clojure.lang.IReduceInit coll xf init)
               (clojure.core.protocols/coll-reduce coll xf init))]
     (xf ret))))
```

Example 5.9: The transduce function

The transduce function has two arities. The 4-arity form of the transduce function calls the .reduce method of the transducible context coll if it is an instance of the clojure.lang.IReduceInit interface. This interface defines a single method reduce that represents how a data source is reduced using a given function and an initial value. If the variable coll does not implement this interface, the transduce function will fall back on the coll-reduce function to process the data source represented by coll. In a nutshell, the transduce function will try to process a transducible context in the fastest possible way. The clojure.lang.IReduceInit interface must be implemented by all data sources that must support the use of transduce.

The 3-arity form of the transduce function produces the initial value for the transduction by invoking the supplied function f without any arguments. Thus, this arity of the transduce function can only be used with functions that provide an identity value.

> The definitions of the map, filter, take, and take-while functions, as shown in this section, are simplified versions of their actual definitions. However, the transduce function is shown exactly as it is implemented in the clojure.core namespace.

This depicts how transducers and the transduce function are implemented. If we need to implement our own transducible source of data, the implementations described in this section can be used as a guideline.

Summary

So far, we have seen how we can process data using sequences, reducers, and transducers. In this chapter, we described how transducers can be used for performant computations. We also briefly studied how transducers are implemented in the Clojure language.

In the following chapter, we will explore algebraic data structures, such as functors, applicatives, and monads, in Clojure. These concepts will deepen our understanding of functional composition, which is the keystone of functional programming.

6
Exploring Category Theory

On a journey into functional programming, a programmer will eventually stumble upon *category theory*. First off, let's just say that the study of category theory is not really needed to write better code. It's more prevalent in the internals of pure functional programming languages, such as Haskell and Idris, in which functions are *pure* and more like mathematical functions that do not have implicit side effects such as I/O and mutation. However, category theory helps us reason about a very fundamental and practical aspect of computation: *composition*. Functions in Clojure, unlike in pure functional programming languages, are quite different from mathematical functions as they can perform I/O and other side effects. Of course, they can be pure under certain circumstances, and thus concepts from category theory are still useful in Clojure for writing reusable and composable code based on pure functions.

Category theory can be thought of as a mathematical framework for modeling composition. In this chapter, we will discuss a few concepts from category theory using Clojure. We will also study a few algebraic types, such as functors, monoids, and monads.

Demystifying category theory

Category theory has its own share of quirky notations and conventions. Let's start off by exploring some of the terminology used in category theory, in a language understandable by us mortal programmers.

A *category* is formally defined as a collection of **objects** and **morphisms**. In simple terms, objects represent abstract types, and morphisms represent functions that convert between these types. A category is thus analogous to a programming language that has a few types and functions, and has two basic properties:

- There exists an *identity morphism* for each object in the category. In practice, a single identity function can be used to represent the identity morphism for all given objects, but this is not mandatory.

- Morphisms in a category can be composed together into a new morphism. In fact, a composition of two or more morphisms is an optimization of applying the individual morphisms one at a time. In this way, the composition of several morphisms is said to *commute* with applying the constituting morphisms.

Morphisms in a category can be composed as illustrated by the following diagram:

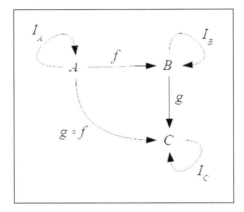

In the preceding diagram, the vertices A, B, and C are the objects and the arrows are morphisms between these objects. The morphisms I_A, I_B, and I_C are identity morphisms that map the objects A, B, and C to themselves. The morphism f maps A to B, and similarly the morphism g maps B to C. These two morphisms can be composed together, as represented by the morphism $g \circ f$ that maps A directly to C, and hence the morphism $g \circ f$ *commutes* with the morphisms f and g. For this reason, the preceding diagram is termed as a *commutative diagram*. Note that identity morphisms in a commutative diagram are generally not shown, unlike in the preceding diagram.

 The following examples can be found in `src/m_clj/c6/demystifying_cat_theory.clj` of the book's source code.

Now, let's translate the previous diagram to Clojure. We shall use the built-in string, symbol and keyword types to depict how morphisms, or rather functions, between these types can be composed together using the comp function:

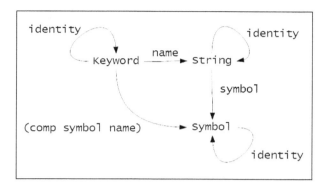

As shown in the preceding diagram, the name function converts a keyword to a string, and the symbol function converts a string to a symbol. These two functions can be composed into a function that converts a keyword directly to a symbol, represented by the (comp symbol name) function. Also, the identity morphisms for each category translate to the identity function.

Internally, the string, symbol, and keyword types are represented by the java.lang.String, clojure.lang.Symbol and clojure.lang.Keyword classes respectively.

We can verify that the name and symbol functions can be composed together using the comp form, as shown in the following REPL output:

```
user> (name :x)
"x"
user> (symbol "x")
x
user> ((comp symbol name) :x)
x
```

This establishes the fact that concepts from category theory have equivalent representations in Clojure, and other programming languages as well. Although it is perfectly valid to think about objects in a category as concrete types like we just described, *algebraic structures* are a more practical substitute for objects. Algebraic structures describe abstract properties of types, rather than what data is contained in a type or how data is structured by a type, and are more like abstract types. Thus, category theory is all about composing functions that operate on abstract types with certain properties.

In Clojure, algebraic structures can be thought of as protocols. Concrete types can implement protocols, and hence a type can represent more than one algebraic structure. The `cats` library (`https://github.com/funcool/cats`) takes this approach and provides protocol-based definitions of a few interesting algebraic structures. The `cats` library also provides types that implement these protocols. Additionally, this library extends some of the built-in types through these protocols allowing us to treat them as algebraic structures. Although there are several alternatives, `cats` is the only library compatible with ClojureScript.

The following library dependencies are required for the upcoming examples:

```
[funcool/cats "1.0.0"]
```

Also, the following namespaces must be included in your namespace declaration:

```
(ns my-namespace
  (:require [cats.core :as cc]
            [cats.builtin :as cb]
            [cats.applicative.validation :as cav]
            [cats.monad.maybe :as cmm]
            [cats.monad.identity :as cmi]
            [cats.monad.exception :as cme]))
```

Now, let's study some of the algebraic structures from the `cats` library.

Using monoids

Let's start by exploring **monoids**. In order to define a monoid, we must first understand what a semigroup is.

The following examples can be found in `src/m_clj/c6/monoids.clj` of the book's source code.

A *semigroup* is an algebraic structure that supports an associative binary operation. A binary operation, say $\oplus$, is termed *associative* if the operation $((a \oplus b) \oplus c)$ produces the same result as the operation $(a \oplus (b \oplus c))$. A monoid is in fact a semigroup with an additional property, as we will see ahead.

The `mappend` function from the `cats.core` namespace will associatively combine a number of instances of the same type and return a new instance of the given type. If we are dealing with strings or vectors, the `mappend` operation is implemented by the standard `concat` function. Thus, strings and vectors can be combined using the `mappend` function, as shown here:

```
user> (cc/mappend "12" "34" "56")
"123456"
user> (cc/mappend [1 2] [3 4] [5 6])
[1 2 3 4 5 6]
```

As strings and vectors support the associative `mappend` operation, they are semigroups. They are also *monoids*, which are simply semigroups that have an *identity element*. It's fairly obvious that the identity element for strings is an empty string, and for vectors it's an empty vector.

This is a good time to introduce a versatile concrete type from the world of functional programming—the `Maybe` type. The `Maybe` type represents an optional value, and can either be empty or contain a value. It can be thought of as a value in a context or a container. The `just` and `nothing` functions from the `cats.monads.maybe` namespace can be used to construct an instance of the `Maybe` type. The `just` function constructs an instance with a contained value, and the `nothing` function creates an empty `Maybe` value. The value contained in a `Maybe` instance can be obtained by either passing it to the `cats.monads.maybe/from-maybe` function, or dereferencing it (using the `deref` form or the `@` reader macro).

Incidentally, the `Maybe` type is also a monoid, since an empty `Maybe` value, created using the `nothing` function, is analogous to an identity element. We can use the `mappend` function to combine values of the `Maybe` type, just like any other monoid, as shown here:

```
user> @(cc/mappend (cmm/just "123")
                    (cmm/just "456"))
"123456"
user> @(cc/mappend (cmm/just "123")
                    (cmm/nothing)
                    (cmm/just "456"))
"123456"
```

The `mappend` function can thus be used to associatively combine any values that are monoids.

Using functors

Next, let's take a look at **functors**. A functor is essentially a value in a container or a computational context. The `fmap` function must be implemented by a functor. This function applies a supplied function to the value contained in a functor. In object-oriented terminology, a functor can be thought of as a generic type with a single abstract method `fmap`. In a way, reference types, such as refs and atoms, can be thought of as functors that save results, as a reference type applies a function to its contained value in order to obtain the new value that should be stored in it.

> The following examples can be found in `src/m_clj/c6/functors.clj` of the book's source code.

The `fmap` function from the `cats.core` namespace takes two arguments: a function and a functor. A functor itself defines what happens when an instance of the functor is passed to the `fmap` function. The `cats` library extends vectors as functors. When a vector is passed to the `fmap` function along with a function, the supplied function is applied to all elements in the vector. Wait a minute! Isn't that what the `map` function does? Well, yes, but the `map` function always returns a lazy sequence. On the other hand, the `fmap` function will return a value with the same concrete type as the functor that is passed. The behavior of the `map` and `fmap` functions can be compared as follows:

```
user> (map inc [0 1 2])
(1 2 3)
user> (cc/fmap inc [0 1 2])
[1 2 3]
```

As shown above, the `map` function produces a lazy sequence, which gets realized into a list in the REPL, when it is passed a vector along with the `inc` function. The `fmap` function, however, produces a vector when passed the same arguments. We should note that the `fmap` function is also aliased as `<$>`. Lazy sequences and sets can also be treated as functors, as shown here:

```
user> (cc/<$> inc (lazy-seq '(1)))
(2)
user> (cc/<$> inc #{1})
#{2}
```

The `Maybe` type is also a functor. The `fmap` function returns a *maybe* when it is passed a *maybe*, as shown here:

```
user> (cc/fmap inc (cmm/just 1))
#<Just@ff5df0: 2>
user> (cc/fmap inc (cmm/nothing))
#<Nothing@d4fb58: nil>
```

The `fmap` function applies the function `inc` to a `Maybe` value only when it contains a value. This behavior of the `fmap` function can be illustrated by the following diagram:

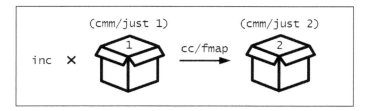

The preceding diagram depicts how the `fmap` function is passed the `inc` function and the expression `(cmm/just 1)`, and returns a new functor instance. The `fmap` function extracts the value from this `Maybe` value, applies the `inc` function to the value, and creates a new `Maybe` value with the result. On the other hand, the `fmap` function will simply return an empty `Maybe` instance, created using the `nothing` function, without touching it, as shown in the following diagram:

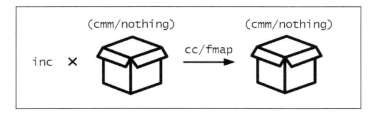

This behavior of the `fmap` function is defined by the implementation of the `Maybe` type. This is because a functor itself gets to define how the `fmap` function behaves with it. Of course, implementing the `fmap` function is not enough to qualify a type as a functor. There are also functor laws that have to be satisfied by any plausible implementation of a functor. The functor laws can be described as follows:

1. Passing an identity morphism and a functor *F* to `fmap` must return the functor *F* without any modification. We can translate this into Clojure using the `identity` function, as follows:

```
user> (cc/<$> identity [0 1 2])
[0 1 2]
```

2. Passing a functor *F* and a morphism *f* to `fmap`, followed by passing the result and another morphism *g* to `fmap`, must be equivalent to calling `fmap` with the functor *F* and the composition $g \circ f$. We can verify this using the `comp` function, as shown here:

```
user> (->> [0 1 2]
          (cc/<$> inc)
          (cc/<$> (partial + 2)))
[3 4 5]
user> (cc/<$> (comp (partial + 2) inc) [0 1 2])
[3 4 5]
```

The first law describes identity morphisms, and the second law upholds the composition of morphisms. These laws can be thought of as optimizations that can be performed by the `fmap` function when used with valid functors.

Using applicative functors

Applicative functors are a subset of functors with a few additional requirements imposed on them, thus making them a bit more useful. Similar to functors, applicative functors are computational contexts that are capable of applying a function to the value contained in them. The only difference is that the function to be applied to an applicative functor must itself be wrapped in the context of an applicative functor. Applicative functors also have a different interface of functions associated with them. An applicative functor, in `cats`, is manipulated using two functions: `fapply` and `pure`.

 The following examples can be found in `src/m_clj/c6/applicatives.clj` of the book's source code.

The `fapply` function from the `cats.core` namespace can be called with an applicative functor, as follows:

```
user> @(cc/fapply (cmm/just inc)
                  (cmm/just 1))
2
```

Here, we again use the `Maybe` type, this time as an applicative functor. The `fapply` function unwraps the `inc` function and the value 1 from the `Maybe` values, combines them and returns the result 2 in a new `Maybe` instance. This can be illustrated with the following diagram:

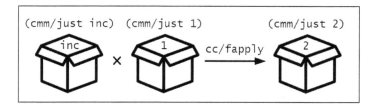

The `cats.core/pure` function is used to create a new instance of an applicative functor. We must pass an implementation-specific context, such as `cats.monads.maybe/context`, and a value to the `pure` function, as follows:

```
user> (cc/pure cmm/context 1)
#<Just@cefb4d: 1>
```

The `cats` library provides an `alet` form to easily compose applicative functors. Its syntax is similar to that of the `let` form, as follows:

```
user> @(cc/alet [a (cmm/just [1 2 3])
                 b (cmm/just [4 5 6])]
          (cc/mappend a b))
[1 2 3 4 5 6]
```

The value returned by the body of the `alet` form, shown previously, is wrapped in a new applicative functor instance and returned. The surrounding `alet` form is dereferenced, and thus the entire expression returns a vector.

The `<*>` function from the `cats.core` namespace is a variadic form of the `fapply` function. It accepts a value representing an applicative functor followed by any number of functions that produce applicative functors. The `cats` library also provides the `Validation` applicative functor type for validating properties of a given object. This type can be constructed using the `ok` and `fail` forms in the `cats.applicative.validation` namespace. Let's say we want to validate a map representing a page with some textual content. A page must have a page number and an author. This validation can be implemented as shown in *Example 6.1*:

```
(defn validate-page-author [page]
  (if (nil? (:author page))
    (cav/fail {:author "No author"})
    (cav/ok page)))

(defn validate-page-number [page]
  (if (nil? (:number page))
    (cav/fail {:number "No page number"})
    (cav/ok page)))
```

```
(defn validate-page [page]
  (cc/alet [a (validate-page-author page)
            b (validate-page-number page)]
    (cc/<*> (cc/pure cav/context page)
            a b)))
```

Example 6.1: The cats.applicative.validation type

The `validate-page-author` and `validate-page-number` functions in *Example 6.1* check whether a map contains the `:author` and `:number` keys respectively. These functions create an instance of the `Validation` type using the `ok` function, and similarly use the `fail` function to create a `Validation` instance that represents a validation failure. Both the `validate-page-author` and `validate-page-number` functions are composed together using the `<*>` function. The first argument passed to `<*>` will have to be an instance of the `Validation` type created using the `pure` function. The `validate-page` function can thus validate maps representing pages, as shown here:

```
user> (validate-page {:text "Some text"})
#<Fail@1203b6a: {:author "No author", :number "No page number"}>
user> (validate-page {:text "Some text" :author "John" :number 1})
#<Ok@161b2f8: {:text "Some text", :author "John", :number 1}>
```

A successful validation will return a `Validation` instance containing the page object, and an unsuccessful one will return an instance of the `Validation` type with the appropriate validation messages as a map. The concrete types for these two cases are `Ok` and `Fail`, as shown in the preceding output.

Applicative functors must themselves define the behavior of the `fapply` and `pure` functions with them. Of course, there are laws that applicative functors must obey too. In addition to the identity and composition laws of functors, applicative functors also conform to the *homomorphism* and *interchange* laws. The reader is encouraged to find out more about these laws before implementing their own applicative functors.

Using monads

Finally, let's take a look at an algebraic structure that helps us build and compose a sequence of computations: a **monad**. There are countless tutorials and articles on the web that explain monads and how they can be used. In this section, we will look at monads in our own unique and Clojure-y way.

In category theory, a monad is a morphism between functors. This means that a monad transforms the context of a contained value into another context. In pure functional programming languages, monads are data structures used to represent computations that are defined in steps. Each step is represented by an operation on a monad, and several of these steps can be chained together. Essentially, a monad is a composable abstraction of a step of any computation. A distinct feature of monads is that they allow us to model impure side effects, which may be performed in the various steps of a given computation, using pure functions.

Monads abstract the way a function binds values to arguments and returns a value. Formally, a monad is an algebraic structure that implements two functions: bind and return. The bind function is used to apply a function to the value contained in a monad, and the return function can be thought of as a construct for wrapping values in a new monad instance. The type signatures of the bind and return functions can be described by the following pseudo code:

```
bind : (Monad A a, [A -> Monad B] f) -> Monad B
return : (A a) -> Monad A
```

The type signature of the bind function states that it accepts a value of type Monad A and a function that converts a value of type A to another value of type Monad B, which is simply a monad containing a value of type B. Also, the bind function returns a type Monad B. The return function's type signature shows that it takes a value of type A and returns a type Monad A. Implementing these two functions allows a monad to execute any code, defined in its bind implementation, before the supplied function f is applied to the value contained in the monad. A monad can also define code to be executed when the supplied function f returns a value, as defined by the monad's implementation of the return function.

Due to the fact that a monad can do more than just call a function over its contained value when passed to the bind function, a monad is used to indicate side effects in pure functional programming languages. Let's say, we have a function that maps type A to B. A function that maps type A to Monad B can be used to model the side effects that can occur when a value of type A is converted to another value of type B. In this way, monads can be used to represent side effects, such as IO, change of state, exceptions, and transactions.

Some programmers may even argue that monads are unnecessary in a language with macros. This is true in some sense, because macros can encapsulate side effects in them. However, monads help us to be explicit about any side-effects, which is quite useful. In fact, monads are the only way to model side effects in pure functional programming languages. Because monads can represent side effects, they allow us to write imperative-style code, which is all about mutation of state, in a pure functional programming language.

The following examples can be found in `src/m_clj/c6/` `monads.clj` of the book's source code.

Let's now look at how the `Maybe` type from the `cats` library can take the form of a monad. We can pass a `Maybe` value along with a function to the `cats.core/bind` function to call the supplied function with the contained value in the monad. This function is aliased as `>>=`. The behavior of the `bind` function with a `Maybe` type is shown here:

```
user> (cc/bind (cmm/just 1) inc)
2
user> (cc/bind (cmm/nothing) inc)
#<Nothing@24e44b: nil>
```

In this way, we can *bind* the `inc` function to a `Maybe` monad. The expression shown in the preceding output can be depicted by the following diagram:

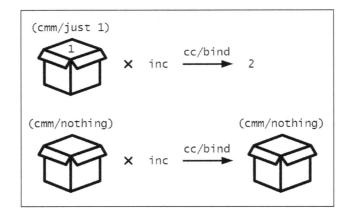

The `inc` function is applied to a `Maybe` monad only if it contains a value. When a `Maybe` monad does contain a value, applying the `inc` function to it using the `bind` function will simply return 2, and not a monad containing 2. This is because the standard `inc` function does not return a monad. On the other hand, an empty `Maybe` value is returned untouched. To return a monad in both the preceding cases, we can use the `return` function from the `cats.core` namespace, as shown here:

```
user> (cc/bind (cmm/just 1) #(-> % inc cc/return))
#<Just@208e3: 1>
user> (cc/bind (cmm/nothing) #(-> % inc cc/return))
#<Nothing@1e7075b: nil>
```

The `lift-m` form can be used to *lift* a function that returns a type A to return a monad containing a type A. The concrete type of the return value of a lifted function depends on the monad context passed to it. If we pass a `Maybe` monad to a lifted version of `inc`, it will return a new instance of the `Maybe` monad, as shown here:

```
user> ((cc/lift-m inc) (cmm/just 1))
#<Just@1eaaab: 2>
```

We can also compose several calls to the `bind` function, as long as the function passed to the `bind` function produces a monad, as shown here:

```
user> (cc/>>= (cc/>>= (cmm/just 1)
                      #(-> % inc cmm/just))
              #(-> % dec cmm/just))
#<Just@91ea3c: 1>
```

Of course, we can also compose calls to the `bind` function to change the type of monad. For example, we can map a `Maybe` monad to an `Identity` monad, which is constructed using the `cats.monads.identity/identity` function. We can modify the preceding expression to return an `Identity` monad as shown here:

```
user> (cc/>>= (cc/>>= (cmm/just 1)
                      #(-> % inc cmm/just))
              #(-> % dec cmi/identity))
#<Identity@dd6793: 1>
```

As shown in the preceding output, calling the `bind` function multiple times can get a bit cumbersome. The `mlet` form lets us compose expressions that return monads, as shown in *Example 6.2*:

```
(defn process-with-maybe [x]
  (cc/mlet [a (if (even? x)
                (cmm/just x)
                (cmm/nothing))
            b (do
                (println (str "Incrementing " a))
                (-> a inc cmm/just))]
    b))
```

Example 6.2. The mlet form

In short, the `process-with-maybe` function defined in *Example 6.2* checks whether a number is even, then prints a line and increments the number. As we use the `Maybe` type, the last two steps of printing a line and incrementing a value are performed only if the input x is even. In this way, an empty `Maybe` monad, created using the `nothing` function, can be used to short-circuit a composition of monads. We can verify this behavior of the `process-with-maybe` function in the REPL, as shown here:

```
user> (process-with-maybe 2)
Incrementing 2
3
user> (process-with-maybe 3)
#<Nothing@1ebd3fe: nil>
```

As shown here, the `process-with-maybe` function prints a line only when the supplied value x is an even number. If not, an empty `Maybe` monad instance is returned.

The previous examples describe how we can use the `Maybe` monad. The `cats` library also provides implementations of the `Either` and `Exception` monads, in the `cats.monads.either` and `cats.monads.exception` namespaces respectively. Let's explore a few constructs from the `cats.monads.exception` namespace.

We can create a new `Exception` monad instance using the `success` and `failure` functions. The `success` form can be passed any value, and it returns a monad that represents a successful step in a computation. On the other hand, the `failure` function must be passed a map containing an `:error` key that points to an exception, and returns a monad that represents a failure in a computation. The value or exception contained in an `Exception` monad can be obtained by dereferencing it (using the `deref` form or the `@` reader macro). Another way to create an `Exception` monad instance is by using the `try-on` macro. The following output describes how these constructs can be used to create an instance of the `Exception` monad:

```
user> (cme/success 1)
#<Success@441a312 [1]>
user> (cme/failure {:error (Exception.)})
#<Failure@4812b43 [#<java.lang.Exception>]>
user> (cme/try-on 1)
#<Success@5141a5 [1]>
user> @(cme/try-on 1)
1
```

The `try-on` macro will return a failure instance of the `Exception` monad if the expression passed to it throws an error, as shown here:

```
user> (cme/try-on (/ 1 0))
#<Failure@bc1115 [#<java.lang.ArithmeticException>]>
user> (cme/try-on (-> 1 (/ 0) inc))
#<Failure@f2d11a [#<java.lang.ArithmeticException>]>
```

A failure instance of an `Exception` monad can be used to short-circuit a composition of monads. This means that binding an `Exception` monad to a function will not call the supplied function if the monad contains an error. This is similar to how exceptions are used to halt computations. We can verify this using the `bind` function, as shown here:

```
user> (cc/bind (cme/try-on (/ 1 1)) #(-> % inc cc/return))
#<Success@116ea43 [2]>
user> (cc/bind (cme/try-on (/ 1 0)) #(-> % inc cc/return))
#<Failure@0x1c90acb [#<java.lang.ArithmeticException>]>
```

Instances of the `Exception` monad can also be created using the `try-or-else` and `try-or-recover` macros from the `cats.monads.exception` namespace. The `try-or-else` form must be passed an expression and a default value. If the expression passed to this form throws an exception, the default value is wrapped in an `Exception` monad instance and returned. The `try-or-recover` form must be passed a 1-arity function in place of the default value. In case an error is encountered, the `try-or-recover` macro will invoke the supplied function and relay the value returned by it. The `try-or-else` and `try-or-recover` f3orms are demonstrated as follows:

```
user> (cme/try-or-else (/ 1 0) 0)
#<Success@bd15e6 [0]>
user> (cme/try-or-recover (/ 1 0)
                          (fn [e]
                            (if (instance? ArithmeticException e)
                              0
                              :error)))
0
```

In this way, monads can be used to model side effects using pure functions. We've demonstrated how we can use the `Maybe` and `Exception` monad types. The `cats` library also implements other interesting monad types. There are monad laws as well, and any monad that we implement must conform to these laws. You are encouraged to learn more about the monad laws on your own.

Summary

In this chapter, we talked about the notations and terminology used in category theory. We also discussed several algebraic types from category theory. Each of these abstractions have laws that must be satisfied by their implementations, and these laws can be thought of as optimizations for computations that use these algebraic types.

In the next chapter, we will look at a different paradigm of programming altogether — logic programming.

7
Programming with Logic

We will now take a step back from the realm of functional programming and explore a completely different paradigm—**logic programming**. Logic programming has its own unique way of solving computational problems. Of course, logic programming isn't the only way to solve a problem, but it's interesting to see what kind of problems can be easily solved with it.

Although logic programming and functional programming are two completely different paradigms, they do have a few commonalities. Firstly, both of these paradigms are forms of *declarative programming*. Studies and papers have also shown that it is possible to implement the semantics of logic programming within a functional programming language. Hence, logic programming operates at a much higher degree of abstraction than functional programming. Logic programming is more suited for problems in which we have a set of rules, and we intend to find all the possible values that conform to these rules.

In this chapter, we look at logic programming in Clojure through the `core.logic` library. We will also study a few computational problems and how we can solve them in a concise and elegant manner using logic programming.

Diving into logic programming

In Clojure, logic programming can be done using the `core.logic` library (`https://github.com/clojure/core.logic/`). This library is a port of **miniKanren**, which is a domain-specific language for logic programming. miniKanren defines a set of simple constructs for creating logical relations and generating results from them.

 miniKanren was originally implemented in the Scheme programming language. You can find out more about miniKanren at `http://minikanren.org/`.

A program written using logic programming can be thought of as a set of logical relations. **Logical relations** are the elementary building blocks of logic programming, just as functions are for functional programming. The terms *relation* and *constraint* are used interchangeably to refer to a logical relation. The core.logic library is in fact an implementation of constraint-based logic programming.

A relation can be thought of as a function that returns a goal, and a goal can either be a success or a failure. In the core.logic library, a goal is represented by the succeed and fail constants. Another interesting aspect of relations is that they can return multiple results, or even no results. This is analogous to a function that produces a sequence of values, which could be empty, as a result. Functions such as keep and filter fit this description perfectly.

The following library dependencies are required for the upcoming examples:

```
[org.clojure/core.logic "0.8.10"]
```

Also, the following namespaces must be included in your namespace declaration:

```
(ns my-namespace
  (:require [clojure.core.logic :as l]
            [clojure.core.logic.fd :as fd]))
```

The following examples can be found in src/m_clj/c7/diving_into_logic.clj of the book's source code.

Solving logical relations

As a convention, relations have their name suffixed with an "o". For example, the conso construct from the clojure.core.logic namespace is a relation that represents the behavior of the cons function. Logical programming constructs that use multiple logical relations, such as conde and matche, end with an "e". We will explore these constructs later on in this chapter. Let's now focus on how we can solve problems with logical relations.

The run* macro, from the clojure.core.logic namespace, processes a number of goals to generate all possible results. The semantics of the run* form allow us to declare a number of logical variables that can be used in relations to return goals. The run* form returns a list of possible values for the logical variables it defines. An expression using the run* form and a set of relations is essentially a way of asking the question "What must the universe look like for these relations to be true?" to a computer and asking it to find the answer.

An equality test can be performed using the `run*` macro in combination with the `clojure.core.logic/==` form, as shown here:

```
user> (l/run* [x]
        (l/== x 1))
(1)
user> (l/run* [x]
        (l/== 1 0))
()
```

Both the statements using the `run*` form in the preceding output find all possible values of the logical variable x. The relation `(l/== x 1)` returns a goal that succeeds when the value of x is equal to 1. Obviously, the only value that x can have for this relation to succeed is 1. The `run*` form evaluates this relation to return 1 in a list. On the other hand, the relation `(l/== 1 0)` is logically false, and thus produces no results when passed to the `run*` form. This means that there are no values of x for which 1 is equal to 0.

A relation built using the `==` form from the `clojure.core.logic` namespace is called *unification*. Unification is often used in logic programming like variable assignment from other paradigms, as it's used to assign values to variables. Conversely, a *disequality* represents a relation in which a logical variable cannot be equal to a given value. The `clojure.core.logic/!=` form is used to construct a disequality relation, as shown here:

```
user> (l/run* [x]
        (l/!= 1 1))
()
user> (l/run* [x]
        (l/== 1 1))
(_0)
```

The first statement in the preceding output produces no results since the relation `(l/!= 1 1)` is logically false. An interesting quirk is that the second statement, which has a goal that always succeeds produces a single result _0, which represents an *unbound* logical variable. As we don't assign a value to x through unification, its value is said to be unbound. The symbols _0, _1, _2, and so on (also written as _.0, _.1, _.2, and so on) represent unbound logical variables in the context of a `run*` form.

The `clojure.core.logic/conso` form is useful in modeling the behavior of the standard `cons` function as a relation. It takes three arguments, of which two are the same as the `cons` function. The first two arguments passed to a `conso` form represent the head and tail of a sequence.

The third argument is a sequence that is expected to be returned on applying the `cons` function on the first two arguments. The `conso` relation can be demonstrated as follows:

```
user> (l/run* [x]
        (l/conso 1 [2 x]
                 [1 2 3]))
(3)
```

The expression using a `conso` relation, in the preceding output, will solve for values of x that produce the value [1 2 3] when a `cons` form is applied to the values 1 and [2 x]. Obviously, x must be 3 for this relation to be true, and hence the result 3 is produced.

Logical variables can be created without the use of a `run*` form using the `lvar` function from the `clojure.core.logic` namespace. Within a `run*` form, we can create local logical variables using the `clojure.core.logic/fresh` macro. Variables declared using a `fresh` form will not be part of the final result produced by the surrounding `run*` form. For example, consider the expressions using the `run*` forms in the following output:

```
user> (l/run* [x y]
        (l/== x y)
        (l/== y 1))
([1 1])
user> (l/run* [x]
        (l/fresh [y]
          (l/== x y)
          (l/== y 1)))
(1)
```

The first expression shown previously produces the vector [1 1] as a result, whereas the second expression produces 1 as the result. This is because we specify a single logical variable x and use a `fresh` form to internally declare the logical variable y in the second expression.

The `run*` form searches for results exhaustively from the set of relations provided to it. If we intend to find a limited number of results and avoid performing any additional computation to find any more results, we should use the `run` macro from the `clojure.core.logic` namespace instead. The `run` form has the same semantics of a `run*` form, but additionally requires the number of desired results to be passed to it as the first argument.

The `clojure.core.logic.fd` namespace provides us with several constructs to deal with relations that are constrained over a finite range of values. For example, suppose we wanted to find values within the range of 0 to 100 that are greater than 10. We can easily express this relation using the `>`, `in`, and `interval` forms from the `clojure.core.logic.fd` namespace and extract the first five values from it using a `run` form, as shown here:

```
user> (l/run 5 [x]
         (fd/in x (fd/interval 0 100))
         (fd/> x 10))
(11 12 13 14 15)
```

The preceding expression uses the `in` and `interval` forms to constrain the value of the variable x. The expression using these two forms ensures that x is within the range of 0 and 100. Also, the `clojure.core.logic.fd/>` function defines a relation in which x must be greater than 10. The surrounding `run` form simply extracts the first five possible values of x from the relations supplied to it. There are also several other arithmetic comparison operators, namely `<`, `<=`, and `>=`, implemented in the `clojure.core.logic.fd` namespace. Instead of specifying a range of values to the `in` macro, we can also enumerate the possible values of a variable by using the `clojure.core.logic.fd/domain` form.

The `firsto` form can be used to describe a relation in which the value in a given variable must be the first element in a collection. We can try out both the `domain` and `firsto` forms in the REPL as shown here:

```
user> (l/run 1 [v a b x]
         (l/== v [a b])
         (fd/in a b x (fd/domain 0 1 2))
         (fd/< a b)
         (l/firsto v x))
([[0 1] 0 1 0])
```

In the preceding expression, we solve for the first set of values of v, a, b, and x that satisfy the following relations. The value of a must be less than that of b, which is shown using the `<` form, and both a and b must constitute the elements of a vector v, which is shown using the `==` form. Also, a, b, and x must be equal to either 0, 1, or 2, as described by a composition of the `in` and `domain` forms. Lastly, the first element of the vector v must be equal to the value x. These relations generate the vector [0 1] and the values 0, 1, and 0 for a, b, and x respectively. Note the arity of the `in` form in the previous expression that allows multiple logical variables to be passed to it along with a constraint.

Combining logical relations

The `clojure.core.logic/conde` form allows us to specify multiple relations, and is a bit similar to the standard `cond` form. For example, consider the following expression that uses the `conde` form:

```
user> (l/run* [x]
        (l/conde
          ((l/== 'A x) l/succeed)
          ((l/== 'B x) l/succeed)
          ((l/== 'C x) l/fail)))
(A B)
```

The preceding expression, which uses a `conde` form, performs equality checks for the symbols A, B, and C against the logical variable x. Only two of these checks produce a goal that succeeds, which is described using the `succeed` and `fail` constants in the clauses of the `conde` form. This logical branching by the `conde` form in the preceding expression can be illustrated through the following diagram:

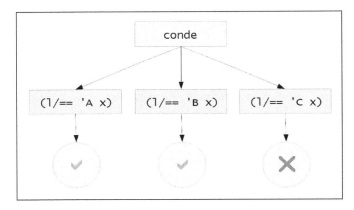

The `conde` form in our previous example creates a conditional check for three clauses. Out of these three clauses, only two succeed, and hence the symbols A and B are returned as results. We should note that the clauses defined in a `conde` form can take any number of relations. Also, the use of the `l/succeed` constant is implicit, and we only need to use the `l/fail` constant to represent a goal that fails.

Another way to perform equality checks is by pattern matching. This can be done using the `clojure.core.logic/matche` form. The `matche` form is thus a more idiomatic way to define conditional branches involving logical variables, as shown here:

```
user> (l/run* [x]
        (l/conde
          ((l/== 'A x) l/succeed)
```

```
        ((1/== 'B x) 1/succeed))))
(A B)
user> (1/run* [x]
        (1/matche [x]
          (['A] 1/succeed)
          (['B] 1/succeed)))
(A B)
```

Both of the preceding expressions produce the same result. The only difference between these expressions is that the first one uses a conde form and the second one performs a pattern match using a matche form. Also, the 1/succeed constant is implicit and does not need to be specified, similar to a conde form. The _ wildcard is also supported by the matche form, as shown here:

```
user> (1/run* [x]
        (1/matche [x]
          (['A])
          ([_] 1/fail)))
(A)
```

In the preceding expression, we solve for all values of x that match the pattern 'A. All other cases fail, which is described using the _ wildcard and the 1/fail constant. Of course, the pattern using the _ wildcard is implicit and is only shown to describe how it can be used in a matche form.

The matche construct also supports destructuring of sequences. A sequence can be destructured by a matche form using a dot (.) to delimit the head and tail of the sequence, as shown here:

```
user> (1/run* [x]
        (1/fresh [y]
          (1/== y [1 2 3])
          (1/matche [y]
            ([[1 . x]]))))
((2 3))
```

In the preceding expression, the logical variable x must be (2 3) for the relation defined using the matche form to succeed. We can define relations using a syntax similar to the defn form using the defne macro from the clojure.core.logic namespace. The defne form allows us to define relations in pattern matching style. Incidentally, a lot of constructs in the core.logic library are defined using the defne form. For example, consider the definition of the membero relation in *Example 7.1*:

```
(1/defne membero [x xs]
  ([_ [x . ys]])
  ([_ [y . ys]]
   (membero x ys)))
```

Example 7.1: Defining the membero relation using the defne macro

The `membero` relation is used to ensure that a value `x` is a member of the collections `xs`. The implementation of this relation destructures the collection `xs` into its head and tail parts. If the value `x` is the head of the collection `xs`, the relation succeeds, otherwise the relation is called recursively with the value `x` and the tail of the destructured list `ys`. We can try out this relation with the `run*` form in the REPL, as shown here:

```
user> (l/run* [x]
        (membero x (range 5))
        (membero x (range 3 10)))
(3 4)
```

The preceding expression solves for values of `x` that are contained in the range 0 to 5 as well as in the range 3 to 10. The results 3 and 4 are produced from these two relations that use the `membero` form.

While dealing with logical variables, it's important to note that we cannot use standard functions to perform any computation with them. In order to extract values from a bunch of logical variables, we have to use the `clojure.core.logic/project` form. For example, consider the following statement:

```
user> (l/run 2 [x y]
        (l/membero x (range 1 10))
        (l/membero y (range 1 10))
        (l/project [x y]
          (l/== (+ x y) 5)))
([1 4] [2 3])
```

The preceding statement solves for two values of x and y such that they are both in the range 1 to 10 and their sum is equal to 5. The values [1 4] and [2 3] are returned as results. The `project` form is used to extract the values of x and y, or else the + function would throw an exception.

Thus, the `core.logic` library provides us with a handful of constructs that can be used to define logical relations, combine them, and generate results from them.

Thinking in logical relations

Now that we are well versed with the various constructs from the `core.logic` library, let's look at some real world problems that can be solved through logic programming.

Solving the n-queens problem

The **n-queens problem** is an interesting problem that can be implemented using logical relations. The objective of the n-queens problem is to place *n* queens on an *n* x *n* sized chessboard such that no two queens are a threat to each other. This problem is a generalization of the *eight queens problem* published by Max Bezzel in 1848, which involves eight queens. In fact, we can actually solve the n-queens problem for any number of queens, as long as we are dealing with four or more queens. Traditionally, this problem can be solved using an algorithmic technique called *backtracking*, which is essentially an exhaustive search for all possible solutions to a given problem. However, in this section, we will solve it using logical relations.

Let's first define how a queen can be used. As we all know, a queen can move as she wishes! A queen can move horizontally, vertically, or diagonally on a chessboard. If any other chess piece is on the same path on which a queen can be moved, then the queen is a threat to it. The position of a chess piece on the chessboard can be specified using a pair of integers, just like how Cartesian coordinates can be used to represent the position of a point on a plane. Suppose the pairs (x_1, y_1) and (x_2, y_2) represent the positions of two queens on the chessboard. As they can threaten each other horizontally, vertically, or diagonally, there are three distinct cases we must avoid:

- The queens cannot be on the same vertical path, that is, x_1 equal to x_2.
- Similarly, the queens cannot be on the same horizontal path, that is, y_1 equal to y_2.
- The queens cannot be on the same diagonal path, in which case the ratio vertical and horizontal distance between them is either 1 or -1. This is actually a trick from coordinate geometry, and its proof is way out of the scope of our discussion. This case can be concisely represented by the following equations:

$$\frac{y_2 - y_1}{x_2 - x_1} = 1 \ or \ \frac{y_2 - y_1}{x_2 - x_1} = -1$$

These are the only rules that determine whether two queens threaten each other. Yet if you think about them from a procedural or object-oriented perspective, implementing them could require a good amount of code. On the contrary, if we think in terms of relations, we can implement these three rules fairly easily using the core.logic library, as shown in the following *Example 7.2*:

The following examples can be found in `src/m_clj/c7/` `nqueens.clj` of the book's source code. This example is based on code from *n-queens with core.logic* by Martin Trojer (http://martinsprogrammingblog.blogspot.in/2012/07/n-queens-with-corelogic-take-2.html).

```
(l/defne safeo [q qs]
  ([_ ()])
  ([[x1 y1] [[x2 y2] . t]]
     (l/!= x1 x2)
     (l/!= y1 y2)
     (l/project [x1 x2 y1 y2]
       (l/!= (- x2 x1) (- y2 y1))
       (l/!= (- x1 x2) (- y2 y1)))
     (safeo [x1 y1] t)))

(l/defne nqueenso [n qs]
  ([_ ()])
  ([n [[x y] . t]]
     (nqueenso n t)
     (l/membero x (range n))
     (safeo [x y] t)))

(defn solve-nqueens [n]
  (l/run* [qs]
    (l/== qs (map vector (repeatedly l/lvar) (range n)))
    (nqueenso n qs)))
```

Example 7.2: The n-queens problem

In *Example 7.2*, we define two relations, namely `safeo` and `nqueenso`, to describe the n-queens problem. Both of these relations must be passed a list `qs` as an argument, where `qs` contains coordinate pairs that represent the positions of queens placed on the chessboard. They are interestingly recursive relations, and the termination is specified by the case in which `qs` is empty.

The `safeo` relation is an implementation of the three rules that determine whether two queens threaten each other. Note the way this relation uses a `project` form to extract the values `x1`, `y1`, `x2`, and `y2` to handle the case in which two queens are on the same diagonal path. The `nqueenso` relation processes all positions of queens from the list `qs` and ensures that each queen is safe. The `solve-queens` function initializes n logical variables using the `clojure.core.logic/lvar` form.

The value `qs` is initialized a list of vector pairs that each contain a logical variable and a number within the range of *0* to *n*. In effect, we initialize the *y* coordinates of all pairs, and solve for the *x* coordinates. The reasoning behind this is that as we are solving for *n* queens on a board with *n* columns and *n* rows, and each row will have a queen placed on it.

The `solve-nqueens` function returns a list of solutions that each contain a list of coordinate pairs. We can print this data in a more intuitive representation by using the `partition` and `clojure.pprint/pprint` functions, as shown in *Example 7.3*:

```
(defn print-nqueens-solution [solution n]
  (let [solution-set (set solution)
        positions (for [x (range n)
                        y (range n)]
                    (if (contains? solution-set [x y]) 1 0))]
    (binding [clojure.pprint/*print-right-margin* (* n n)]
      (clojure.pprint/pprint
        (partition n positions)))))

(defn print-all-nqueens-solutions [solutions n]
  (dorun (for [i (-> solutions count range)
               :let [s (nth solutions i)]]
           (do
             (println (str "\nSolution " (inc i) ":"))
             (print-nqueens-solution s n)))))

(defn solve-and-print-nqueens [n]
  (-> (solve-nqueens n)
      (print-all-nqueens-solutions n)))
```

Example 7.3: The n-queens problem (continued)

Now, we just need to call the `solve-and-print-nqueens` function by passing it the number of queens. Let's try to use this function to solve the n-queens problem for four queens, as shown here:

```
user> (solve-and-print-nqueens 4)

Solution 1:
((0 1 0 0)
 (0 0 0 1)
 (1 0 0 0)
 (0 0 1 0))
```

```
Solution 2:
((0 0 1 0)
 (1 0 0 0)
 (0 0 0 1)
 (0 1 0 0))
nil
```

The `solve-and-print-nqueens` function prints two solutions for four queens. Each solution is printed as a bunch of nested lists, in which each inner list represents a row on the chessboard. The value `1` indicates that a queen is placed on that position on the chessboard. As you can see, none of the four queens threaten each other in either of the two solutions.

In this way, the `solve-nqueens` function uses relations to solve the n-queens problem. We mentioned earlier that the n-queens problem originally involved eight queens. There are totally 92 distinct solutions for eight queens, and the `solve-nqueens` function can find every single one of them. You are encouraged to try this out by passing the value `8` to the `solve-and-print-nqueens` function and verifying the solutions it prints.

Solving a Sudoku puzzle

Some of us may already be in love with the intuitive and mesmerizing Sudoku puzzles that we find in newspapers and magazines. This is another problem that involves logical rules. A Sudoku board is a *9* x *9* grid on which we can place digits. The grid is divided into nine smaller grids, each of which is further divided into *3* x *3* grids that contain digits. These smaller grids are also called *squares* or *boxes*. Some of the squares will be filled with boxes. The goal is to place digits on all positions on the grid such that each row, each column, and each of the smaller grids all contain distinct digits in the range 1 through 9.

Let's implement the rules of a Sudoku puzzle in this way. We will create a logical variable for every possible position of a digit on a Sudoku board and solve for their values using the rules of the puzzle. The initial values of the digits on a Sudoku board can be provided as a single vector comprising of 81 numbers. In this implementation, we introduce a couple of new constructs that are useful in concisely describing the rules of a Sudoku puzzle. The `everyg` function from the `clojure.core.logic` namespace can be used to apply a relation over a list of logical variables, thus ensuring that a relation is true for all the supplied logical variables. We must also ensure that the logical variables in a row, column, and *3* x *3* sized grid in a Sudoku puzzle are distinct. This can done by using the `clojure.core.logic.fd/distinct` function. An implementation of this design of a Sudoku solver is shown in *Example 7.4*.

The following examples can be found in `src/m_clj/c7/sudoku.clj` of the book's source code.

```
(l/defne init-sudoku-board [vars puzzle]
  ([[] []])
  ([[_ . vs] [0 . ps]] (init-sudoku-board vs ps))
  ([[n . vs] [n . ps]] (init-sudoku-board vs ps)))

(defn solve-sudoku [puzzle]
  (let [board (repeatedly 81 l/lvar)
        rows (into [] (map vec (partition 9 board)))
        cols (apply map vector rows)
        val-range (range 1 10)
        in-range (fn [x]
                   (fd/in x (apply fd/domain val-range)))
        get-square (fn [x y]
                     (for [x (range x (+ x 3))
                           y (range y (+ y 3))]
                       (get-in rows [x y])))
        squares (for [x (range 0 9 3)
                      y (range 0 9 3)]
                  (get-square x y))]
    (l/run* [q]
      (l/== q board)
      (l/everyg in-range board)
      (init-sudoku-board board puzzle)
      (l/everyg fd/distinct rows)
      (l/everyg fd/distinct cols)
      (l/everyg fd/distinct squares)))))
```

Example 7.4: A Sudoku solver

In *Example 7.4*, the init-sudoku-board relation initializes the logical variables vars from the puzzle puzzle, and the solve-sudoku function finds all possible solutions of the given puzzle. The solve-sudoku function creates the logical variables through a composition of the repeatedly and clojure.core.logic/lvar forms. These variables are then partitioned into rows, columns, and squares, represented by the variables rows, cols, and squares respectively. The solve-sudoku function then initializes the logical variables using the init-sudoku-board form, and uses a composition of the everyg and distinct forms to ensure that the rows, columns, and squares of a solution contain distinct values. All the logical variables are also bound to the range 1 through 9 using the internally defined in-range function.

The `solve-sudoku` function defined in *Example 7.4* takes a vector of values representing the initial state of a Sudoku board as an argument and returns a list of solutions in which each solution is a vector. As a plain vector isn't really an intuitive representation of a Sudoku board, let's define a simple function to find all solutions of a given puzzle and print the solutions, as shown in *Example 7.5*:

```
(defn solve-and-print-sudoku [puzzle]
  (let [solutions (solve-sudoku puzzle)]
    (dorun (for [i (-> solutions count range)
                 :let [s (nth solutions i)]]
             (do
               (println (str "\nSolution " (inc i) ":"))
               (clojure.pprint/pprint
                (partition 9 s)))))))
```

Example 7.5: A Sudoku solver (continued)

The `solve-and-print-sudoku` function in *Example 7.5* calls the `solve-sudoku` function to determine all possible solutions to a given Sudoku puzzle and prints the results using the `partition` and `clojure.pprint/pprint` functions. Now, let's define a simple Sudoku puzzle to solve, as shown in *Example 7.6*.

```
(def puzzle-1
  [0 9 0 0 0 0 0 5 0
   6 0 0 0 5 0 0 0 2
   1 0 0 8 0 4 0 0 6
   0 7 0 0 8 0 0 3 0
   8 0 3 0 0 0 2 0 9
   0 5 0 0 3 0 0 7 0
   7 0 0 3 0 2 0 0 5
   3 0 0 0 6 0 0 0 7
   0 1 0 0 0 0 0 4 0])
```

Example 7.6: A Sudoku solver (continued)

Now, let's pass the vector `puzzle-1` to the `solve-and-print-sudoku` function to print all possible solutions to it, as shown here:

```
user> (solve-and-print-sudoku puzzle-1)

Solution 1:
((4 9 8 6 2 3 7 5 1)
 (6 3 7 9 5 1 4 8 2)
 (1 2 5 8 7 4 3 9 6)
 (9 7 1 2 8 6 5 3 4)
 (8 4 3 5 1 7 2 6 9)
 (2 5 6 4 3 9 1 7 8)
 (7 6 9 3 4 2 8 1 5)
 (3 8 4 1 6 5 9 2 7)
 (5 1 2 7 9 8 6 4 3))
nil
```

The `solve-sudoku` function finds a single solution to the Sudoku puzzle represented by the vector `puzzle-1` as shown previously. The puzzle represented by `puzzle-1` and its solution are shown on a Sudoku board in the following illustration:

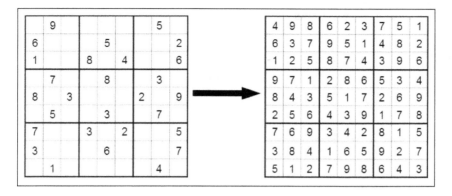

It is very likely that a Sudoku puzzle has multiple solutions. For example, the Sudoku puzzle represented by `puzzle-2` in *Example 7.7* has eight distinct solutions. You're more than welcome to find the solutions to this puzzle using the `solve-and-print-sudoku` function:

```
(def puzzle-2
  [0 8 0 0 0 9 7 4 3
   0 5 0 0 0 8 0 1 0
   0 1 0 0 0 0 0 0 0
   8 0 0 0 0 5 0 0 0
   0 0 0 8 0 4 0 0 0
   0 0 0 3 0 0 0 0 6
   0 0 0 0 0 0 0 7 0
   0 3 0 5 0 0 0 8 0
   9 7 2 4 0 0 0 5 0])
```

Example 7.7: A Sudoku solver (continued)

In conclusion, we can implement the rules of a Sudoku puzzle as logical relations using the `core.logic` library.

Summary

In this chapter, we looked at how Clojure can be used for logic programming. We introduced the `core.logic` library by exploring the various constructs provided by this library. We also studied how we can implement solutions to the n-queens problem and a Sudoku puzzle using the `core.logic` library.

In the following chapter, we will get back on our journey through functional programming and talk about handling asynchronous tasks in Clojure.

8

Leveraging Asynchronous Tasks

The term **asynchronous programming** refers to defining tasks that are executed *asynchronously* on different threads of execution. While this is similar to multithreading, there are a few subtle differences. Firstly, a thread or a future will remain allocated to a single operating system thread until completion. This leads to the fact that is there can only be a limited number of futures that can be executed concurrently, depending on the number of processing cores available. On the other hand, asynchronous tasks are scheduled for execution on threads from a thread pool. This way, a program can have thousands, or even millions of asynchronous tasks running concurrently. An asynchronous task can be suspended at any time, or *parked*, and the underlying thread of execution can be reallocated to another task. Asynchronous programming constructs also allow the definition of an asynchronous task to look like a sequence of synchronous calls, but each call could potentially be executed asynchronously.

In this chapter, we will explore various libraries and constructs that can be used for asynchronous programming in Clojure. First off, we will take a look at *processes* and *channels* in the `core.async` library for asynchronous programming. Later, we will explore *actors* from the *Pulsar* library. Processes and channels are constructs similar to *go-routines* in the Go programming language. On the other hand, actors were first popularized in the Erlang programming language. All of these techniques are different ways of structuring code that executes asynchronously. We must understand that the theory behind these concepts isn't really novel, and more implementations of these theories have been springing up since the rise of distributed and multi-core architectures. With that in mind, let's start off on our journey into asynchronous programming.

Using channels

The `core.async` library (`https://github.com/clojure/core.async`) facilitates asynchronous programming in Clojure. Through this library, we can use asynchronous constructs that run on both the JVM and web browsers without dealing with how they are scheduled for execution on low-level threads. This library is an implementation of the theory in the paper **Communicating Sequential Processes (CSPs)**, originally published in the late '70s by C. A. R. Hoare. The bottom line of CSPs is that any system that processes some input and provides an output can be comprised of smaller subsystems, and each subsystem can be defined in terms of *processes* and *queues*. A queue simply buffers data, and a process can read from and write to several queues. Here, we shouldn't confuse the term *process* with an operating system process. In the context of CSPs, a process is simply a sequence of instructions that interacts with some data stored in queues. Several processes may exist in a given system and queues are a means of conveying data between them. A process that takes data from a single queue and outputs data to another queue can be illustrated as follows:

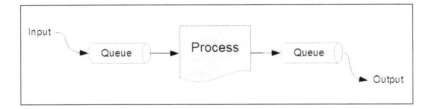

As shown in the preceding diagram, input data goes into a queue, a process manipulates this data through the queue, and finally, writes the output data to another queue. The `core.async` library essentially provides first-class support for creating processes and queues. Queues are dubbed as **channels** in the `core.async` library, and can be created using the `chan` function. Processes can be created using `go` and `thread` macros. Let's dive a bit deeper into the details.

The following library dependencies are required for the upcoming examples:

```
[org.clojure/core.async " 0.1.346.0-17112a-alpha"]
```

Also, the following namespaces must be included in your namespace declaration:

```
(ns my-namespace
  (:require [clojure.core.async :as a]))
```

Processes, created using the thread and go forms, are scheduled for execution on thread pools. In fact, we can create several thousands of these processes in a program as they do not require their own dedicated thread. On the other hand, creating a large number of threads or futures would result in the excessive jobs being queued for execution. This imposes a practical limit on the number of threads or futures we can run concurrently. Hence, the core.async library, and CSPs in general, allows us to model a system as a large number of lightweight and concurrent processes.

Channels can be thought of as data structures for managing the state between processes. The chan function from the core.async namespace returns a channel that can be read from and written to by several concurrent processes. Channels are *unbuffered* by default, which means a write operation to a channel will not complete until a read operation is invoked on it concurrently and vice versa. We can also create a *buffered* channel by specifying a number to the chan function to indicate the buffer size. A buffered channel will allow a certain number of values to be written to it without blocking, and the buffered values can then be read. A channel can be closed using the close! function from the core.async namespace.

We can also create a buffered channel by passing a buffer object to the chan function. A buffer object can be created using the buffer, dropping-buffer, or sliding-buffer functions, and these functions require a number, indicating the size of the buffer, as an argument. Either of the expressions (a/chan (a/buffer n)) or (a/chan n) can be used to create a channel that can buffer n values, and the channel will block write operations to it once it is filled with n values. The dropping-buffer function creates a buffer that drops newly added values once it's full. Conversely, a buffer created using the sliding-buffer function will drop the oldest values added to it once it is completely filled.

The core.async library provides a handful of constructs for reading from and writing to channels, and the values passed to and returned by these constructs conform to a few simple rules. A read operation on a channel returns a value from the channel, or nil if the channel is closed. A write operation will return true if it succeeds, or false if the channel is closed and the write operation couldn't be completed. We can read the buffered data from a closed channel, but once the channel is exhausted of data, a read operation on it will return nil. The arguments to the read and write operations for channels conform to the following pattern:

1. The first argument to any operation is a channel.

2. A write operation must be passed a value to put onto a channel in addition to the channel itself.

At this point, we should note that in the context of channels, the terms "write" and "put" can be used interchangeably, and similarly, the terms "read" and "take" refer to the same operation. The `take!` and `put!` functions take data and put data onto a queue. Both these functions return immediately, and can be passed a callback function as an argument in addition to the usual parameters. Similarly, the `<!!` and `>!!` functions can be used to read from and write to a channel, respectively. However, the `<!!` operation can block the calling thread if there is no data in the supplied channel and the `>!!` operation will be blocked if there is no more buffer space available in a given channel. These two operations are meant to be used within a `thread` form. Finally, the parking read and write functions, namely `<!` and `>!`, can be used within a `go` form to interact with a channel. Both the `<!` and `>!` operations will park the state of the task and release the underlying thread of execution if an operation cannot be completed immediately.

Let's move on to the details of creating processes using the `core.async` library. The `core.async/thread` macro is used to create a single-threaded process. It is similar to the `future` form in the sense that the body of a `thread` form is executed on a new thread and a call to a `thread` form returns immediately. A `thread` form returns a channel from which the output of its body can be read. This makes the `thread` form a bit more convenient than the standard `future` form for interacting with channels, and is thus preferred over a `future` form. The `<!!` and `>!!` functions can be used within a `thread` form to interact with a channel.

To create an asynchronous process that can be parked and scheduled for execution, we must use the `go` macro from the `core.async` namespace. Similar to the `thread` form, it returns a channel from which the output of its body can be read. All channel operations within the body of the `go` form will park, rather than blocking the underlying thread of execution. This implies that the executing thread will not be blocked and can be reallocated to another asynchronous process. Thus, the execution of a number of `go` forms can be interleaved over a much lesser number of actual threads. We must ensure that no thread-specific operations, such as `Thread/sleep`, are made within a `go` form, as such operations affect the underlying thread of execution. Within a `go` form, we must always use the `<!` and `>!` parking forms to read from and write to a channel.

Visit `https://clojure.github.io/core.async/` for the complete documentation on all the functions and macros in the `core.async` library.

The go-loop macro is an asynchronous version of the loop form, and accepts a vector of bindings as its first argument, followed by any number of forms that must be executed. The body of a go-loop form will be internally executed within a go form. The go-loop construct is often used to create asynchronous event loops that have their own localized state. As an example, let's consider the simple wait-and-print function that sets off a process that reads from a given channel, as shown in *Example 8.1*.

 The following examples can be found in src/m_clj/c8/async.clj of the book's source code.

```
(defn wait-and-print [c]
  (a/go-loop [n 1]
    (let [v (a/<! c)]
      (when v
        (println (str "Got a message: " v))
        (println (str "Got " n " messages so far!"))
        (recur (inc n)))))
  (println "Waiting..."))
```

Example 8.1: A function that asynchronously reads from a channel

The wait-and-print function shown previously will repeatedly read from the channel c passed to it. The when form is used to check if the value read from channel, represented by v, is not nil, since nil could be returned from the <! form if the channel c is closed. The go-loop form in the previous example also counts the number of values read from the channel using the variable n. On receiving a value from the channel, some information is printed and the body is looped over using a recur form. We can create a channel, pass it to the wait-and-print function and observe the output of sending values to the channel, as shown here:

```
user> (def c (a/chan))
#'user/c
user> (wait-and-print c)
Waiting...
nil
user> (a/>!! c :foo)
true
Got a message: :foo
Got 1 messages so far!
user> (a/>!! c :bar)
true
Got a message: :bar
Got 2 messages so far!
```

As shown previously, a call to the `wait-and-print` function starts an asynchronous event loop that reads from the channel `c`. On sending a value to the channel `c` using a `>!!` form, the value gets printed along with a total count of values sent to the channel. Also, calls to the `>!!` form return the value `true` immediately. Now, let's see what happens when we close the channel `c` using the `close!` function, shown as follows:

```
user> (a/close! c)
nil
user> (a/>!! c :foo)
false
```

After closing the channel `c`, the `>!!` form returns `false` when it is applied to the channel, which implies that the channel `c` doesn't allow any more values to be put into it. Also, nothing gets printed, which means that the asynchronous routine that was trying to take values from the channel `c` has terminated.

Another way to send values into a channel is by using the `onto-chan` function from the `core.async` namespace. This function must be passed a channel and a collection of values to put *onto* the channel, as shown here:

```
user> (def c (a/chan 4))
#'user/c
user> (a/onto-chan c (range 4))
#<ManyToManyChannel@0x86f03a>
user> (repeatedly 4 #(-> c a/<!!))
(0 1 2 3)
```

The `onto-chan` function will close the channel it has been passed once the supplied collection of values is entirely put onto the channel. To avoid closing the channel, we can specify `false` as an additional argument to the `onto-chan` function.

The `alts!` and `alts!!` functions from the `core.async` namespace can be used to wait for completion of one of several channel operations. The main distinction between these functions is that the `alts!` function is intended for use within a `go` form and will park the current thread, unlike the `alts!!` function that blocks the current thread and must be used in a `thread` form. Both these functions must be passed a vector of channels and return a vector of two elements. The first element in the returned vector represents the value for a take operation or a Boolean value for a put operation, and the second one indicates the channel on which the operation completed. We can also specify a default value as a keyword argument with the key `:default` to the `alts!` and `alts!!` functions. The default value will be returned if none of the operations supplied to the `alts!` or `alts!!` forms have completed.

The `core.async` library provides two versatile macros, namely `alt!` and `alt!!`, to wait for one among several channel operations to be complete. As you may have already guessed, an `alt!` form parks the current task, and an `alt!!` form blocks the current thread. Both these forms can also return a default value when used with the `:default` keyword argument. We can pass several clauses to the `alt!` and `alt!!` forms for reading from and writing to several channels. The `alt!` form in *Example 8.2* describes the clauses supported by the `alt!` and `alt!!` macros:

```
(defn process-channels [c0 c1 c2 c3 c4 c5]
  (a/go
    (a/alt!
      ;; read from c0, c1, c2, c3
      c0 :r
      c1 ([v] (str v))
      [c2 c3] ([v c] (str v))
      ;; write to c4, c5
      [[c4 :v1] [c5 :v2]] :w)))
```

Example 8.2: An asynchronous process implemented using the alt! form

The preceding `process-channels` function takes six channels as its arguments, and uses an `alt!` form within a `go` form to perform asynchronous operations on these channels. The channels c0, c1, c2, and c3 are read, and the channels c4 and c5 are written to. The `alt!` form tries to read from the channel c0 and returns the keyword `:r` if the operation completes first. The channel c1 is also read from, but the right hand side of its clause contains a parameterized expression with the argument v, where v is the value read from the channel. The channels c2 and c3 are passed as a vector in one of the clauses of the `alt!` form shown previously, and this clause uses a parameterized expression with the arguments v and c, where c is the channel on which the read operation completed first and v is the value read from the channel. Write operations are specified in an `alt!` form as a nested vector, where each inner vector contains a channel and a value to put onto the channel. The channels c4 and c5 are written to in the previous `alt!` form, and the value `:w` is returned if either of the two write operations completes. In this way, we can specify clauses to the `alt!` and `alt!!` forms to read to and write from several channels, and return a value based on which channel operation completes first.

Another facility that is often required in asynchronous programming is the ability to specify a *timeout* with a given operation. By the term *timeout*, we mean a specified amount of time after which the current operation is aborted. The `core.async` has an intuitive method for specifying operations with timeouts. This is done using the `core.async/timeout` function, which must be supplied a time interval in milliseconds and returns a channel that closes after the specified amount of time. If we intend to perform an operation with a timeout, we use one of the `alt*` forms with a channel returned by the `timeout` function.

This way, an operation with a channel returned by a `timeout` form will surely complete after the specified amount of time. The `timeout` form is also useful in parking or blocking the current thread of execution for a given amount of time. For example, a blocking read operation from a channel returned by a `timeout` form will block the current thread for the specified time interval, as shown here:

```
user> (time  (a/<!! (a/timeout 1000)))
"Elapsed time: 1029.502223 msecs"
nil
```

We have now covered the basics of processes and channels in the `core.async` library.

Customizing channels

Channels can also be programmed to modify or compute values from those put into them. A read operation, for instance, on a channel could invoke a computation using the values buffered in the same channel, or even other channels. The `reduce` function from the `core.async` namespace can be used to compute values from channels and has more-or-less the same semantics as that of the standard `reduce` function. This variant of the `reduce` function requires a reducing operation, an initial value for the reduction operation and a channel to be passed to it, and it will return a channel from which the result can be read. Also, this function only produces values once the channel passed to it is closed. For example, consider the following code that computes a string from the values in a channel using the `core.async/reduce` function:

```
user> (def c (a/chan 5))
#'user/c
user> (a/onto-chan c (range 5))
#<ManyToManyChannel@0x4adadd>
user> (def rc (a/reduce #(str %1 %2 " ") "" c))
#'user/rc
user> (a/<!! rc)
"0 1 2 3 4 "
```

In the preceding example, the sequence generated by the expression `(range 5)` is put onto the channel `c` using an `onto-chan` form, and values from the channel are computed over using the channel-based variant of the `reduce` function. A single value is read from the resulting channel `rc`, thus producing a string containing all the values from the channel `c`. Note that the `reduce` form in this example produced a result without explicitly calling the `close!` function, as the `onto-chan` function closes the supplied channel after it completes putting values onto it.

A more powerful and intuitive way to compute values from a channel is by using a transducer. We have already discussed transducers in some detail in *Chapter 5, Composing Transducers,* and we will now have a look at how transducers can be used with channels. Essentially, a channel can be associated with a transducer by specifying the transducer as a second argument to the `core.async/chan` function. Let's consider the simple transducer `xform` shown in *Example 8.3*.

```
(def xform
  (comp
    (map inc)
    (map #(* % 2)))))
```

Example 8.3: A simple transducer to use with a channel

The transducer `xform` shown is a trivial composition of mapping the functions `inc` and `#(* % 2)`. It will simply increment all values in a source of data, or rather a channel, and then double all of the results from the previous step. Let's create a channel using this transducer and observe its behavior, as shown here:

```
user> (def xc (a/chan 10 xform))
#'user/xc
user> (a/onto-chan xc (range 10) false)
#<ManyToManyChannel@0x17d6a37>
user> (repeatedly 10 #(-> xc a/<!!))
(2 4 6 8 10 12 14 16 18 20)
```

The channel `xc` will apply the transducer `xform` to each value contained in it. The result of repeatedly taking values from the channel `xc` is thus a sequence of even numbers, which is produced by applying the functions `inc` and `#(* % 2)` to each number in the range `(range 10)`. Note that the `onto-chan` form in the previous example does not close the channel `xc` as we pass `false` as its last argument.

A transducer associated with a channel could encounter an exception. To handle errors, we can pass a function as an additional argument to the `chan` form. This function must take exactly one argument, and will be passed any exception that is encountered by a transducer while transforming the values in a channel. For example, the expression `(a/chan 10 xform ex-handler)` creates a channel with a transducer `xform` and an exception handler `ex-handler`.

In this way, the `core.async/reduce` form and transducers can be used to perform computations on the values contained in channels.

Connecting channels

Now that we are familiar with the basics of channels and processes in the `core.` `async` library, let's explore the different ways in which channels can be connected together. Connecting two or more channels is useful for aggregating and distributing data among them. A connection between two or more channels is called a *joint fitting*, or simply a *joint*. We will use diagrams to describe some of the more complex joint fittings in this section. Keep in mind that the arrows in these diagrams indicate the direction of the flow of data in a given channel.

The simplest way to connect two channels is by using a *pipe*, which is implemented by the `core.async/pipe` function. This function will take values from the first channel provided to it, and supplies these values to the second channel passed to it. In this way, a pipe between channels is similar to UNIX-style pipes between streams. For example, the expression `(a/pipe from to)` will take values from the channel `from` and put them onto the channel `to`. The `pipe` function also takes an optional third argument, which indicates whether the destination channel will be closed when the source channel closes, and this argument defaults to `true`. We can also connect two channels using a *pipeline*, using the `pipeline` function from the `core.async` namespace. The `pipeline` function will essentially apply a transducer to the values in a channel before they are put into another channel. The supplied transducer will also be invoked in parallel for each element in the supplied channel by the `pipeline` function.

The `merge` function from the `core.async` namespace can be used to combine several channels. This function must be passed a vector of channels, and returns a channel from which the values from all of the supplied channels can be read. The returned channel is unbuffered by default, and we specify the size of the channel's buffer by passing a number as an additional argument to the `merge` function. Also, the channel returned by a `merge` form will be closed once all the source channels have been closed. The operation of the `merge` function with two channels can be illustrated as follows:

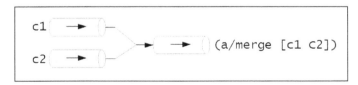

A channel can be split into two channels using the `core.async/split` function. The `split` function must be passed a predicate p? and a channel c, and returns a vector of two channels. The predicate p? is used to decide the channel on which a value from the channel c must be put. All values from the channel c that return a truthy value when passed to the predicate p? will be put onto the first channel in the vector returned by the `split` function.

Conversely, the second channel in the returned vector will contain all values that return `false` or `nil` when `p?` is applied to these values. Both the channels returned by this function will be unbuffered by default, and the buffer size of both these channels can be specified as additional arguments to a `split` form. The `split` function can be depicted by the following illustration:

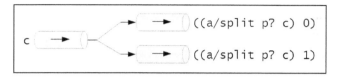

A more dynamic way to combine several channels, compared to the `merge` function, is by using the `mix`, `admix`, and `unmix` functions from the `core.async` namespace. The `mix` function creates a *mix*, to which channels with incoming data can be connected to using the `admix` function. The `mix` function takes a channel as an argument, and the supplied channel will contain values from all the source channels added by the `admix` function. A source channel can be removed from a mixer by using the `unmix` function. The `admix` and `unmix` functions both accept a mix, which is returned by the `mix` function, and a source channel as arguments. To remove all channels from a mix, we simply pass the mix as an argument to the `unmix-all` function. The gist of a mix is that it allows us to dynamically add and remove source channels that send data to a given output channel. A mix, its output channel, and source channels can be illustrated as follows:

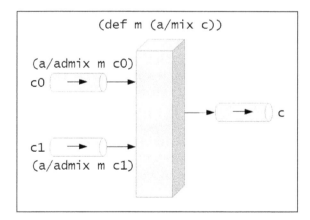

In the preceding illustration, the channel `c` is used as the output channel of the mix `m`, and the channels `c0` and `c1` are added as source channels to the mix `m` using the `admix` function.

The core.async/mult function creates a *multiple* of a given channel. The data from a multiple can be *tapped into* from another channel using the tap function. The channel supplied to the tap function will receive copies of all data sent to the source channel of a multiple. The untap function is used to disconnect a channel from a multiple, and the untap-all function will disconnect all channels from a multiple. A multiple essentially allows us to dynamically add and remove output channels that read values from a given source channel. The mult and tap functions can be described by the following diagram:

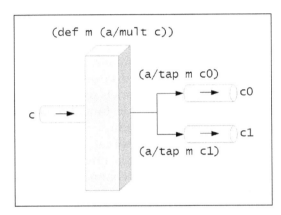

In the preceding illustration, the channel c is used as the source channel by the multiple m, and the channels c0 and c1 are passed to the tap function so that they effectively receive copies of the data sent to the channel c.

The core.async library also supports a *publish-subscribe* model of transferring data. This can be done using a *publication*, which is created using the core.async/pub function. This function must be supplied a source channel and a function to decide the topic of a given value in the publication. Here, a topic can be any literal value, such as a string or a keyword, which is returned by the function supplied to the pub form. Channels can subscribe to a publication and a topic via the sub function, and a channel can unsubscribe from a publication using the unsub function. The sub and unsub functions must be passed a publication, a topic value and a channel. Also, the unsub-all function can be used to disconnect all channels that have subscribed to a publication. This function can optionally be passed a topic value, and will disconnect all channels that have subscribed to the given topic. A publication with two channels subscribed to it is depicted in following diagram:

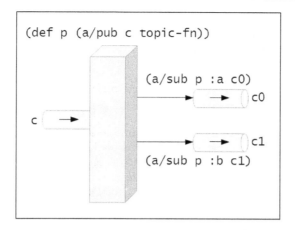

```
(def p (a/pub c topic-fn))

                            (a/sub p :a c0)
                                        → c0
c        →

                                        → c1
                            (a/sub p :b c1)
```

In the preceding illustration, the publication p is created using the channel c and the function topic-fn. The channel c0 subscribes to the publication p and the topic :a, while the channel c1 subscribes to the same publication but for the topic :b. When a value is received on the channel c, it will either be sent to the channel c0 if the function topic-fn returns :a for the given value, or to channel c1 if the function topic-fn returns :b for the given value. Note that the values :a and :b in the preceding diagram are just arbitrary literals, and we could have used any other literal values just as easily.

In summary, the core.async library provides several constructs to create joints between channels. These constructs help in modelling different ways in which data flows from any number of source channels into any number of output channels.

Revisiting the dining philosophers problem

Now, let's try to implement a solution to the **dining philosophers problem** using the core.async library. We have already implemented two solutions to the dining philosophers problem in *Chapter 2, Orchestrating Concurrency and Parallelism* of which one solution used refs and the other one used agents. In this section, we will use channels to implement a solution to the dining philosophers problem.

The dining philosophers problem can be concisely described as follows. Five philosophers are seated on a table with five forks placed between them. Each philosopher requires two forks to eat. The philosophers must somehow share access to the forks placed in between them to consume the food allocated to them, and none of the philosophers must starve due to being unable to acquire two forks. In this implementation, we will use channels to maintain the state of the forks as well as the philosophers on the table.

The following namespaces must be included in your namespace declaration for the upcoming examples:

```
(ns my-namespace
  (:require [clojure.core.async :as a]
            [m-clj.c2.refs :as c2]))
```

The following examples can be found in `src/m_clj/c8/dining_philosophers_async.clj` of the book's source code. Some of these examples are based on code from *A Dining Philosophers solver* by Pepijn de Vos (`http://pepijndevos.nl/2013/07/11/dining-philosophers-in-coreasync.html`).

Let's first define a couple of functions to initialize all the philosophers and forks we are dealing with, as shown in *Example 8.4*:

```
(defn make-philosopher [name forks food]
  {:name name
   :forks forks
   :food food})

(defn make-forks [nf]
  (let [forks (repeatedly nf #(a/chan 1))]
    (doseq [f forks]
      (a/>!! f :fork))
    forks))
```

Example 8.4: The dining philosophers problem

The `make-philosopher` function defined in *Example 8.4* creates a map representing the state of a philosopher. The argument `name` will be a string, the argument `forks` will be a vector of two fork channels, and the argument `food` will be a number indicating the amount of food served to a philosopher. The two forks represent the forks on the left- and right-hand side of a philosopher. These forks will be allocated and passed to the `make-philosopher` function by the `init-philosophers` function that we previously defined in *Chapter 2, Orchestrating Concurrency and Parallelism*. The `make-forks` function shown previously creates a specified number of channels, puts the value `:fork` onto each of them, and finally returns the new channels.

Next, let's define the routine of a philosopher as a process. A philosopher must try to acquire the forks on his left and right side, eat his food if he acquires both forks, and finally release any forks that he successfully acquired. Also, since the state of all the philosophers in our simulation is captured in a channel, we will have to take a philosopher out of a channel, perform the routine of a philosopher, and then put the philosopher's state back onto the channel. This routine is implemented by the `philosopher-process` function in *Example 8.5*:

```
(defn philosopher-process [p-chan max-eat-ms max-think-ms]
  (a/go-loop []
    (let [p (a/<! p-chan)
          food (:food p)
          fork-1 ((:forks p) 0)
          fork-2 ((:forks p) 1)
          ;; take forks
          fork-1-result (a/alt!
                          (a/timeout 100) :timeout
                          fork-1 :fork-1)
          fork-2-result (a/alt!
                          (a/timeout 100) :timeout
                          fork-2 :fork-2)]
      (if (and (= fork-1-result :fork-1)
               (= fork-2-result :fork-2))
        (do
          ;; eat
          (a/<! (a/timeout (rand-int max-eat-ms)))
          ;; put down both acquired forks
          (a/>! fork-1 :fork)
          (a/>! fork-2 :fork)
          ;; think
          (a/<! (a/timeout (rand-int max-think-ms)))
          (a/>! p-chan (assoc p :food (dec food))))
        (do
          ;; put down any acquired forks
          (if (= fork-1-result :fork-1)
            (a/>! fork-1 :fork))
          (if (= fork-2-result :fork-2)
            (a/>! fork-2 :fork))
          (a/>! p-chan p)))
      ;; recur
      (when (pos? (dec food)) (recur)))))
```

Example 8.5: The dining philosophers problem (continued)

The preceding `philosopher-process` function starts an asynchronous process using the `go-loop` macro. The arguments p-chan, max-eat-ms, and max-think-ms represent the channel containing the state of all philosophers, the maximum amount of time a philosopher can spend eating, and the maximum amount of time a philosopher can think, respectively. The asynchronous task started by the `philosopher-process` function will try to take values from the forks fork-1 and fork-2 of a philosopher with a timeout of 100 milliseconds. This is done using a combination of the alt! and timeout functions. If a philosopher is able to acquire two forks, he will eat for some time, put down or release both forks, spend some time thinking, and repeat the same process. If he is unable to get two forks, the philosopher will release any acquired forks and restart the same process. The state of the philosopher is always put back onto the channel p-chan. This asynchronous process is repeated until a philosopher has any remaining food. Next, let's define a couple of functions to start and print the philosophers in our simulation, as shown in *Example 8.6*:

```
(defn start-philosophers [p-chan philosophers]
  (a/onto-chan p-chan philosophers false)
  (dorun (repeatedly (count philosophers)
                     #(philosopher-process p-chan 100 100))))

(defn print-philosophers [p-chan n]
  (let [philosophers (repeatedly n #(a/<!! p-chan))]
    (doseq [p philosophers]
      (println (str (:name p) ":\t food=" (:food p)))
      (a/>!! p-chan p))))
```

Example 8.6: The dining philosophers problem (continued)

The preceding `start-philosophers` function will put a sequence of philosophers, represented by the argument philosophers, onto the channel p-chan, and then call the `philosopher-process` function for each philosopher in the sequence philosophers. The print-philosophers function uses the blocking channel read and write functions, namely <!! and >!!, to read n philosophers from the channel p-chan and print the amount of food remaining on each philosopher's plate.

Finally, let's create some instances of philosophers and associated forks by using the make-philosopher and make-forks functions. We will also use the init-philosophers function from *Chapter 2, Orchestrating Concurrency and Parallelism*, to create philosopher objects, using the make-philosopher function, and assign two forks to each philosopher. These top-level definitions of the philosophers and forks in our simulation are shown in *Example 8.7*.

```
(def all-forks (make-forks 5))
(def all-philosophers
  (c2/init-philosophers 5 1000 all-forks make-philosopher))

(def philosopher-chan (a/chan 5))
```

Example 8.7: The dining philosophers problem (continued)

As shown here, we define five forks and philosophers, and create a channel to represent the state of all philosophers we have created. Note that the channel we use for the philosophers has a buffer size of 5. The simulation can be started by calling the `start-philosophers` function, and the state of the philosophers can be printed using the `print-philosophers` function, as shown here:

```
user> (start-philosophers philosopher-chan all-philosophers)
nil
user> (print-philosophers philosopher-chan 5)
Philosopher 3:    food=937
Philosopher 2:    food=938
Philosopher 1:    food=938
Philosopher 5:    food=938
Philosopher 4:    food=937
nil
user> (print-philosophers philosopher-chan 5)
Philosopher 4:    food=729
Philosopher 1:    food=729
Philosopher 2:    food=729
Philosopher 5:    food=730
Philosopher 3:    food=728
nil
```

As the preceding output shows us, the five philosophers share access to the forks among themselves and consume their food at the same rate. All philosophers get a chance to eat their food, and thus no one starves. Note that the order of the philosophers printed by the `print-philosophers` function may differ from time to time, and some philosophers may also be printed twice by this function.

In this way, we can solve a given problem using channels and processes from the `core.async` library. Also, we can create any number of such processes without bothering about the available number of operating system level threads.

Using actors

Actors are another way of modeling a system as a large number of concurrently running processes. Each process in *the actor model* is termed as an actor, and this model is based on the philosophy that every piece of logic in a system can be represented as an actor. The theory behind actors was first published by Carl Hewitt in the early '70s. Before we explore actors, we must note that the core Clojure language and libraries do not provide an implementation of the actor model. In fact, it is a widely accepted notion in the Clojure community that processes and channels are a much better methodology to model concurrently running processes compared to actors. That aside, actors can be used to provide more resilient error handling and recovery, and it is possible to use actors in Clojure through the Pulsar library (`https://github.com/puniverse/pulsar`).

 To find out more about why processes and channels are preferred over actors in Clojure, take a look at *Clojure core.async Channels* by Rich Hickey (`http://clojure.com/blog/2013/06/28/clojure-core-async-channels`).

The actor model describes actors as concurrent processes that perform some computation on receiving messages. An actor can also send messages to other actors, create more actors, and change its own behavior depending on the messages it receives. Actors can also have their own internal state. In fact, actors were originally described as independent processors with their own local memory that interact with each other through a high-speed communication network. Every actor has its own *mailbox* to receive messages, and messages are the only means of conveying data between actors. The following diagram depicts an actor as an entity that receives some input as messages and performs computations to produce some output:

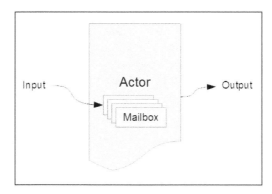

The Pulsar library provides a comprehensive implementation of the actor model. In this library, actors are scheduled to execute on **fibers**, which are similar to asynchronous tasks created using the `go` form from the `core.async` library. Fibers are scheduled to run on fork-join thread pools, unlike regular thread pools that are used in the `core.async` library. Due to this design, the Pulsar library is available only on the JVM, and not in the browser through ClojureScript.

Fibers communicate with each other through the Pulsar library's own implementation of *promises* and *channels*. Interestingly, the Pulsar library also has several thin wrappers around its implementation of channels, to provide an API that is fully compatible with that of the `core.async` library. Although we won't discuss fibers, promises, and channels from the Pulsar library any further in this section, we must understand that channels are quite relevant to actors, since an actor's mailbox is implemented using a channel. Now, let's explore the basics of actors in the Pulsar library.

Creating actors

The `spawn` macro, from the `co.paralleluniverse.pulsar.actors` namespace, creates a new actor and must be passed a function that takes no arguments. We can specify the buffer size of an actor's mailbox using the `:mailbox-size` keyword argument of the `spawn` macro. There are several other interesting keyword arguments that can be passed to the `spawn` form, and you are encouraged to find out more about them on your own.

The following library dependencies are required for the upcoming examples:

```
[co.paralleluniverse/quasar-core "0.7.3"]
[co.paralleluniverse/pulsar "0.7.3"]
```

Your `project.clj` file must also contain the following entries:

```
:java-agents
[[co.paralleluniverse/quasar-core "0.7.3"]]
:jvm-opts
["-Dco.paralleluniverse.pulsar.instrument.auto=all"]
```

Also, the following namespaces must be included in your namespace declaration:

```
(ns my-namespace
   (:require [co.paralleluniverse.pulsar.core :as pc]
             [co.paralleluniverse.pulsar.actors :as pa]))
```

The function supplied to the `spawn` macro must use the `receive` macro, from the `co.paralleluniverse.pulsar.actors` namespace, to process messages received by the actor. Within this supplied function, we can use the expression `@self` to refer to the actor executing it. The `receive` form also supports pattern matching, which is implemented through the `core.match` library. We can also call the `receive` macro with no arguments, in which case it will return a message from the actor's mailbox. The `receive` form will also park the fiber on which it is executed.

To send messages to actors, we can use either the `!` or `!!` macros from the `co.paralleluniverse.pulsar.actors` namespace. Both these macros must be passed an actor and an expression that returns a value, and both of these forms return `nil`. The only difference between these two forms is that `!` is asynchronous, while `!!` is synchronous and may block the current thread of execution if the actor's mailbox is full. An actor may terminate on receiving a particular message, and we can check whether an actor is still active using the `done?` function from the `co.paralleluniverse.pulsar.actors` namespace. Once an actor terminates, we can obtain the final value returned by the actor using the `join` function from the `co.paralleluniverse.pulsar.core` namespace. For example, consider the actor created using the `spawn` and `receive` forms in *Example 8.8*.

The following examples can be found in `src/m_clj/c8/actors.clj` of the book's source code. Some of these examples are based on code from the official Pulsar documentation (`http://docs.paralleluniverse.co/pulsar/`).

```
(def actor (pa/spawn
             #(pa/receive
                :finish (println "Finished")
                m (do
                    (println (str "Received: " m))
                    (recur)))))
```

Example 8.8: An actor created using the spawn macro

The actor, represented by the preceding variable `actor`, will receive a message, print it and loop using a `recur` form. If the message `:finish` is received, it will print a string and terminate. The following code demonstrates how we can send a message to the actor:

```
user> (pa/! actor :foo)
nil
Received: :foo
user> (pa/done? actor)
false
```

As shown here, sending the value `:foo` to the actor returns `nil` immediately, and the message gets printed from another thread. As the `done?` function returns `false` when passed the variable `actor`, it is evident that the actor does not terminate on receiving the value `:foo` as a message. On the other hand, if we send the value `:finish` to the actor, it will terminate, as shown here:

```
user> (pa/! actor :finish)
nil
Finished
user> (pa/done? actor)
true
```

After being sent the value `:finish`, the `done?` function returns `true` when applied to the actor, which implies that the actor has terminated. The value returned by an actor before termination can be obtained using the `join` function from the `co.paralleluniverse.pulsar.core` namespace. We must note that the `join` function actually returns the result of any fiber, and will block the calling thread of execution until the fiber completes or terminates. For example, consider the actor in *Example 8.9* that divides a number by another number:

```
(def divide-actor
  (pa/spawn
   #(loop [c 0]
      (pa/receive
       :result c
       [a b] (recur (/ a b)))))))
```

Example 8.9: An actor that performs division of a number by another

We can send messages to the actor `divide-actor` defined in *Example 8.9*, and obtain the final result from it using the `join` function, as shown here:

```
user> (pa/! divide-actor 30 10)
nil
user> (pa/! divide-actor :result)
nil
user> (pc/join divide-actor)
3
```

The preceding code shows that we can send two numbers to the actor `divide-actor`, and send it the value `:result` to terminate it. After termination, we can obtain the result of the actor, that is 3, by passing the actor to the `join` function.

Actors can be registered with meaningful names that can be used to locate them. This is done using the `register!` function from the `co.paralleluniverse.pulsar.actors` namespace, which must be passed an actor instance and a name to register for the supplied actor. We can then send messages to a registered actor by specifying the actor's name to either the `!` or `!!` functions. For example, suppose the variable `actor` represents an actor instance created using the `spawn` macro. After registering the actor with the name `:my-actor` by calling `(pa/register! actor :my-actor)`, we can send the value `:foo` to the actor by calling `(pa/! :my-actor :foo)`.

Passing messages between actors

Now, let's build a simple simulation of a ping pong game with two actors. These two actors will send the messages `:ping` and `:pong` to each other for a specified number of times. The code for this simulation is shown in *Example 8.10* as follows:

```
(defn ping-fn [n pong]
  (if (= n 0)
    (do
      (pa/! pong :finished)
      (println "Ping finished"))
    (do
      (pa/! pong [:ping @pa/self])
      (pa/receive
       :pong (println "Ping received pong"))
      (recur (dec n) pong))))

(defn pong-fn []
  (pa/receive
   :finished (println "Pong finished")
   [:ping ping] (do
                  (println "Pong received ping")
                  (pa/! ping :pong)
                  (recur))))

(defn start-ping-pong [n]
  (let [pong (pa/spawn pong-fn)
        ping (pa/spawn ping-fn n pong)]
    (pc/join pong)
    (pc/join ping)
    :finished))
```

Example 8.10: Two actors playing a game of ping-pong

The `ping-fn` and `pong-fn` functions shown in *Example 8.10* implement the logic of two actors playing a game of ping pong. The `ping-fn` will essentially send a vector containing the keyword `:ping` and the current actor instance to the actor represented by the argument `pong`. This is done n times, and finally the message `:finished` is sent to the actor `pong`. The function `pong-fn` will receive the vector `[:ping ping]`, where `ping` will be the actor sending the message. An actor created with the `pong-fn` will terminate once it receives the message `:finished`. The `start-ping-pong` function simply creates two actors using the functions `ping-fn` and `pong-fn` and waits until they are both finished using the `join` function. We can call the `start-ping-pong` function by passing in the number of times each of the two actors must send messages to each other, as shown here:

```
user> (start-ping-pong 3)
Pong received ping
Ping received pong
Pong received ping
Ping received pong
Pong received ping
Ping received pong
Ping finished
Pong finished
:finished
```

The two actors created by the `start-ping-pong` function pass messages between themselves to simulate a game of ping pong, as demonstrated by the preceding output. In conclusion, actors from the Pulsar library can be used to implement concurrently executing processes.

Handling errors with actors

Actors support some interesting methods for error handling. If an actor encounters an error while processing a received message, it will terminate. The exception that was raised within the fiber executing the actor will be saved and thrown again when we pass the actor to the `join` function. In effect, we don't need to handle exceptions within the function passed to the `spawn` macro, and instead we must catch exceptions when the `join` function is called.

This brings us to an interesting consequence of actors. If an actor could encounter an error and fail, we can have another actor that monitors the first actor, and restart it in case of failure. Thus, an actor can be notified when another actor in the system terminates. This principle allows actors to recover from errors in an automated fashion. In the Pulsar library, this sort of error handling is done through the `watch!` and `link!` functions from the `co.paralleluniverse.pulsar.actors` namespace.

An actor can *watch* or *monitor* another actor by calling the `watch!` function from within its body. For example, we must call `(watch! A)` within the body of an actor to watch the actor `A`. If the actor being watched encounters an exception, the same exception will be thrown from the `receive` form of the monitoring actor. The monitoring actor must catch the exception, or else it will be terminated along with the actor from which the exception originated. Also, the monitoring actor could restart the terminated actor by calling the `spawn` macro. To stop watching an actor, we must pass the watched actor to the `unwatch!` function from within the body of the monitoring actor.

Two actors could also be *linked* by passing them to the `link!` function. If two actors are linked together, an exception encountered in either of the two actors will be caught by the other one. In this way, linking two actors is a symmetrical way of monitoring them for errors. The `link!` function can also be called within the function passed to a `spawn` form, in which case it must be passed the actor to be linked. To unlink two actors, we can use the `unlink!` function.

Thus, the Pulsar library provides some interesting ways to watch and link actors to perform error handling and recovery.

Managing state with actors

As we mentioned earlier, actors can have their own internal mutable state. Of course, accessing this state from other actors is not allowed, and immutable messages are the only way an actor can communicate with other actors. Another way that an actor can maintain or manage its state is by changing its behavior depending on the messages it receives, and this technique is called a *selective receive*.

Every actor created using the `spawn` function can read its internal state using the expression `@state`, and can also write to this state using the `set-state!` function. The `set-state!` function will also return the new state of the actor, as returned by the expression `@state`. Note that both of these forms are implemented in the `co.paralleluniverse.pulsar.actors` namespace.

Consider the `add-using-state` function in *Example 8.11* that uses an actor to add two numbers. Of course, we would never really need such a function in the real world, and it is only demonstrated here to depict how an actor can change its internal state.

```
(defn add-using-state [a b]
  (let [actor (pa/spawn
                #(do
                   (pa/set-state! 0)
                   (pa/set-state! (+ @pa/state (pa/receive)))))
```

```
              (pa/set-state! (+ @pa/state (pa/receive))))))]
    (pa/! actor a)
    (pa/! actor b)
    (pc/join actor)))
```

Example 8.11: A function to add two numbers using an actor

The `add-using-state` function shown in *Example 8.11* creates an actor that sets its state to 0, and adds the first two messages it receives to its state. The actor will return the latest state of the actor, as returned by the last call to `set-state!` in the function passed to the `spawn` macro. On calling the `add-using-state` function with two numbers, it produces their sum as its output, shown as follows:

```
user> (add-using-state 10 20)
30
```

Another way in which an actor can modify its state is through a selective receive, in which the actor modifies its behavior on receiving a particular message. This is done by calling a `receive` form within the body of another `receive` form, as shown in *Example 8.12*:

```
(defn add-using-selective-receive [a b]
  (let [actor (pa/spawn
                #(do
                   (pa/set-state! 0)
                   (pa/receive
                    m (pa/receive
                        n (pa/set-state! (+ n m))))))]
    (pa/! actor a)
    (pa/! actor b)
    (pc/join actor)))
```

Example 8.12: A function to add two numbers using an actor with selective receive

The `add-using-selective-receive` function shown previously will set its state to 0, receive the messages m and n through a selective receive, and add these messages. This function produces identical results as the `add-using-state` function from *Example 8.11*, as shown here:

```
user> (add-using-selective-receive 10 20)
30
```

In this way, actors can change their internal state and behavior based on the messages sent to them.

Comparing processes and actors

CSPs and actors are two distinct approaches to modeling a system as a large number of concurrent processes that execute and interact asynchronously. The logic of an asynchronous task can reside within a process created using a go block, or within the function passed to the spawn macro that creates an actor. However, there are some subtle contrasts between these two approaches:

- Processes created using the go and thread forms encourage us to put all states onto channels. Actors, on the other hand, can have their own internal state, in addition to the state in the form of messages sent to them. Thus, actors are more like objects with encapsulated state, while processes are more like functions that operate on states stored in channels.

- Tasks created using the go or thread macros have no implicit error handling, and we must handle exceptions using the try and catch forms in the body of the go and thread macros. Of course, channels do support error handlers, but only when combined with a transducer. Actors, however, will save any exception they run into until we apply the join function on the actor. Also, actors can be linked and monitored to provide a form of automated error recovery. In this way, actors are more focused on building fault-tolerant systems.

These distinguishing factors between CSPs and the actor model give us an idea about which approach is more suitable for implementing asynchronous tasks in a given problem.

Summary

In this chapter, we looked at how we can create concurrent and asynchronous tasks using the core.async and Pulsar libraries. The core.async library provides an implementation of CSPs, and is supported in both Clojure and ClojureScript. We studied the various constructs in the core.async library and also demonstrated how a solution to the dining philosophers problem can be implemented using this library. Later on, we explored actors through the Pulsar library.

We will explore reactive programming in the following chapter. As we will see ahead, reactive programming can be thought of as an extension of asynchronous programming for handling data and events.

9
Reactive Programming

One of the many interesting applications of programming with asynchronous tasks is *reactive programming*. This methodology of programming is all about asynchronously reacting to changes in state. In reactive programming, code is structured in such a way that it *reacts* to changes. Generally, this is implemented using asynchronous data streams, in which data and events are propagated asynchronously through a program. In fact, there are quite a few interesting variants of reactive programming.

Reactive programming is particularly useful in designing graphical user interfaces in frontend development, where changes in the internal state of an application must asynchronously trickle down to the user interface. A program is thus segregated into events and logic that is executed on those events. For programmers used to imperative and object-oriented programming techniques, the hardest part of reactive programming is thinking in reactive abstractions and letting go of old habits like using the mutable state. However, if you've been paying attention so far and have started thinking with immutability and functions, you'll find reactive programming quite natural. In the JavaScript world, reactive programming with *observables* can be thought of as a contrasting alternative to using promises to manage asynchronous events and actions.

In this chapter, we will explore a few interesting forms of reactive programming through Clojure and ClojureScript libraries. Later on, we will also demonstrate how we can build dynamic user interfaces using reactive programming.

Reactive programming with fibers and dataflow variables

Dataflow programming is one of the simplest forms of reactive programming. In dataflow programming, computations are described by composing variables without bothering about when these variables are set to a value. Such variables are also called **dataflow variables**, and they will trigger computations that refer to them once they are set. The *Pulsar* library (`https://github.com/puniverse/pulsar`) provides a few useful constructs for dataflow programming. These constructs can also be used with Pulsar **fibers**, which we briefly talked about in *Chapter 8, Leveraging Asynchronous Tasks*. In this section, we will explore the basics of fibers and dataflow variables from the Pulsar library.

The following library dependencies are required for the upcoming examples:

```
[co.paralleluniverse/quasar-core "0.7.3"]
[co.paralleluniverse/pulsar "0.7.3"]
```

Your `project.clj` file must also contain the following entries:

```
:java-agents
[[co.paralleluniverse/quasar-core "0.7.3"]]
:jvm-opts
["-Dco.paralleluniverse.pulsar.instrument.auto=all"]
```

Also, the following namespaces must be included in your namespace declaration:

```
(ns my-namespace
  (:require [co.paralleluniverse.pulsar.core :as pc]
            [co.paralleluniverse.pulsar.dataflow
             :as pd]))
```

The elementary abstraction of an asynchronous task in the Pulsar library is a fiber. Fibers are scheduled for execution on fork-join based thread pools, and we can create a large number of fibers without bothering about the number of available processing cores. Fibers can be created using the `spawn-fiber` and `fiber` macros from the `co.paralleluniverse.pulsar.core` namespace. The `spawn-fiber` macro must be passed a function that takes no arguments, and the `fiber` form must be passed a body of expressions. The body of both these forms will be executed on a new fiber. The `join` function from the `co.paralleluniverse.pulsar.core` namespace can be used to retrieve the value returned by a fiber.

An important rule we must keep in mind while dealing with fibers is that we must never call methods or functions that manipulate the current thread of execution from within a fiber. Instead, we must use fiber-specific functions from the `co.paralleluniverse.pulsar.core` namespace to perform these operations. For example, calling the `java.lang.Thread/sleep` method in a fiber must be avoided. Instead, the `sleep` function from the `co.paralleluniverse.pulsar. core` namespace can be used to suspend the current fiber for a given number of milliseconds.

The following examples can be found in `src/m_clj/c9/fibers. clj` of the book's source code. Some of these examples are based on code from the official Pulsar documentation (`http://docs. paralleluniverse.co/pulsar/`).

For example, we can add two numbers using a fiber as shown in *Example 9.1*. Of course, using a fiber for such a trivial operation has no practical use, and it is only shown here to demonstrate how we can create a fiber and obtain its return value:

```
(defn add-with-fiber [a b]
  (let [f (pc/spawn-fiber
            (fn []
              (pc/sleep 100)
              (+ a b)))]
    (pc/join f)))
```

Example 9.1: Adding two numbers with a fiber

The preceding `add-with-fiber` function creates a fiber `f` using the `spawn-fiber` macro and fetches the return value of the fiber using the `join` function. The fiber `f` will suspend itself for `100` milliseconds using the `sleep` function and then return the sum of `a` and `b`.

Let's talk a bit about dataflow variables. We can create dataflow variables using the `df-val` and `df-var` functions from the `co.paralleluniverse.pulsar.dataflow` namespace. A dataflow variable created using these functions can be set by calling it like a function and passing it a value. Also, the value of a dataflow variable can be obtained by dereferencing it using the `@` operator or the `deref` form. A dataflow variable declared using the `df-val` function can only be set once, whereas one created using the `df-var` function can be set several times.

The df-var function can also be passed a function that takes no arguments and refers to other dataflow variables in the current scope. This way, the value of such a dataflow variable will be recomputed when the values of referenced variables are changed. For example, two numbers can be added using dataflow variables as shown in the df-add function defined in *Example 9.2*:

```
(defn df-add [a b]
  (let [x (pd/df-val)
        y (pd/df-val)
        sum (pd/df-var #(+ @x @y))]
    (x a)
    (y b)
    @sum))
```

Example 9.2: Adding two numbers with dataflow variables

The value of the dataflow variable sum, declared in the preceding df-add function, will be recalculated when the referenced dataflow variables x and y are set to a value. The variables x and y are set by calling them like functions. Similarly, we can add a number to each element in a range of numbers using the df-val and df-var functions as shown in the following *Example 9.3*:

```
(defn df-add-to-range [a r]
  (let [x (pd/df-val)
        y (pd/df-var)
        sum (pd/df-var #(+ @x @y))
        f (pc/fiber
            (for [i r]
              (do
                (y i)
                (pc/sleep 10)
                @sum)))]
    (x a)
    (pc/join f)))
```

Example 9.3: Adding a number to a range of number with dataflow variables

The df-add-to-range function shown previously defines the dataflow variables x, y, and sum, where sum is dependent on x and y. The function then creates a fiber f that uses the for macro to return a sequence of values. Within the body of the for macro, the dataflow variable y is set to a value from the range r, and the value @sum is returned. The fiber thus returns the result of adding a to all elements in the range r, as shown in the following output:

```
user> (df-add-to-range 2 (range 10))
(2 3 4 5 6 7 8 9 10 11)
```

In conclusion, we can use the df-val and df-var functions to define dataflow variables, whose value can be recomputed when its referenced variables are changed. Effectively, changing the state of a dataflow variable may cause other dataflow variables to *react* to the change.

We should note that the Pulsar library also implements channels, which are analogous to channels from the core.async library. In a nutshell, channels can be used to exchange data with fibers. The Pulsar library also provides constructs for reactive programming with channels, through the co.paralleluniverse.pulsar. rx namespace. These constructs are termed as *reactive extensions*, and are very similar to transducers, in the sense that they perform some computation on the values in a channel. Reactive extensions are also implemented by the *RxClojure* library. We should note that one of the limitations of both the Pulsar and RxClojure libraries is that they are available only on the JVM, and can't be used in ClojureScript programs. Thus, using core.async channels with transducers is a more feasible option in ClojureScript. Nevertheless, we will briefly explore reactive extensions through the RxClojure library in the following section.

Using Reactive Extensions

Reactive Extensions (written as **Rx**) are a generalized implementation of reactive programming that can be used to model event and data streams. Rx can be thought of as an object-oriented approach to reactive programming, in the sense that an event stream is an object with certain methods and properties. In Rx, asynchronous event streams are termed as *observables*. An entity or object that subscribes to events from an observable is called an *observer*. Reactive extensions are essentially a library of functions, or methods, to manipulate observables and create objects that conform to the observer-observable pattern. For example, an observable can be transformed using the Rx variants of the map and filter functions, as shown in the following illustration:

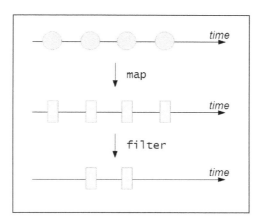

As shown previously, an observable can be described as a collection of values that vary over a period of time. It's quite evident that observables can be treated as a sequence of values using the Rx-flavored variants of the `map` and `filter` functions. An observable can also be subscribed to by an observer, and the observer will be asynchronously invoked for any value produced by an observable.

We will now discuss the various constructs of the RxClojure library (`https://github.com/ReactiveX/RxClojure`). There are several implementations of Rx across multiple languages, such as C#, Java, and PHP. The Java library for reactive extensions is RxJava, and the RxClojure library provides Clojure bindings to RxJava. As we mentioned earlier, it's important to note that RxClojure can only be used on the JVM. Also, the RxClojure library predates the implementation of transducers in Clojure, and thus channels and transducers are a more portable and generic approach to reactive programming.

> The following library dependencies are required for the upcoming examples:
>
> ```
> [io.reactivex/rxclojure "1.0.0"]
> ```
>
> Also, the following namespaces must be included in your namespace declaration:
>
> ```
> (ns my-namespace
>   (:require [rx.lang.clojure.core :as rx]
>             [rx.lang.clojure.blocking :as rxb]
>             [rx.lang.clojure.interop :as rxj]))
> ```

The `rx.lang.clojure.core` namespace contains functions for creating and manipulating observables. Observables are internally represented as collections of values. To extract values from observables, we can use functions from the `rx.lang.clojure.blocking` namespace. However, we must note that functions from the `rx.lang.clojure.blocking` namespace must be avoided in a program and used only for testing purposes. The `rx.lang.clojure.interop` namespace contains functions for performing Java interop with the underlying RxJava library.

> The following examples can be found in `src/m_clj/c9/rx.clj` of the book's source code.

A value can be converted to an observable using the `return` function from the `rx.lang.clojure.core` namespace. An observable can be converted to a vector of values using the `rx.lang.clojure.blocking/into` function, and similarly, we can obtain the first value of an observable using the `rx.lang.clojure.blocking/first` function. These functions are demonstrated in the following output:

```
user> (def o (rx/return 0))
#'user/o
user> (rxb/into [] o)
[0]
user> (rxb/first o)
0
```

A sequence of values can be converted to an observable using the `seq->o` function from the `rx.lang.clojure.core` namespace. To convert the observable back to a sequence, we pass it to the `o->seq` function from the `rx.lang.clojure.blocking` namespace. For example, we can convert the vector `[1 2 3]` to an observable and back to a sequence, as shown here:

```
user> (def o (rx/seq->o [1 2 3]))
#'user/o
user> (rxb/o->seq o)
(1 2 3)
```

Another way of creating an observable is by using the `cons` and `empty` functions from the `rx.lang.clojure.core` namespace. The `empty` function creates an observable with no values, and the `cons` function adds or combines a value and an observable into a new, observable, similar to the standard `cons` function. We can create an observable containing the value `0` using the `cons` and `empty` functions as follows:

```
user> (def o (rx/cons 0 (rx/empty)))
#'user/o
user> (rxb/first o)
0
```

As we mentioned earlier, observers can subscribe to events from observables. Observers can be defined by implementing the `rx.lang.clojure.Observer` interface. This interface defines three methods, namely `onNext`, `onError`, and `onCompleted`. The `onNext` method is called whenever an observable produces a new value, and the `onCompleted` method is called when an observable is done producing values. The `onError` method will be called in case an exception is encountered. Interestingly, all of these methods will be invoked asynchronously from an observable. For example, we can create an observer using the `reify` form to implement the `Observer` interface as shown in *Example 9.4*:

```
(def observer
  (reify rx.Observer
    (onNext [this v] (println (str "Got value: " v "!")))
    (onError [this e] (println e))
    (onCompleted [this] (println "Done!")))))
```

Example 9.4: Implementing the rx.lang.clojure.Observer interface

An observable can call the methods of all its subscribed observers using the `on-next`, `on-error` and `on-completed` functions from the `rx.lang.clojure.core` namespace. We can also define an observable using these functions and the `observable*` form from the `rx.lang.clojure.core` namespace. The `observable*` form must be passed a function that takes a single argument, which represents an observer. For example, we can define a function to create an observable of two values using the `observable*` form as shown in *Example 9.5*:

```
(defn make-observable []
  (rx/observable* (fn [s]
                    (-> s
                        (rx/on-next :a)
                        (rx/on-next :b)
                        rx/on-completed)))))
```

Example 9.5: Creating an observable using the observable* form

The function passed to the `observable*` form, shown previously, calls the `on-next` and `on-completed` functions to produce an observable of two values. We can convert this observable into a vector using the `into` function from the `rx.lang.clojure.blocking` namespace, as shown here:

```
user> (def o (make-observable))
#'user/o
user> (rxb/into [] o)
[:a :b]
```

An observer can also be created using the `subscribe` function from the `rx.lang.clojure.core` namespace. This function must be passed a function that takes a single value, and an observer will be created by implementing the `onNext` method using the supplied function. We can also pass a second argument representing the `onError` method, as well as a third argument that represents the `onCompleted` method, to the `subscribe` function. For example, we can subscribe to an observable using the `subscribe` function, and apply a function to all values in the observable using the `rx.lang.clojure.core/map` function, as shown in *Example 9.6*:

```
(defn rx-inc [o]
  (rx/subscribe o (fn [v] (println (str "Got value: " v "!"))))
  (rx/map inc o))
```

Example 9.6: Subscribing to an observable using the subscribe function

We can create an observable and pass it to the `rx-inc` function defined in *Example 9.6*, as shown here:

```
user> (def o (rx/seq->o [0 1 2]))
#'user/o
user> (rx-inc o)
```

```
Got value: 0!
Got value: 1!
Got value: 2!
#<rx.Observable 0xc3fae8>
```

The function passed to the subscribe form in *Example 9.6* is executed every time the inc function is applied to a value in the observable o. We could as well define the rx-inc function using Java interop with RxJava, as shown in *Example 9.7*:

```
(defn rxj-inc [o]
  (.subscribe o (rxj/action [v]
                  (println (str "Got value: " v "!")))))
  (.map o (rxj/fn [v] (inc v))))
```

Example 9.7: Subscribing to an observable using the Java interop

It's quite clear that using the RxJava library through Java interop isn't pretty, as we would have to wrap all the functions in the action and fn forms from the rx.lang.clojure.interop namespace. The action macro is used to represent a function that performs a side-effect, whereas the fn macro is used to wrap functions that return values. Observables can also be created using the Java interop. This is done using the from static method from the rx.lang.clojure.core.Observable class. The following output demonstrates this method as well as the rxj-inc function defined in *Example 9.7*:

```
user> (def o (rx.Observable/from [0 1 2]))
#'user/o
user> (rxj-inc o)
Got value: 0!
Got value: 1!
Got value: 2!
#<rx.Observable 0x16459ef>
```

Of course, we should prefer to use functions from the rx.lang.clojure.core namespace, and we are using Java interop here only to show that it is possible. Similar to the map function used in *Example 9.6*, there are several other functions in the rx.lang.clojure.core namespace that allow us to treat observables as sequences. Thus, functions such as map, filter, and mapcat comprise the interface of observables, and describe the many ways in which we can interact with them. For example, the following output demonstrates the Rx variants of the take, cycle, and range functions:

```
user> (rxb/into [] (->> (rx/range)
                         (rx/take 10)))
[0 1 2 3 4 5 6 7 8 9]
```

```
user> (rxb/into [] (->> (rx/cycle (rx/return 1))
                        (rx/take 5)))
[1 1 1 1 1]
```

The `rx.lang.clojure.core` namespace also provides a `filter` function that can be used with an observable and a predicate, as shown here:

```
user> (rxb/into [] (->> (rx/seq->o [:a :b :c :d :e])
                        (rx/filter #{:b :c})))
[:b :c]
```

The `group-by` and `mapcat` functions from the `rx.lang.clojure.core` namespace have the same semantics as the standard versions of these functions. For example, let's define a function that uses the `group-by` and `mapcat` functions, as shown in *Example 9.8*:

```
(defn group-maps [ms]
  (->> ms
       (rx/seq->o)
       (rx/group-by :k)
       (rx/mapcat (fn [[k vs :as me]]
                    (rx/map #(vector k %) vs)))
       (rxb/into [])))
```

Example 9.8: Using the group-by and mapcat functions

The `group-maps` function, defined previously, will transform a number of maps into an observable, group the maps by their values for the key `:k`, and create a number of vectors using the `mapcat` and `map` functions. Of course, we wouldn't really need such a function in practice, and it's only shown here to demonstrate how the `group-by` and `mapcat` functions can be used. We can pass a vector of maps to the `group-maps` function to produce a sequence of vectors, as shown here:

```
user> (group-maps [{:k :a :v 1}
                   {:k :b :v 2}
                   {:k :a :v 3}
                   {:k :c :v 4}])
[[[:a {:k :a, :v 1}]
  [:a {:k :a, :v 3}]
  [:b {:k :b, :v 2}]
  [:c {:k :c, :v 4}]]]
```

Several observables can be combined using the `merge` function from the `rx.lang.clojure.core` namespace. The `merge` function can be passed any number of observables, as shown here:

```
user> (let [o1 (rx/seq->o (range 5))
            o2 (rx/seq->o (range 5 10))
            o (rx/merge o1 o2)]
        (rxb/into [] o))
[0 1 2 3 4 5 6 7 8 9]
```

An observable can also be split up into two observables using the `split-with` function from the `rx.lang.clojure.core` namespace. This function must be passed an observable and a predicate function, as shown here:

```
user> (->> (range 6)
           rx/seq->o
           (rx/split-with (partial >= 3))
           rxb/first
           (map (partial rxb/into [])))
([0 1 2 3] [4 5])
```

In summary, the RxClojure library provides us with several constructs for creating and manipulating observables. We can also easily create observers that asynchronously *react* to observables using the `subscribe` function from this library. Also, the constructs from the `rx.lang.clojure.core` namespace have semantics similar to that of standard functions such as `map`, `filter`, and `mapcat`. There are several functions in the `rx.lang.clojure.core` namespace that we haven't talked about in this section, and you're encouraged to explore them on your own.

Using functional reactive programming

A more functional flavor of reactive programming is **functional reactive programming** (abbreviated as **FRP**). FRP was first described in the late '90s by Conal Elliott, who was a member of the Microsoft Graphics Research Group at the time, and Paul Hudak, a major contributor to the Haskell programming language. FRP was originally described as a bunch of functions to interact with *events* and *behaviors*. Both events and behaviors represent values that change over time. The major difference between these two is that events are values that change discretely over time, whereas behaviors are continuously changing values. There is no mention of an observer-observable pattern in FRP. Also, programs in FRP are written as composable transformations of events and behaviors, and are also termed as **compositional event systems (CESs)**.

Modern implementations of FRP provide constructs to create and transform asynchronous event streams. Also, any form of state change is represented as an event stream. In this perspective, a click of a button, a request made to a server, and mutating a variable, can all be treated as event streams. The *Bacon.js* library (`https://github.com/baconjs/bacon.js/`) is a JavaScript implementation of FRP, and the *Yolk* library (`https://github.com/Cicayda/yolk`) provides ClojureScript bindings to the Bacon.js library. In this section, we will briefly study the constructs provided by the Yolk library.

> The following library dependencies are required for the upcoming examples:
>
> ```
> [yolk "0.9.0"]
> ```
>
> Also, the following namespaces must be included in your namespace declaration:
>
> ```
> (ns my-namespace
>   (:require [yolk.bacon :as y]))
> ```
>
> In addition to the preceding dependencies, the following examples also use the set-html! and by-id functions from src/m_clj/c9/common.cljs. These functions are defined as follows:
>
> ```
> (defn ^:export by-id [id]
>   (.getElementById js/document id))
>
> (defn ^:export set-html! [el s]
>   (set! (.-innerHTML el) s))
> ```
>
> Ensure that the code in the following ClojureScript examples is compiled, using the following command:
>
> ```
> $ lein cljsbuild once
> ```

The `yolk.bacon` namespace provides several functions to create event streams, such as the `later` and `interval` functions. The `later` function creates an event stream that produces a single value after a given delay. The `interval` function can infinitely repeat a value with a given time interval. Both these functions must be passed a number of milliseconds as the first argument and a value to produce as the second argument.

Event streams in the Yolk library may produce an infinite number of values. We can limit the number of values produced by an event stream by using the `yolk.bacon/sliding-window` function, which creates an event stream that drops older values once it's full. This function must be passed an event stream and a number indicating the capacity of the event stream returned by it.

We can also create an *event bus*, onto which we can arbitrarily push values, using the bus function from the `yolk.bacon` namespace. The push function puts a value onto an event bus, and the `plug` function connects an event bus to another event stream.

To listen to values produced from event streams, we can use the `on-value`, `on-error`, and `on-end` functions. The `on-value` and `on-error` functions will call a supplied 1-arity function whenever a given event stream produces a value or an error, respectively. The `on-end` function will call a supplied function that takes no arguments whenever a stream ends. This function is often used with the `yolk.bacon/never` function, which creates an event stream that ends immediately without producing a value.

Event streams can also be combined in several ways. The `merge-all` function combines a vector of several event streams into a single one. Another function that can collect values from several event streams in this way is the `flat-map` function. Alternatively, the `combine-array` function can be used to create a single event stream that produces arrays of the values from the supplied streams. The `yolk.bacon/when` function can be used to conditionally combine several channels. This function must be passed a number of clauses, similar to the `cond` form. Each clause must have two parts—a vector of event streams and an expression that will be invoked when all the supplied event streams produce values.

The `yolk.bacon` namespace also provides event stream based variants of the standard `map`, `filter`, and `take` functions. These functions take an event stream as the first argument, which is a little different from the semantics of the standard versions of these functions.

Using these functions from the Yolk library, we can implement a simplified ClojureScript based solution to the dining philosophers problem, which we described in the previous chapters. For a detailed explanation of the dining philosophers problem and its solution, refer to *Chapter 2, Orchestrating Concurrency and Parallelism* and *Chapter 8, Leveraging Asynchronous Tasks*.

The following examples can be found in `src/m_clj/c9/yolk/core.cljs` of the book's source code. Also, the HTML page for the following ClojureScript examples can be found in `resources/html/yolk.html`. The following scripts will be included in this page:

```
<script type="text/javascript" src="../js/bacon.js">
</script>
<script type="text/javascript" src="../js/out/yolk.js">
</script>
```

In this implementation of the dining philosophers problem, we will represent the state of the philosophers and the forks on the table using event buses. The event buses can then be combined using the when function from the Yolk library. We won't maintain much state about the philosophers for the sake of simplicity. Let's first define functions to print the philosophers and represent the routine of a philosopher, as shown in the following *Example 9.9*:

```
(defn render-philosophers [philosophers]
  (apply str
        (for [p (reverse philosophers)]
          (str "<div>" p "</div>"))))

(defn philosopher-fn [i n forks philosophers wait-ms]
  (let [p (nth philosophers i)
        fork-1 (nth forks i)
        fork-2 (nth forks (-> i inc (mod n)))]
    (fn []
      (js/setTimeout
        (fn []
          (y/push fork-1 :fork)
          (y/push fork-2 :fork)
          (y/push p {}))
        wait-ms)
      (str "Philosopher " (inc i) " ate!"))))
```

Example 9.9: Solving the dining philosophers problem with event streams

The preceding render-philosophers function will wrap each philosopher in a div tag, which will be displayed on a web page. The philosopher-fn function returns a function that represents the routine of a philosopher. The function returned by the philosopher-fn function sets off a task, using the setTimeout JavaScript function, to push values representing a particular philosopher and his associated forks into the event buses. This function will finally return a string indicating that the given philosopher was able to eat the food supplied to him. Using these functions, we can create a simulation of the dining philosophers problem in a web page, as shown in the following *Example 9.10*:

```
(let [out (by-id "ex-9-10-out")
      n 5
      [f1 f2 f3 f4 f5 :as forks] (repeatedly n #(y/bus))
      [p1 p2 p3 p4 p5 :as philosophers] (repeatedly n #(y/bus))
      eat #(philosopher-fn % n forks philosophers 1000)
      events (y/when [p1 f1 f2] (eat 0)
                     [p2 f2 f3] (eat 1)
                     [p3 f3 f4] (eat 2)
```

```
                    [p4 f4 f5] (eat 3)
                    [p5 f5 f1] (eat 4))]
(-> events
    (y/sliding-window n)
    (y/on-value
    #(set-html! out (render-philosophers %)))))
(doseq [f forks]
  (y/push f :fork))
(doseq [p philosophers]
  (y/push p {})))
```

Example 9.10: Solving the dining philosophers problem with event streams (continued)

In the `let` form shown in *Example 9.10*, we created the philosophers and forks in our simulation using the `bus` function from the Yolk library. The values produced by these event buses are then combined using a `when` form. The `when` function in the preceding code will check for events from a philosopher and the forks on his left- and right-hand side. The combinations of philosophers and forks are, in fact, hardcoded into the clauses of the `when` form. Of course, we must understand that the clauses of the `when` form shown previously could have easily been generated using a macro. Values are then placed onto the event buses representing the philosophers and forks using the `push` function, to start the simulation. The last five philosophers who could eat are rendered in the web page, as shown here:

```
Philosopher 5 ate!
Philosopher 3 ate!
Philosopher 1 ate!
Philosopher 4 ate!
Philosopher 2 ate!
```

In summary, the Yolk library provides several constructs to handle event streams. There are several functions from this library that we haven't discussed, and you should explore them on your own. In the following section, we will provide examples that demonstrate the other functions from the Yolk library.

 Some of the preceding examples are based on code from *Yolk examples* by Wilkes Joiner (https://github.com/Cicayda/yolk-examples).

Building reactive user interfaces

One of the primary applications of reactive programming is frontend development, where we must create user interface components that react asynchronously to changes in state. In this section, we will describe a few examples implemented using the core.async library and the Yolk library. This is meant to give you a comparison between channels and event streams, and also demonstrate how we can design solutions to problems using both these concepts. Note that only the overall design and code for these examples will be described, and you should be able to fill in the details on your own.

The following library dependencies are required for the upcoming examples:

```
[yolk "0.9.0"]
[org.clojure/core.async "0.1.346.0-17112a-alpha"]
```

Also, the following namespaces must be included in your namespace declaration:

```
(ns my-namespace
  (:require [goog.events :as events]
            [goog.events.EventType]
            [goog.style :as style]
            [cljs.core.async :as a]
            [yolk.bacon :as y])
  (:require-macros [cljs.core.async.macros
                    :refer [go go-loop alt!]]))
```

In addition to the preceding dependencies, the following examples also use the set-html! and by-id functions from src/m_clj/c9/common.cljs. Ensure that the code in the following ClojureScript examples is compiled, using the following command:

```
$ lein cljsbuild once
```

As a first example, let's create three asynchronous tasks that each produce values at different time intervals. We must fetch all the values produced by these tasks and render them on a web page in the same order.

The following examples can be found in `src/m_clj/c9/reactive/core.cljs` of the book's source code. Also, the HTML page for the following ClojureScript examples can be found in `resources/html/reactive.html`. The following scripts will be included in this page:

```
<script type="text/javascript" src="../js/bacon.js">
</script>
<script type="text/javascript"
src="../js/out/reactive.js">
</script>
```

We could implement this using processes and channels from the `core.async` library. In this case, channels will convey the values produced by three processes, and we will use a `merge` operation to combine these channels, as shown in the following *Example 9.11*:

```
(defn render-div [q]
  (apply str
         (for [p (reverse q)]
           (str "<div class='proc-" p "'>Process " p "</div>"))))

(defn start-process [v t]
  (let [c (a/chan)]
    (go (while true
          (a/<! (a/timeout t))
          (a/>! c v)))
    c))

(let [out (by-id "ex-9-11-out")
      c1 (start-process 1 250)
      c2 (start-process 2 1000)
      c3 (start-process 3 1500)
      c (a/merge [c1 c2 c3])
      firstn (fn [v n]
               (if (<= (count v) n)
                 v
                 (subvec v (- (count v) n))))]
  (go-loop [q []]
    (set-html! out (render-div q))
    (recur (-> (conj q (a/<! c))
               (firstn 10)))))
```

Example 9.11: Three asynchronous tasks using channels

The preceding `start-process` function will create a process that periodically produces values using the `go` form, and returns a channel from which the values can be read. The `render-div` function will generate HTML for the values produced by the three tasks. Only the ten most recent values will be shown. This code will produce the following output:

```
Process 1
Process 2
Process 1
Process 1
Process 1
Process 1
Process 2
Process 3
Process 1
Process 1
```

We could also implement the preceding example using FRP, in which values produced by each of the three tasks are represented as event streams. The `merge-all` function from the `yolk.bacon` namespace can be used to combine these event streams, and the `sliding-window` function can obtain the ten most recent values produced by the resulting stream. The `render-div` function from *Example 9.11* can be reused to render the values. This is implemented in *Example 9.12*, and produces the same output as *Example 9.11*:

```
(let [out (by-id "ex-9-12-out")
      events [(y/interval 250 1)
              (y/interval 1000 2)
              (y/interval 1500 3)]]
  (-> events
      y/merge-all
      (y/sliding-window 10)
      (y/on-value
       #(set-html! out (render-div %)))))
```

Example 9.12: Three asynchronous tasks using FRP

Next, let's try to capture mouse events from a particular `div` tag, and display the page offset values of the locations of these events. We can do this with channels, but we would first need a function to convey DOM events onto a channel. We can implement this using the `goog.events/listen` and `cljs.core.async/put!` functions, as shown in *Example 9.13*:

```
(defn listen
  ([el type] (listen el type nil))
```

```
([el type f] (listen el type f (a/chan)))
([el type f out]
 (events/listen el type
              (fn [e] (when f (f e)) (a/put! out e)))
 out))
```

Example 9.13: A function to convey events onto a channel

We can now use the `listen` function defined previously to listen to the `goog.events.EventType.MOUSEMOVE` event type from a particular `div` tag. The values will have to be converted to page offsets, and this can be done using the `getPageOffsetLeft` and `getPageOffsetTop` functions from the `goog.style` namespace. This implementation is described in *Example 9.14*:

```
(defn offset [el]
  [(style/getPageOffsetLeft el) (style/getPageOffsetTop el)])

(let [el (by-id "ex-9-14")
      out (by-id "ex-9-14-out")
      events-chan (listen el goog.events.EventType.MOUSEMOVE)
      [left top] (offset el)
      location (fn [e]
                  {:x (+ (.-offsetX e) (int left))
                   :y (+ (.-offsetY e) (int top))})]
  (go-loop []
    (if-let [e (a/<! events-chan)]
      (let [loc (location e)]
        (set-html! out (str (:x loc) ", " (:y loc)))
        (recur)))))
```

Example 9.14: Mouse events using channels

We can also implement a solution to this problem using the `from-event-stream` and `map` functions from the Yolk library. Interestingly, the events produced by the stream returned by the `from-event-target` function will have page offsets of the event stored as the `pageX` and `pageY` properties. This allows us to have a much simpler implementation, as shown in *Example 9.15*:

```
(let [el (by-id "ex-9-15")
      out (by-id "ex-9-15-out")
      events (y/from-event-target el "mousemove")]
  (-> events
    (y/map (juxt (fn [e] (.-pageX e))
                 (fn [e] (.-pageY e))))
    (y/map (fn [[x y]] (str x ", " y)))
    (y/on-value
     #(set-html! out %))))
```

Example 9.15: Mouse events using FRP

Both of the implementations shown in *Example 9.14* and *Example 9.15* work as expected, and produce the following output:

```
686, 915
```

As a final example, we will simulate several search queries being performed and display the results from the first three queries that return results. The queries can be described as: two queries for web results, two queries for image results, and two queries for video results. We can implement these simulated queries as shown in *Example 9.16*:

```
(defn chan-search [kind]
  (fn [query]
    (go
      (a/<! (a/timeout (rand-int 100)))
      [kind query])))

(def chan-web1 (chan-search :web1))
(def chan-web2 (chan-search :web2))
(def chan-image1 (chan-search :image1))
(def chan-image2 (chan-search :image2))
(def chan-video1 (chan-search :video1))
(def chan-video2 (chan-search :video2))
```

Example 9.16: Simulating search queries with channels

The `chan-search` function returns a function that uses the `cljs.core.async/timeout` function to simulate a search query by parking the current task for a random number of milliseconds. Using the `chan-search` function, we create several queries for the different kinds of results we are interested in. Using these functions, we can implement a function to perform all the queries and return the first three results, as shown in *Example 9.17*:

```
(defn chan-search-all [query & searches]
  (let [cs (for [s searches]
             (s query))]
    (-> cs vec a/merge)))

(defn chan-search-fastest [query]
  (let [t (a/timeout 80)
        c1 (chan-search-all query chan-web1 chan-web2)
```

```
            c2 (chan-search-all query chan-image1 chan-image2)
            c3 (chan-search-all query chan-video1 chan-video2)
            c (a/merge [c1 c2 c3])]
       (go (loop [i 0
                  ret []]
             (if (= i 3)
               ret
               (recur (inc i)
                      (conj ret (alt!
                                  [c t] ([v] v)))))))))))
```

Example 9.17: Simulating search queries with channels (continued)

As shown in the preceding example, the merge function can be used to combine channels that produce the results of the search queries. Note that the queries to all three types of results, namely web, images, and videos, are timed out after 80 milliseconds. We can bind the chan-search-fastest function to the click of a mouse button using the listen function we defined earlier, as shown in *Example 9.18*:

```
(let [out (by-id "ex-9-18-out")
      button (by-id "search-1")
      c (listen button goog.events.EventType.CLICK)]
   (go (while true
         (let [e (a/<! c)
               result (a/<! (chan-search-fastest "channels"))
               s (str result)]
           (set-html! out s)))))
```

Example 9.18: Simulating search queries with channels (continued)

Clicking on the button bound to the chan-search-fastest function will show the following output. Note that the nil value in the following output indicates a timeout of all queries for a particular search result type.

```
[[:image2 "channels"] [:web1 "channels"] nil]
```

We can just as easily implement an FRP version of the simulation of search queries that was previously described. The queries for the various sources of data are defined as shown in the following *Example 9.19*:

```
(defn frp-search [kind]
  (fn [query]
    (y/later (rand-int 100) [kind query])))

(def frp-web1 (frp-search :web1))
```

```
(def frp-web2 (frp-search :web2))
(def frp-image1 (frp-search :image1))
(def frp-image2 (frp-search :image2))
(def frp-video1 (frp-search :video1))
(def frp-video2 (frp-search :video2))
```

Example 9.19: Simulating search queries with FRP

The preceding functions all return event streams for search results. The search results produced can be combined with timeouts using the later, merge, and combine-as-array functions from the yolk.bacon namespace, as shown in *Example 9.20*:

```
(defn frp-search-all [query & searches]
  (let [results (map #(% query) searches)
        events (cons (y/later 80 "nil") results)]
    (-> (apply y/merge events)
        (y/take 1))))

(defn frp-search-fastest [query]
  (y/combine-as-array
   (frp-search-all query frp-web1 frp-web2)
   (frp-search-all query frp-image1 frp-image2)
   (frp-search-all query frp-video1 frp-video2)))
```

Example 9.20: Simulating search queries with FRP (continued)

The frp-search-fastest function can be invoked on clicking a button, as shown in *Example 9.21*:

```
(let [out (by-id "ex-9-21-out")
      button (by-id "search-2")
      events (y/from-event-target button "click")]
  (-> events
      (y/flat-map-latest #(frp-search-fastest "events"))
      (y/on-value
       #(set-html! out %))))
```

Example 9.21: Simulating search queries with FRP (continued)

The preceding example produces the following output when the search button is clicked:

```
nil,[:image2 "events"],[:video2 "events"]
```

In conclusion, we can use both channels and event streams to implement interactive interfaces in web pages. Although the FRP implementations of the preceding examples are slightly shorter, we can say that both the `core.async` and Yolk libraries have their own elegance.

> The preceding examples are based on code from *Communicating Sequential Processes* by David Nolen (`http://swannodette.github.io/2013/07/12/communicating-sequential-processes/`) and *CSP vs. FRP* by Draco Dormiens (`http://potetm.github.io/2014/01/07/frp.html`).

Introducing Om

The *Om* library (`https://github.com/omcljs/om`) is a great tool for building dynamic user interfaces in ClojureScript. In fact, it's an interface to *React.js* (`http://facebook.github.io/react/`), which is a JavaScript library for creating interactive user interface components. Om lets us define a user interface as a hierarchy of components, and each component reactively modifies its appearance based on changes to the component's state. In this way, Om components *react* to changes in their state.

> The following library dependencies are required for the upcoming examples:
>
> ```
> [org.omcljs/om "0.8.8"]
> ```
>
> Also, the following namespaces must be included in your namespace declaration:
>
> ```
> (ns my-namespace
>   (:require [om.core :as om :include-macros true]
>             [om.dom :as dom :include-macros true]))
> ```
>
> In addition to the preceding dependencies, the following examples also use the by-id function from `src/m_clj/c9/common.cljs`. Ensure that the code in the following ClojureScript examples is compiled, using the following command:
>
> ```
> $ lein cljsbuild once
> ```

The Om components are generally defined by implementing the `IRender` and `IRenderState` protocols from the `om.core` namespace. The `IRender` protocol declares a single function `render`, and similarly the `IRenderState` protocol declares the `render-state` function. The `render` and `render-state` functions define how a component that implements either of these protocols is converted to DOM, which can be rendered by a web browser. The implementations of these functions must return a DOM object constructed using functions from the `om.dom` namespace. There are also several other protocols in the `om.core` namespace that allow us to define a component's behavior. Internally, Om uses React.js to perform batched updates to the DOM for the sake of performance, and uses *virtual DOM* to maintain the state of the DOM to be rendered.

The following examples can be found in `src/m_clj/c9/om/core.cljs` of the book's source code. Also, the HTML page for the following ClojureScript examples can be found in `resources/html/om.html`. The following scripts will be included in this page:

```
<script type="text/javascript" src="../js/out/om.js">
</script>
```

Let's now build a simple component using Om. Suppose we want to build a web application. One of the first steps in doing so is creating a login page for our application. As an example, let's create a simple login form with Om. A user will enter their username and password in this form. The only requirement is that the submit button of this form must be enabled only if the user has entered a username and password. Let's start off by defining some functions to create an input field of a form, as shown in *Example 9.22*:

```
(defn update-input-value-fn [owner]
  (fn [e]
    (let [target (.-target e)
          val (.-value target)
          id (keyword (.-id target))]
      (om/set-state! owner id val))))

(defn input-field [text owner attrs]
  (let [handler (update-input-value-fn owner)
        event-attr {:onChange handler}
        js-attrs (-> attrs (merge event-attr) clj->js)]
    (dom/div
     nil
     (dom/div nil text)
     (dom/input js-attrs))))
```

Example 9.22: A login form using Om

The `update-input-value-fn` function defined in *Example 9.22* accepts a component `owner` as an argument and returns a function that we can bind to a DOM event. The returned function updates the state of the component with the value of the `.-value` property using the `set-state!` function from the `om.core` namespace. The `input-field` function returns a DOM object for an input field with some associated properties. The `input-field` function also creates an event handler using the `update-input-value-fn` function and binds it to the `onChange` event of the input field.

> Note that a component can change its state or the global application state by using the `set-state!`, `update-state!`, `update!`, or `transact!` functions from the `om.core` namespace.

Next, let's define a form as a component using the `om.core/IRenderState` protocol and `input-field` function, as shown in *Example 9.23*:

```
(defn form [data owner]
  (reify
    om/IInitState
    (init-state [_]
      {:username "" :password ""})
    om/IRenderState
    (render-state [_ state]
      (dom/form
       nil
       (input-field "Username" owner
                    {:type "text"
                     :id "username"
                     :value (:username state)})
       (input-field "Password" owner
                    {:type "password"
                     :id "password"
                     :value (:password state)})
       (dom/br nil)
       (dom/input
        #js {:type "submit"
             :value "Login"
             :disabled (or (-> state :username empty?)
                           (-> state :password empty?))})))))

(om/root form nil {:target (by-id "ex-9-23")})
```

Example 9.23: A login form using Om (continued)

The preceding `form` function creates a component by implementing the `render-state` function of the `IRenderState` protocol. This component also implements the `IInitState` protocol to define the initial state of the component. The `form` function will render a login form with two input fields, for a username and password, and a login button. The button is enabled only when the username and password are entered. Also, the component is mounted onto a `div` using the `om.core/root` function. The following output in a web page describes the behavior of the component defined by the `form` function:

The preceding output describes two states of the login form component defined by the `form` function. The login button is observed to be disabled when either the username or password fields are empty, and is enabled only when the user enters values in both of these input fields. In this way, the login form *reacts* to changes in the state of its input fields.

 Visit `https://github.com/omcljs/om/wiki/Documentation` for complete documentation on all the protocols, functions, and macros in the Om library.

Thus, the Om library provides us with several constructs for creating interactive and stateful components.

Summary

So far, we have discussed reactive programming through the Pulsar, RxClojure, and Yolk libraries. We have also described several ClojureScript examples that compare channels from the `core.async` library to reactive event streams from the Yolk library. We also demonstrated how we can leverage the Om library to build dynamic user interfaces.

In the following chapter, we will explore how we can test our Clojure programs.

10
Testing Your Code

Testing is an integral part of developing software. Alongside implementing functionality in our software, it is imperative to simultaneously define tests to verify several aspects of it. The Clojure standard library provides several constructs to define tests and mock data. There are also several community libraries that allow us to verify different aspects of the code being tested.

The main advantage of using tests is that they allow us to identify the overall impact of a particular change in a program's code. If we have tests to check the functionality of a program, we can refactor the program with confidence and without the fear of losing any functionality. If there's something that we unavoidably missed while refactoring a program, it will surely be brought to our attention when we run the program's tests. Thus, tests are indispensable tools for keeping code maintainable.

In this chapter, we will study the different ways in which we can write tests in Clojure. We will also discuss how we can perform type checking in Clojure. Although we describe several libraries for writing tests in this chapter, we must note that there are several more available in the Clojure ecosystem. That aside, the libraries described in this chapter are the most mature and battle-hardened tools for testing our code.

Writing tests

Being a thoughtfully designed language, Clojure has a built-in unit testing library, namely `clojure.test`. Apart from that, there are a couple constructs in the core language that are helpful with regard to testing. Of course, these constructs don't allow us to define and run any tests in the formal sense, and the constructs from the `clojure.test` namespace must be preferred for that purpose.

Let's start off by briefly discussing the constructs from the core language that can be used for unit testing. The `assert` function checks whether an expression evaluates to a truthy value at runtime. This function will throw an exception if the expression passed to it does not evaluate to a truthy value, and the message of this exception can be optionally specified as a second argument to the `assert` form. We can effectively disable all the `assert` forms in a given program by using the global `*assert*` compile time `var`. This variable can only be changed by a top-level `set!` form in a given program or namespace.

Another interesting aspect of testing that is easily tackled by the core language is *mocking* and *stubbing*. In a nutshell, these techniques allow us to redefine the behavior of certain functions within the context of a test case. This is useful in preventing functions from performing unwanted side effects or using unavailable resources. In the Clojure language, this can be done using the `with-redefs` function. This form can be used within tests as well as plain functions, but its usage outside of the scope of tests is not really encouraged. Its semantics are similar to that of the standard `let` form, and you are encouraged to go through the Clojure docs for examples on the `with-redefs` form.

Now, let's explore how we can actually define tests using constructs from the `clojure.test` namespace.

Defining unit tests

Clojure has support for defining unit tests baked into it. The `clojure.test` namespace, which requires no additional dependencies whatsoever, provides several constructs for testing our code. Let's explore a few of them.

The following namespaces must be included in your namespace declaration for the upcoming examples:

```
(ns my-namespace
  (:require [clojure.test :refer :all]))
```

The following examples can be found in `test/m_clj/c10/test.clj` of the book's source code.

Tests can be defined using the `deftest` macro. This form must be passed a symbol, indicating the name of the defined test, and any number of expressions. Generally, `is` and `are` forms are used within the `deftest` macro. The `is` form must be passed an expression, and will fail the test if the supplied expression does not return a truthy value. The `are` form must be passed a vector of variable names, a condition to test, and values for the defined variables. For example, the standard `*` function can be tested as shown in *Example 10.1*:

```
(deftest test-*
  (is (= 6 (* 2 3)))
  (is (= 4 (* 1 4)))
  (is (= 6 (* 3 2))))

(deftest test-*-with-are
  (are [x y] (= 6 (* x y))
    2 3
    1 6
    3 2))
```

Example 10.1: Defining tests using the clojure.test namespace

The preceding code defines two tests using the `is` and `are` forms. We can run tests using the `run-tests` and `run-all-tests` functions from the `clojure.test` namespace. The `run-tests` function can be passed any number of namespaces, and will run all the tests defined in them. Also, this form can be called without passing any arguments, in which case it will run all the tests in the current namespace. The `run-all-tests` function will run all the tests in all namespaces of the current project. It can optionally be passed a regular expression, and will only run the tests from matching namespaces if this argument is supplied. In fact, an IDE with integrated support for running tests will call these functions. For example, we can run the tests we defined in *Example 10.1* using the `run-tests` function shown here:

```
user> (run-tests)

Testing ...

Ran 2 tests containing 6 assertions.
0 failures, 0 errors.
{:test 2, :pass 6, :fail 0, :error 0, :type :summary}
```

As shown in the preceding output, the `run-tests` function executes both the tests, and both of them pass. Let's now define a test that will fail, although we shouldn't really be doing this unless we have a good reason:

```
(deftest test-*-fails
  (is (= 5 (* 2 3))))
```

Example 10.2: A test that fails

The test `test-*-fails` shown in *Example 10.2* will fail when it is run, as shown here:

```
user> (run-tests)

Testing ...
```

```
FAIL in (test-*-fails) (test.clj:24)
expected: (= 5 (* 2 3))
  actual: (not (= 5 6))

Ran 3 tests containing 7 assertions.
1 failures, 0 errors.
{:test 3, :pass 6, :fail 1, :error 0, :type :summary}
```

In fact, defining tests that fail should be considered a part and parcel of developing a program. To start a feature or fix a bug in a program, we must first define a test that validates this change (by failing!). We should then proceed to implement the feature or fix, such that all the newly defined tests pass. These two steps are then repeated, until all the requirements of our feature or fix are met. This is the essence of **test-driven development (TDD)**.

 We can also run the tests defined in a given namespace using the following command:

```
$ lein test my-namespace
```

The `clojure.test` namespace must be used for testing programs written strictly in Clojure. For testing ClojureScript programs in the same way, we can use the *doo* library (`https://github.com/bensu/doo`), which provides ClojureScript implementations of the `deftest`, `is`, and `are` constucts.

Using top-down testing

A more powerful way to define tests in Clojure is by using the *Midje* library (`https://github.com/marick/Midje`). This library provides several constructs that allow us to easily define unit tests by describing relationships between several functions, rather than describing the implementation of the functions themselves. This approach is also called *top-down testing*, and Midje champions this kind of testing methodology. Let's dive into the details of the Midje library.

The following library dependencies are required for the upcoming examples:

```
[midje "1.8.2"]
```

We must also include the following dependencies in the :plugins section of your project.clj file:

```
[lein-midje "3.1.3"]
```

Also, the following namespaces must be included in your namespace declaration:

```
(ns my-namespace
  (:require [midje.sweet :refer :all]
            [midje.repl :as mr]))
```

The following examples can be found in test/m_clj/c10/midje.clj of the book's source code.

Firstly, let's define a simple function that we intend to test, as shown in *Example 10.3*:

```
(defn first-element [sequence default]
  (if (empty? sequence)
    default
    (first sequence)))
```

Example 10.3: A simple function to test

We can define tests for the first-element function using the facts and fact constructs from the midje.sweet namespace, as shown in *Example 10.4*.

```
(facts "about first-element"
  (fact "it returns the first element of a collection"
        (first-element [1 2 3] :default) => 1
        (first-element '(1 2 3) :default) => 1)

  (fact "it returns the default value for empty collections"
        (first-element [] :default) => :default
        (first-element '() :default) => :default
        (first-element nil :default) => :default
        (first-element
         (filter even? [1 3 5])
         :default) => :default))
```

Example 10.4: Tests for the first-element function

As shown in the preceding code, the `fact` form describes a test, and can be passed any number of clauses. Each clause is comprised of an expression, a `=>` symbol, and the expected return value of the supplied expression. The `facts` form is simply used to group together several `fact` forms. It's quite apparent that instead of checking logical conditions, we use `fact` forms to check expressions and the values returned by them.

The `provided` form can be used to mock function calls. The Midje library allows us to use *metaconstants* in our tests, and they are often used with the `provided` form. Metaconstants can be thought of as generic placeholders for values and functions. All metaconstants should start and end with two or more dots (`.`) or hyphens (`-`); hyphens are more suitable for metaconstants representing functions. For example, we can test the `first-element` function we defined earlier using metaconstants and the `provided` form as shown in *Example 10.5*:

```
(fact "first-element returns the first element of a collection"
      (first-element ..seq.. :default) => :default
      (provided
       (empty? ..seq..) => true))
```

Example 10.5: Using the provided form and metaconstants

In the test shown previously, the metaconstant `..seq..` is used to indicate the first argument passed to the `first-element` function, and the `provided` form mocks the call to the `empty?` function. This way, we can implement tests without completely implementing the functions being tested. Of course, we should avoid mocking or redefining standard functions in the `provided` form. For example, suppose we have three partially implemented functions, as shown in *Example 10.6*.

```
(defn is-diesel? [car])

(defn cost-of-car [car])

(defn overall-cost-of-car [car]
  (if (is-diesel? car)
    (* (cost-of-car car) 1.4)
    (cost-of-car car)))
```

Example 10.6: Partially implemented functions to test

Notice that only the `overall-cost-of-car` function is completely implemented in the preceding code. Nevertheless, we can still test the relation between these three functions using the Midje library, as shown in *Example 10.7*.

```
(fact
  (overall-cost-of-car ..car..) => (* 5000 1.4)
  (provided
```

```
(cost-of-car ..car..) => 5000
(is-diesel? ..car..) => true))
```

Example 10.7: Testing the is-diesel?, cost-of-car and overall-cost-of-car functions

In the test shown previously, the `cost-of-car` and `is-diesel?` functions are mocked using the `provided` form and the `..car..` metaconstant, and the value returned by the `overall-cost-of-car` function is checked. We can run all of the tests we have defined so far using the `autotest` function from the `midje.repl` namespace, as shown here:

```
user> (mr/autotest :files "test")


=====================================================================
Loading ( ... )
>>> Output from clojure.test tests:

0 failures, 0 errors.
>>> Midje summary:
All checks (8) succeeded.
[Completed at ... ]
```

We can also run the tests defined in a given namespace using the following command. Note that the following command will watch your project for file changes, and will run the tests in any files once they are changed:

```
$ lein midje :autotest test
```

In this way, we can use the Midje library to write tests, even for functions that haven't been completely implemented. Midje allows us to describe tests as relations between functions using metaconstants. In summary, the `clojure.test` and Midje libraries are great tools for defining unit tests.

Testing with specs

We will now take a look at the Speclj, pronounced *speckle*, library (`https://github.com/slagyr/speclj`), which is used to write *specs*. Specs are similar to unit tests, but are focused on the behavior of functions being tested, rather than their internal implementation. In fact, **behavior-driven development (BDD)** is centered about writing specs.

The main difference between TDD and BDD is that BDD focuses on the behavior or specifications of functions, rather than their implementation. From this perspective, if we change the internal implementation of a function that has been previously tested, there is a smaller chance that we have to modify the tests, or rather specs, associated with the function. BDD can also be thought of as a refined approach to TDD, in which the interface and behavior of a function is more important than its internal implementation. Now, let's study the various constructs of the Speclj library.

The following library dependencies are required for the upcoming examples. We must also include the following dependencies in the `:plugins` section of your `project.clj` file:

```
[speclj "3.3.1"]
```

Also, the following namespaces must be included in your namespace declaration:

```
(ns my-namespace
  (:require [speclj.core :refer :all]))
```

The `describe`, `it`, and `should` forms, from the `speclj.core` namespace, are used to define specs for a given function. The `it` form represents a single specification for the function being tested, and the `describe` form is used to group together several specs together. Assertions within an `it` form can be expressed using the `should` form and its variants. For example, we can write a spec for the behavior of the standard `*` function, as shown in the following *Example 10.8*.

The following examples can be found in `spec/m_clj/c10/speclj.clj` of the book's source code.

```
(describe "*"
  (it "2 times 3 is 6"
    (should (= 6 (* 2 3)))))
```

Example 10.8: A spec for the * function

The spec shown previously checks a single condition using the `should` and `=` forms. There are several variants of the `should` form, such as `should=`, `should-not`, `should-fail`, and `should-throw`. These forms are pretty much self-explanatory, and you are encouraged to go through the Speclj docs for more details. We can describe some specs for the standard `/` function, as shown in *Example 10.9*.

```
(describe "/"
  (it "5 divided by 5 is 1"
    (should= 1 (/ 5 5)))
  (it "5 divided by 5 is not 0"
```

```
    (should-not= 0 (/ 5 5)))
  (it "fail if 5 divided by 5 is not 1"
    (if (not= 1 (/ 5 5))
      (should-fail "divide not working")))
  (it "throw an error if 5 is divided by 0"
    (should-throw ArithmeticException
      (/ 5 0)))))
```

Example 10.9: Specs for the / function using several it forms

Within a `describe` form, we can use the `before` and `after` forms to execute arbitrary code before or after each `it` form is checked. Similarly, the `before-all` and `after-all` forms can specify what to execute before and after all the specs are checked in a `describe` form.

Input and output performed by a certain function can be described using specs. This is done using the `with-out-str` and `with-in-str` forms. The `with-out-str` form returns whatever data is sent to standard output by a given expression. Conversely, the `with-in-str` form must be passed a string and an expression, and the supplied string will be sent to the standard input once the supplied expression is called. For example, let's say we have a simple function that reads a string and prints it. We can write a spec for such a function using the `with-out-str` and `with-in-str` forms as shown in *Example 10.10*:

```
(defn echo []
  (let [s (read-line)]
    (println (str "Echo: " s))))

(describe "echo"
  (it "reads a line and prints it"
    (should= "Echo: Hello!\r\n"
      (with-out-str
        (with-in-str "Hello!"
          (echo))))))
```

Example 10.10: A spec for a function that reads a string and prints it

We can also mock function calls within an `it` form using the standard `with-redefs` macro we described earlier. For example, we can write a spec for the `echo` function described in *Example 10.10* by mocking the `read-line` and `println` functions as shown in *Example 10.11*. Obviously, it's not advisable to mock standard functions, and it's only done here to depict the usage of the `with-redefs` macro within a spec.

```
(describe "echo"
  (it "reads a line and prints it"
    (with-redefs [read-line (fn [] "Hello!")
```

```
                  println (fn [x] x)]
        (should= "Echo: Hello!" (echo)))))
```

Example 10.11: Using the with-redefs macro within a spec

To run all the specs defined in a given project, we can call the `run-specs` macro, as shown here:

```
user> (run-specs)
...

Finished in 0.00547 seconds
7 examples, 0 failures
#<speclj.run.standard.StandardRunner 0x10999>
```

 We can also run the specs defined in a given namespace using the following command. Note that the following command will watch your project for file changes, and will run the specs in any files once they are changed:

```
$ lein spec -a
```

To summarize, the Speclj library provides us with several constructs to define specs for BDD. Specs for a given function should be modified only when the required functionality or behavior of a function must be changed. With specs, there's less of a chance that modifying the underlying implementation of a function will require a change in its associated specs. Of course, the question of whether you should use specs or tests in your project is a subjective one. Some projects do fine with simple tests, and others prefer to use specs.

Generative testing

Another form of testing is **generative testing**, in which we define properties of functions that must hold true for all inputs. This is quite different compared to enumerating the expected inputs and outputs of functions, which is essentially what unit tests and specs do. In Clojure, generative testing can be done using the `test.check` library (`https://github.com/clojure/test.check`). This library is inspired by Haskell's QuickCheck library, and provides similar constructs for testing properties of functions.

The following library dependencies are required for the upcoming examples:

```
[org.clojure/test.check "0.9.0"]
```

Also, the following namespaces must be included in your namespace declaration:

```
(ns my-namespace
    (:require [clojure.test.check :as tc]
              [clojure.test.check.generators :as gen]
              [clojure.test.check.properties :as prop]
              [clojure.test.check.clojure-test
               :refer [defspec]]))
```

The following examples can be found in `src/m_clj/c10/check.clj` of the book's source code.

To define a property to check, we can use the `for-all` macro from the `clojure.test.check.properties` namespace. This macro must be passed a vector of generator bindings, which can be created using constructs from the `clojure.test.check.generators` namespace, along with a property to verify. For example, consider the properties defined in *Example 10.12*:

```
(def commutative-mult-prop
  (prop/for-all [a gen/int
                 b gen/int]
    (= (* a b)
       (* b a))))

(def first-is-min-after-sort-prop
  (prop/for-all [v (gen/not-empty (gen/vector gen/int))]
    (= (apply min v)
       (first (sort v)))))
```

Example 10.12: Simple properties defined using the test.check library

In the preceding code, we have defined two properties, namely `commutative-mult-prop` and `first-is-min-after-sort-prop`. The `commutative-mult-prop` property asserts that a multiplication operation using the `*` function is commutative, and the `first-is-min-after-sort-prop` function checks whether the first element of a vector of integers sorted using the `sort` function is the smallest value in the vector. Note the use of the `int`, `vector` and `non-empty` functions from the `clojure.test.check.generators` namespace. We can verify that these properties are true using the `quick-check` function from the `clojure.test.check` namespace, as shown here:

```
user> (tc/quick-check 100 commutative-mult-prop)
{:result true, :num-tests 100, :seed 1449998010193}
```

```
user> (tc/quick-check 100 first-is-min-after-sort-prop)
{:result true, :num-tests 100, :seed 1449998014634}
```

As shown previously, the quick-check function must be passed the number of checks to run and a property to verify. This function returns a map describing the checks performed on the supplied properties, in which the value of the :result key indicates the outcome of the test. It's fairly evident that both of the properties commutative-mult-prop and first-is-min-after-sort-prop hold true for the specified type of inputs. Now, let's define a property that is not true, as shown in *Example 10.13*:

```
(def commutative-minus-prop
  (prop/for-all [a gen/int
                 b gen/int]
    (= (- a b)
       (- b a))))
```

Example 10.13: A property that won't be true defined using the test.check library

Running the preceding check will obviously fail, as shown in the following output:

```
user> (tc/quick-check 100 commutative-minus-prop)
{:result false, :seed 1449998165908,
 :failing-size 1, :num-tests 2, :fail [0 -1],
 :shrunk {:total-nodes-visited 1, :depth 0, :result false,
              :smallest [0 -1]}}
```

We can also define specs based on generative testing using the defspec macro from the clojure.test.check.clojure-test namespace. This form must be passed the number of checks to perform and a property, which is analogous to the quick-check function. Specs defined using the defspec form will be checked by the standard clojure.test runner. For example, we can define the commutative-mult-prop property as a spec as shown in *Example 10.14*:

```
(defspec commutative-mult 100
  (prop/for-all [a gen/int
                 b gen/int]
    (= (* a b)
       (* b a))))
```

Example 10.14: A spec defined using the defspec macro

The spec defined in the preceding code can be verified by calling the run-tests or run-all-tests functions from the clojure.test namespace, or by running the lein test Leiningen command. In conclusion, generative testing through the test.check library is yet another way to test our code. It focuses on specifying properties of functions rather than describing the expected output of functions for some input.

Testing with types

Type checking is something that is often taken for granted in statically typed languages. With type checking, type errors can be found at compile time, rather than during runtime. In some dynamic languages such as Clojure, type signatures can be declared wherever and whenever they are required, and this technique is termed as *optional typing*. Type checking can be done using the `core.typed` library (`https://github.com/clojure/core.typed`). Using `core.typed`, the type signature of a var can be checked using *type annotations*. Type annotations can be declared for any var, which includes values created using a `def` form, a `binding` form, or any other construct that creates a var. In this section, we will explore the details of this library.

The following library dependencies are required for the upcoming examples.

```
[org.clojure/core.typed "0.3.0"]
```

Also, the following namespaces must be included in your namespace declaration.

```
(ns my-namespace
    (:require [clojure.core.typed :as t]))
```

The following examples can be found in `src/m_clj/c10/typed.clj` of the book's source code.

Type annotations for vars are declared using the `ann` macro from the `clojure.core.typed` namespace. This form must be passed an expression to annotate and a vector of types. For example, a type annotation for a function that accepts two numbers as arguments and returns a number is shown in *Example 10.15*.

```
(t/ann add [Number Number -> Number])
(defn add [a b]
  (+ a b))
```

Example 10.15: A type annotation for a function that accepts two numbers and returns a number

To check all the type annotations in the given namespace, we must call the `clojure.core.typed/check-ns` function by passing it the namespace to be checked, as shown here:

```
user> (t/check-ns 'my-namespace)
Start collecting my-namespace
Finished collecting my-namespace
Collected 2 namespaces in 200.965982 msecs
Start checking my-namespace
Checked my-namespace in 447.580402 msecs
Checked 2 namespaces  in 650.979682 msecs
:ok
```

As shown previously, the `check-ns` function prints some information about the
namespaces being checked, and returns the keyword `:ok` if all type checks in
the specified namespace have passed. Now, let's change the definition of the `add`
function we previously defined as shown in *Example 10.16*:

```
(defn add [a b]
  (str (+ a b)))
```

Example 10.16: Redefining the add function

Although the preceding definition is valid, it will not be passed by the type checker,
as shown here:

```
user> (t/check-ns 'my-namespace)
Start collecting my-namespace
Finished collecting my-namespace
Collected 2 namespaces in 215.705251 msecs
Start checking my-namespace
Checked my-namespace in 493.669488 msecs
Checked 2 namespaces  in 711.644548 msecs
Type Error (m_clj/c1/typed.clj:23:3) Type mismatch:

Expected:    Number

Actual:    String
in: (str (clojure.lang.Numbers/add a b))


ExceptionInfo Type Checker: Found 1 error  clojure.core/ex-info
(core.clj:4403)
```

The `check-ns` function throws an error stating that a `String` type was found where
a `Number` type was expected. In this way, the `check-ns` function can find type errors
in functions that have been annotated with the `ann` macro. Functions with multiple
arities can be annotated using the `IFn` construct from the `clojure.core.typed`
namespace, as shown in *Example 10.17*:

```
(t/ann add-abc
       (t/IFn [Number Number -> Number]
              [Number Number Number -> Number]))
(defn add-abc
  ([a b]
   (+ a b))
  ([a b c]
   (+ a b c)))
```

Example 10.17: Annotating functions with multiple arities

We can also annotate functions with variadic arguments using the * symbol in the vector of types passed to the ann macro, as shown in *Example 10.18*.

```
(t/ann add-xs [Number * -> Number])
(defn add-xs [& xs]
  (apply + xs))
```

Example 10.18: Annotating functions with variadic arguments

In the REPL, we can determine the inferred type of an expression or a value using the cf macro from the clojure.core.typed namespace. This macro can also be passed the expected type as the second argument. Note that the cf form is only for experimentation and should not be used in type annotations. The cf form returns an inferred type, along with a structure called a *filter set*, which is represented as a map. For example, the type and filter sets of the values nil, true, and false can be inferred using the cf form as shown here:

```
user> (t/cf nil)
[nil {:then ff, :else tt}]
user> (t/cf true)
[true {:then tt, :else ff}]
user> (t/cf false)
[false {:then ff, :else tt}]
```

In the preceding output, the second value in each of the vectors returned by the cf macro represents the filter set derived from the supplied expression. A filter set can be described as a collection of the two filters:

- The :then filter, which is true if the expression is a truthy value
- The :else filter, which is true if the expression is not a truthy value

In the context of filter sets, there are two *trivial filters*, namely tt and ff, which can be described as follows:

- tt, which translates to trivially true and means the value is truthy.
- ff, which translates to *forever false* and means the value is not truthy. This filter is also termed as the *impossible filter*.

In this perspective, the filter set {:then tt, :else ff} translates into "the expression could be a truthy value, but it is impossible for it to be a non-truthy value". Thus, false values such as nil and false are never true as inferred by the cf form, which agrees with the semantics of these values in Clojure. Truthy values will always have tt as the :then filter, as shown in the following output:

```
user> (t/cf "Hello")
[(t/Val "Hello") {:then tt, :else ff}]
user> (t/cf 1)
```

```
      [(t/Val 1) {:then tt, :else ff}]
user> (t/cf :key)
      [(t/Val :key) {:then tt, :else ff}]
```

The cf macro can also be used to check the type signature of functions, as shown here:

```
user> (t/cf str)
[t/Any * -> String]
user> (t/cf +)
(t/IFn [Long * -> Long]
       [(t/U Double Long) * -> Double]
       [t/AnyInteger * -> t/AnyInteger]
       [Number * -> Number])
```

A form or expression can be annotated with an expected type using the ann-form macro, as shown here:

```
user> (t/cf (t/ann-form #(inc %) [Number -> Number]))
[[Number -> Number] {:then tt, :else ff}]
user> (t/cf (t/ann-form #(str %) [t/Any -> String]))
[[t/Any -> String] {:then tt, :else ff}]
```

Aggregate types such as lists and vectors also have types defined for them in the clojure.core.typed namespace. We can infer the types of these data structures using the cf macro, as shown here:

```
user> (t/cf (list 0 1 2))
(PersistentList (t/U (t/Val 1) (t/Val 0) (t/Val 2)))
user> (t/cf [0 1 2])
[(t/HVec [(t/Val 0) (t/Val 1) (t/Val 2)]) {:then tt, :else ff}]
```

The types PersistentList and HVec in the preceding output are concrete types for a list and a vector respectively. We can also pass the expected type as an extra argument to the cf form as shown here:

```
user> (t/cf (list 0 1 2) (t/List t/Num))
(t/List t/Num)
user> (t/cf [0 1 2] (t/Vec t/Num))
(t/Vec t/Num)
user> (t/cf {:a 1 :b 2} (t/Map t/Keyword t/Int))
(t/Map t/Keyword t/Int)
user> (t/cf #{0 1 2} (t/Set t/Int))
(t/Set t/Int)
```

The core.typed library also supports *parameterized types, union types,* and *intersection types*. Union types are declared using the U construct, and intersection types are declared using the I construct. Intersection types are meant to be used with protocols, which implies that the intersection type (I A B) must implement both the protocols A and B. On the other hand, union types can be defined using concrete types. For example, the clojure.core.typed namespace defines a parameterized Option type, which is simply a union of nil and the parameterized type. In other words, the type (Option x) is defined as the union type (U x nil). Another good example of a union type is the AnyInteger type, which represents a whole number, and is defined in the clojure.core.typed namespace as shown in *Example 10.19*.

```
(defalias AnyInteger
  (U Integer Long clojure.lang.BigInt BigInteger Short Byte))
```

Example 10.19: The AnyInteger union type

Polymorphic types are also supported by the core.typed library, which allow us to specify generalized types. For example, the identity and iterate functions have polymorphic type signatures, as shown here:

```
user> (t/cf identity)
(t/All [x] [x -> x :filters ... ])
user> (t/cf iterate)
(t/All [x] [[x -> x] x -> (t/ASeq x)])
```

We can annotate functions with polymorphic type signatures using the All construct from the clojure.core.typed namespace, as shown in *Example 10.20*.

```
(t/ann make-map (t/All [x] [x -> (t/Map t/Keyword x)]))
(defn make-map [a]
  {:x a})
```

Example 10.20: Defining a polymorphic type signature

In conclusion, the core.typed library provides several constructs to define and verify type signatures of vars. There are also several constructs for determining the type signature of a given expression. Using core.typed, you can find logical type errors in your code before it is executed at runtime. Type annotations can also be thought of as a form of documentation, which concisely describe the types of functions and vars. Thus, there are several benefits of using types through the core.typed library in Clojure.

Summary

So far, we have discussed several libraries that can help us test and verify our code. We talked about the `clojure.test` and Midje libraries for defining tests. We also explored how we can define specs in the spirit of BDD using the Speclj library. Generative testing is another approach to testing, and we demonstrated how it can be done using the `test.check` library. Lastly, we talked about how we can perform type checking in Clojure using the `core.typed` library. Hence, there is a wide array of options for testing our code in Clojure.

In the next and final chapter, we will talk about how we can troubleshoot our code, as well as some good practices for developing applications in Clojure.

11

Troubleshooting and Best Practices

By now, you must be aware of all the features and most of the constructs of the Clojure language. Before you start building your own applications and libraries in Clojure, we will briefly discuss a few techniques to troubleshoot your code and some practices that you should incorporate in your projects.

Debugging your code

Along your journey of building applications and libraries in Clojure, you'll surely run into situations where it would be helpful to debug your code. The usual response to such a situation is to use an **Integrated Development Environment** (**IDE**) with a debugger. And while Clojure IDEs such as *CIDER* (`https://github.com/clojure-emacs/cider`) and *Counterclockwise* (`http://doc.ccw-ide.org`) do support debugging, there are a few simpler constructs and tools that we can use to troubleshoot our code. Let's have a look at a few of them.

One of the easiest ways to debug your code is by printing the value of some variables used within a function. We could use the standard `println` function for this purpose, but it doesn't always produce the most readable output for complex data types. As a convention, we should use the `clojure.pprint/pprint` function to print variables to the console. This function is the standard pretty-printer of the Clojure language.

 Macros can be quite bewildering to debug. As we mentioned in *Chapter 4, Metaprogramming with Macros*, macros should be used sparingly and we can debug macros using macroexpansion constructs such as `macroexpand` and `macroexpand-all`.

Apart from these built-in constructs, there are a couple of useful libraries that we can add to our debugging toolkit.

 The following examples can be found in `test/m_clj/c11/debugging.clj` of the book's source code.

Using tracing

Tracing can be used to determine when and how a form is called. The `tools.trace` contrib library (`https://github.com/clojure/tools.trace`) provides some handy constructs for tracing our code.

 The following library dependencies are required for the upcoming examples:

```
[org.clojure/tools.trace "0.7.9"]
```

Also, the following namespaces must be included in your namespace declaration:

```
(ns my-namespace
  (:require [clojure.tools.trace :as tr]))
```

The `trace` function, from the `clojure.tools.trace` namespace, is the most elementary way to trace an expression. It will simply print the value returned by the expression passed to it. The `trace` construct can also be passed a string, with which the trace can be tagged, as an additional argument. For example, suppose we have to trace the function defined in *Example 11.1*:

```
(defn make-vector [x]
  [x])
```

Example 11.1: A simple function to trace

We can trace the expression `(make-vector 0)` using the `trace` function shown here:

```
user> (tr/trace (make-vector 0))
TRACE: [0]
[0]
user> (tr/trace "my-tag" (make-vector 0))
TRACE my-tag: [0]
[0]
```

We can trace all the functions defined in a namespace by passing the namespace to the `trace-ns` macro, which is defined in the `clojure.tools.trace` namespace. Similarly, specific functions or vars in a namespace can be traced using the `trace-vars` macro. Traces added using these forms can be removed using the `untrace-ns` and `untrace-vars` marcos. If we want to determine which expression among several ones is failing, we can pass the expressions to the `trace-forms` macro, shown here:

```
user> (tr/trace-forms (+ 10 20) (* 2 3) (/ 10 0))
ArithmeticException Divide by zero
  Form failed: (/ 10 0)
clojure.lang.Numbers.divide (Numbers.java:158)
```

As the preceding output shows, the `trace-forms` macro will print the form that causes the error. A more informative way to trace a function is by replacing the `defn` symbol in its definition by `clojure.tools.trace/deftrace`, which simply defines a function whose arguments and return value will be traced. For example, consider the function defined in the following *Example 11.2*:

```
(tr/deftrace add-into-vector [& xs]
  (let [sum (apply + xs)]
    [sum]))
```

Example 11.2: Tracing a function using the deftrace macro

On calling the `add-into-vector` function defined previously, the following trace will be printed:

```
user> (add-into-vector 10 20)
TRACE t9083: (add-into-vector 10 20)
TRACE t9083: => [30]
[30]
```

In this way, tracing can be used to find the value returned by an expression during the execution of a program. The tracing constructs from the `tools.trace` namespace allow us to determine when a function is called, as well as what its return value and arguments are.

Using Spyscope

As you may have already been thinking, you can easily implement your own debugging constructs using macros. The Spyscope library (https://github.com/dgrnbrg/spyscope) takes this approach and implements a few reader macros for debugging code. The use of reader macros for debugging is a more favorable approach for languages with the parentheses-flavored syntax of Lisps. This is because, in these languages, reader macros that print debugging information can be added more easily to an existing program compared to forms such as trace and deftrace. Let's explore the constructs of the Spyscope library to get a clearer idea of the advantage of debugging code with reader macros.

The Spyscope library provides the #spy/p, #spy/d, and #spy/t reader macros, which can all be used by writing them immediately before expressions that have to be debugged. It is a common practice to have these forms made available in the REPL using the :injections section of the project.clj file in a Leiningen project.

The following library dependencies are required for the upcoming examples:

```
[spyscope "0.1.5"]
```

We must also include the following forms as a vector in the :injections section of your project.clj file:

```
(require 'spyscope.core)
```

Also, the following namespaces must be included in your namespace declaration:

```
(ns my-namespace
  (:require [spyscope.repl :as sr]))
```

The #spy/p reader macro can be used to print a value that is used within an expression. An interesting point about this construct is that it is implemented using the clojure.pprint/pprint function. For example, we can print out the intermediate values produced by a take form shown here:

```
user> (take 5 (repeatedly
               #(let [r (rand-int 100)]
                  #spy/p r)))
95
36
61
99
73
(95 36 61 99 73)
```

To produce more detailed information, such as the call stack and the form that returns a value, we can use the #spy/d reader macro. For example, we can use this construct to produce the following information:

```
user> (take 5 (repeatedly
                #(let [r (rand-int 100)]
                  #spy/d (/ r 10.0))))
user$eval9408$fn___9409.invoke(form-init1..0.clj:2) (/ r 10.0) =>
4.6
user$eval9408$fn___9409.invoke(form-init1..0.clj:2) (/ r 10.0) =>
4.4
user$eval9408$fn___9409.invoke(form-init1..0.clj:2) (/ r 10.0) =>
5.0
user$eval9408$fn___9409.invoke(form-init1..0.clj:2) (/ r 10.0) =>
7.8
user$eval9408$fn___9409.invoke(form-init1..0.clj:2) (/ r 10.0) =>
3.1
(4.6 4.4 5.0 7.8 3.1)
```

The #spy/d reader macro also supports several options, which can be passed to it as metadata. The :fs key of this metadata map specifies the number of stack frames to display. Also, the :marker key can be used to declare a string tag for a form. We can use these options to display information from the call stack of a form, shown here:

```
user> (take 5 (repeat #spy/d ^{:fs 3 :marker "add"}
                  (+ 0 1 2)))
----------------------------------------
clojure.lang.Compiler.eval(Compiler.java:6745)
clojure.lang.Compiler.eval(Compiler.java:6782)
user$eval9476.invoke(form-init1..0.clj:1) add (+ 0 1 2) => 3
(3 3 3 3 3)
```

The preceding output shows the top three stack frames of a call to the + form. We can also filter out stack frames from the call stack information using the :nses key with a regular expression, shown here:

```
user> (take 5 (repeat #spy/d ^{:fs 3 :nses #"core|user"}
                  (+ 0 1 2)))
----------------------------------------
clojure.core$apply.invoke(core.clj:630)
clojure.core$eval.invoke(core.clj:3081)
user$eval9509.invoke(form-init1..0.clj:1) (+ 0 1 2) => 3
(3 3 3 3 3)
```

To skip printing the form being debugged, we can specify the `:form` key with a `false` value in the metadata map specified to the `#spy/d` reader macro, and this key defaults to `true`. We can also print out the time at which a form is called using the `:time` key. The value for this key can either be `true`, in which case the default time format is used, or a string such as `"hh:mm:ss"`, which represents the timestamp format with which the time must be displayed.

The `#spy/t` reader macro is used for tracing a form, and this construct supports the same options as the `#spy/d` reader macro. The trace is not printed immediately, and can be displayed using the `trace-query` function from the `spyscope.repl` namespace. For example, consider the function in *Example 11.3* that adds a number of values in a future:

```
(defn add-in-future [& xs]
  (future
    #spy/t (apply + xs))))
```

Example 11.3: Tracing a function that adds numbers in a future

Once the `add-in-future` function is called, we can display a trace of the call using the `trace-query` function, shown here:

```
user> (sr/trace-next)
nil
user> (def f1 (add-in-future 10 20))
#'user/f1
user> (def f2 (add-in-future 20 30))
#'user/f2
user> (sr/trace-query)
user$add_in_future$fn__..7.invoke(debugging.clj:66) (apply + xs) =>
30
----------------------------------------
user$add_in_future$fn__..7.invoke(debugging.clj:66) (apply + xs) =>
50
nil
```

In the preceding output, the `trace-next` function is used to start a new *generation* of traces. Traces in the Spyscope library are grouped into generations, and a new generation can be started using the `spyscope.repl/trace-next` function. All trace information from all generations can be cleared using the `trace-clear` function from the `spyscope.repl` namespace. We can also pass an argument to the `trace-query` function to filter out results. This argument can be either a number, which represents the number of recent generations to show, or a regex to filter traces by their namespaces.

To summarize, there are several ways to debug your code in Clojure without the use of a debugger. The `tools.trace` and Spyscope libraries have several useful and simple constructs for debugging and tracing the execution of Clojure code.

Logging errors in your application

Another way to analyze what went wrong in an application is by using logs. Logging can be done using the `tools.logging` contrib library. This library lets us use multiple logging implementations through an agnostic interface, and the implementations to choose from include `slf4j`, `log4j`, and `logback`. Let's quickly skim over how we can add logging to any Clojure program using the `tools.logging` library and `logback`, which is arguably the most recent and configurable implementation to use with this library.

The following library dependencies are required for the upcoming examples:

```
[org.clojure/tools.logging "0.3.1"]
[ch.qos.logback/logback-classic "1.1.3"]
```

Also, the following namespaces must be included in your namespace declaration:

```
(ns my-namespace
  (:require [clojure.tools.logging :as log]))
```

The following examples can be found in `test/m_clj/c11/logging.clj` of the book's source code.

All the logging macros implemented in the `clojure.tools.logging` namespace fall into two categories. The first category of macros require arguments like those which are passed to the `println` form. All of these arguments are concatenated and written to the log. The other category of macros must be passed a format string and values to interpolate into the specified format. This second category of macros are generally suffixed with an `f` character, such as `debugf` or `infof`. The logging macros in the `tools.logging` library can be passed an exception followed by the other usual arguments.

The macros in the `tools.logging` library write log messages at differing log levels. For example, the `debug` and `debugf` forms write log messages at the `DEBUG` level, and similarly, the `error` and `errorf` macros log at the `ERROR` level. In addition, the `spy` and `spyf` macros will evaluate and return the value of an expression, and may log the result if the current log level is equal to or below the log level specified to it, which defaults to `DEBUG`.

For example, the `divide` function, shown in the following *Example 11.4*, logs some information, using the `info`, `spyf`, and `error` macros, while performing integer division:

```
(defn divide [a b]
  (log/info "Dividing" a "by" b)
  (try
    (log/spyf "Result: %s" (/ a b))
    (catch Exception e
      (log/error e "There was an error!"))))
```

Example 11.4: A function that logs information using the tools.logging library

The following log messages will be written when the `divide` function is called:

```
user> (divide 10 1)
INFO  - Dividing 10 by 1
DEBUG - Result: 10
10
user> (divide 10 0)
INFO  - Dividing 10 by 0
ERROR - There was an error!
java.lang.ArithmeticException: Divide by zero
at clojure.lang.Numbers.divide(Numbers.java:158) ~[clojure-
1.7.0.jar:na]
...
at java.lang.Thread.run(Thread.java:744) [na:1.7.0_45]
nil
```

As shown previously, the `divide` function writes several log messages at different log levels when it is called. The logging configuration for `logback` must be saved in a file named `logback.xml`, which can reside in either the `src/` or `resources/` directories of a Leiningen project. We can specify the default log level and several other options for `logback` in this file.

> If you're interested in the logging configuration for the previous examples, take a look at the `src/logback.xml` file in the book's source code. For detailed configuration options, visit `http://logback.qos.ch/manual/configuration.html`.

It is also handy to have a global exception handler that logs exceptions for all threads in a program. This can be particularly useful for checking errors that are encountered during the execution of `go` and `thread` macros from the `core.async` library. Such a global exception handler can be defined using the `setDefaultUncaughtExceptionHandler` method from the `java.lang.Thread` class, as shown in *Example 11.5*:

```
(Thread/setDefaultUncaughtExceptionHandler
  (reify Thread$UncaughtExceptionHandler
    (uncaughtException [_ thread ex]
      (log/error ex "Uncaught exception on" (.getName thread)))))
```

Example 11.5: A global exception handler that logs all errors

 You can also use *Timbre* (`https://github.com/ptaoussanis/timbre`) for logging, which can be configured without the use of XML and is also supported on ClojureScript.

In conclusion, there are several options for logging available to us through the `tools.logging` library. This library also supports several logging implementations that each have their own set of configuration options.

Thinking in Clojure

Let's briefly discuss a handful of good practices for building real world applications in Clojure. Of course, these practices are only guidelines, and you should eventually try to establish your own set of rules and practices for writing code in Clojure:

- **Minimize state and use pure functions**: Most applications must inevitably use some form of state. You must always strive to reduce the amount of state you're dealing with, and implement most of the heavy lifting in pure functions. State can be managed using reference types, channels, or even monads in Clojure, thus giving us a lot of proven options. In this way, we can reduce the number of conditions that can cause any unexpected behavior in a program. Pure functions are also easier to compose and test.

- **Don't forget about laziness**: Laziness can be used as an alternative to solve problems that have solutions based on recursion. Although laziness does tend to simplify several aspects of functional programming, it also incurs additional memory usage in certain situations, such as holding on to the head of a lazy sequence. Take a look at `http://clojure.org/reference/lazy#_don_t_hang_onto_your_head` for more information on how laziness can increase the memory usage of your program. Most of the standard functions in Clojure return lazy sequences as results, and you must always consider laziness when working with them.

- **Model your program as transformations of data**: It is unavoidable to think in steps as humans, and you must always try to model your code as steps of transforming data. Try to avoid thinking in steps that mutate state, but rather in transformations of data. This leads to a more composable design, which makes combining a handful of transformations very easy.

- **Use the threading macros -> and ->> to avoid nesting expressions**: You must have seen quite a few examples in this book that have used these macros, and have probably started enjoying their presence in your own code as well. The `->` and `->>` macros improve readability greatly, and must be used wherever possible. Don't hesitate to use these macros even if it avoids a couple of levels of nesting. There are several other threading macros, such as `cond->` and `as->`, that can often be useful.

- **Parallelism is at your fingertips**: There are several ways to write programs that benefit through the use of parallelism in Clojure. You can choose between futures, reducers, `core.async` processes, and several other constructs to model concurrent and parallel operations. Also, most of the state management constructs, such as atoms, agents, and channels, have been designed with concurrency in mind. So, don't hesitate to use them when you're dealing with concurrent tasks and state.

- **Live in the REPL**: It's an indispensable tool for experimenting with code and prototyping your programs. After writing a function or a macro, the first thing you should do is play with it in the REPL. You can use the `load-file` function to quickly reload changes in your source files without ever restarting the REPL. Keep in mind that reloading a source file with the `load-file` form will erase any modifications or redefinitions in the namespace of the source file that have been made through the REPL.

- **Embed a Clojure REPL in your application**: It is possible to embed the REPL into an application, thus allowing us to connect to it and modify its behavior at runtime as we desire. For more information on how to do this, take a look at the constructs in the `clojure.core.server.repl` namespace or the `tools.nrepl` library (`https://github.com/clojure/tools.nrepl`). But, this is a possible security risk, and should be used with caution.

- **Use the standard coding style with consistency**: Maintaining a good coding style is important in any project or programming language. All of the examples in this book are formatted in a standard way, as defined by the Clojure style guide (`https://github.com/bbatsov/clojure-style-guide`).

Summary

So far, we talked about several ways to troubleshoot our code. The `tools.trace` and Spyscope libraries are useful in interactive debugging, while the `tools.logging` library can be used to log information in running applications. We also discussed a handful of good practices for developing applications and libraries in Clojure.

You must be quite anxious by now to write your own applications in Clojure. If you've been paying attention so far, you must have noticed that Clojure is indeed a simple language. Yet, through its simplicity, we are empowered to create elegant and scalable solutions to a lot of interesting problems. On your journey with Clojure ahead, always strive to make things simpler, if they aren't simple enough already. We'll leave you with a few thought provoking quotes as you go onwards to realize the possibilities of this elegant, powerful, and simple programming language.

"Composing simple components is the way we write robust software."

– Rich Hickey

"Simplicity is prerequisite for reliability."

– Edsger W. Dijkstra

"Simplicity is the ultimate sophistication."

– Leonardo da Vinci

References

- *Anatomy of a Reducer*, Rich Hickey (2012): `http://clojure.com/blog/2012/05/15/anatomy-of-reducer.html`

- *Transducers are Coming*, Rich Hickey (2014): `http://blog.cognitect.com/blog/2014/8/6/transducers-are-coming`

- *Introduction to Logic Programming with Clojure*, Ambrose Bonnaire-Sergeant (2011): `http://github.com/frenchy64/Logic-Starter/wiki`

- *N-Queens with core.logic*, Martin Trojer (2012): `http://martinsprogrammingblog.blogspot.in/2012/07/n-queens-with-corelogic-take-2.html`

- *Clojure core.async Channels*, Rich Hickey (2013): `http://clojure.com/blog/2013/06/28/clojure-core-async-channels`

- *Communicating Sequential Processes*, C. A. R. Hoare (1978): `http://www.cs.ucf.edu/courses/cop4020/sum2009/CSP-hoare.pdf`

- *Communicating Sequential Processes*, David Nolen (2013): `http://swannodette.github.io/2013/07/12/communicating-sequential-processes/`

- *A Dining Philosophers solver*, Pepijn de Vos (2013): `http://pepijndevos.nl/2013/07/11/dining-philosophers-in-coreasync.html`

- *CSP vs. FRP*, Draco Dormiens (2014): `http://potetm.github.io/2014/01/07/frp.html`

- *Functional Reactive Animation*, Conal Elliott and Paul Hudak (1997): `http://conal.net/papers/icfp97/icfp97.pdf`

- *Yolk examples*, Wilkes Joiner (2013): `https://github.com/Cicayda/yolk-examples`

- *The Clojure docs*: `http://clojure.org/`

- *Cats Documentation*: `http://funcool.github.io/cats/latest`

- *The core.logic wiki*: http://github.com/clojure/core.logic/wiki
- *The Pulsar docs*: http://docs.paralleluniverse.co/pulsar/
- *The Midje wiki*: http://github.com/marick/Midje/wiki
- *Getting Started with Speclj*: http://speclj.com/tutorial
- *The core.typed wiki*: http://github.com/clojure/core.typed/wiki

Index

I

identity element 133
identity morphism 130
identity value 83
infix notation 102
Input 178
Integrated Development Environment
    (IDE) 231
interning 44
iota library
  URL 85

J

joint 170
joint fitting 170

L

lazy sequences 7, 22-4
Lisps 89
list comprehension
  creating 17
local vars 45
logging configuration
  reference link 238
logical relations
  about 146
  combining 150-152
  n-queens problem, solving 153-156
  solutions, to problems 152
  solving 146-148
  Sudoku puzzle, solving 156-159
logic programming
  about 145
  exploring 145, 146
  logical relations, combining 150-152
  logical relations, solving 146-149

M

macros
  about 231
  avoiding 111
  creating 101-105
  expanding 99-101
  issues 111

patterns, encapsulating 106-108
  thumb rules 111
map function
  characteristics 72
MapReduce frameworks 69
metaconstants 218
metaprogramming 89
Midje library
  reference link 216
miniKanren
  about 145
  reference link 145
mix function 171
mocking 214
monads
  using 139-143
monoids
  about 83, 133
  using 132, 133
morphisms 130
multithreading 36
mutable state, modeling
  identity 42
  state 42
  time 42

N

n-queens problem
  reference link 154
  solving 153-156

O

objects 130
observables 187, 191
Om library
  about 209-212
  reference link 209
optional typing 225
Output 178

P

parallelism
  about 62-64
  controlling, with thread pools 64-66